Basic
Spanish
Grammar

Basic
Spanish
Grammar

Fourth Edition

Ana C. Jarvis

Chandler-Gilbert Community College

Raquel Lebredo

California Baptist College

Francisco Mena-Ayllón

University of California, Riverside

D.C. Heath and Company
Lexington, Massachusetts   Toronto

Address editorial correspondence to:

D. C. Heath
125 Spring Street
Lexington, MA 02173

Cover: We Know They Made Pottery and Lived in Elaborately Decorated Rooms, 48" × 55", watercolor, © 1988, by Lisa Houck.

Text Photograph Credits: p. 1, Ulrike Welsh; p. 7, David Kupferschmid; p. 15, Arvind Garg / Photo Researchers, Inc.; p. 25, Beryl Goldberg; p. 35, Camermann International, Ltd; p. 47, Beryl Goldberg; p. 61, Peter Menzel; p. 79, Monkmeyer Press Photo Service / Renate Hiller; p. 91, Joe Viesti / Viesti Associates, Inc.; p. 103, Joe Viesti / Viesti Associates, Inc; p. 117, Bill Aron / Photo-Edit; p. 133, Beryl Goldberg; p. 153, Chip and Rosa Maria Peterson; p. 165, Beryl Goldberg; p. 175, Joe Viesti / Viesti Associates, Inc.; p. 185, Larry Mangino / The Image Works; p. 195, Chip and Rosa Maria Peterson; p. 217, Victor Englebert; p. 227, Camermann International, Ltd.; p. 237, D. Donne Bryant; p. 247, Robert Frerck / Woodfin Camp & Associates; p. 257, Victor Englebert / Photo Researchers, Inc.

Published simultaneously in Canada.

Printed in the United States of America.

International Standard Book Number: 0–669–24286–1

Library of Congress Catalog Number: 90–86146

10 9 8 7 6 5 4 3 2 1

Preface

Basic Spanish Grammar, Fourth Edition, presents the essential points of Spanish grammar to students whose personal or professional goals include a working knowledge of Spanish. This text clearly and concisely explains grammatical structures that are indispensable for communication and follows up each explanation with practice exercises. Fundamental vocabularly is developed and expanded throughout each lesson.

New features in the fourth edition

While retaining the solid, proven framework of previous editions, *Basic Spanish Grammar* has been substantially revised.

- A vocabulary list now opens each *Basic Spanish Grammar* lesson, introducing students to words and phrases used in the explanation and practice of grammar points. Each vocabulary list relates thematically to a corresponding lesson in the communication manuals.
- In response to reviewers' requests, grammar explanations have been revised, with an earlier introduction of the familiar (*tú*) command (*Lección 11*). Exercises on key grammar points have been expanded for additional practice. Definitions of important grammatical terms, formerly located in an appendix, now appear within related grammar presentations to help students understand key concepts.
- Expanded *En el laboratorio* sections provide audiocassette practice of vocabulary, pronunciation, and grammatical structures, with additional material for listening comprehension at the end of each lesson.
- Revised appendixes contain useful guides to Spanish pronunciation patterns, verb conjugations, and career terminology. Answers to the *¿Cuánto sabe usted ahora?* self-tests are also included. The Spanish-English / English-Spanish end vocabulary has been revised to reflect changes in the individual lesson vocabularies.
- Maps, to help increase students' knowledge of the Spanish-speaking world, apppear after the Table of Contents for easy reference.

Components of Basic Spanish Grammar, Fourth Edition

- Two preliminary lessons: one dealing with very basic grammatical concepts (gender, number, etc.), and one dealing with very basic vocabulary concepts (personal data, greetings and farewells, etc.).
- Twenty core lessons, each containing the following:

  A list of new vocabulary terms. Since this vocabulary is used in the grammar explanation and practice sections, students should familiarize themselves with the terms before proceeding to the grammar sections. Substantially revised for this new edition, the vocabulary lists include high-frequency words and expressions, with cognates featured in a separate section.

  Grammar explanations that focus on three to five main structural points per lesson in succinct, accessible presentations.

  Mini-dialogues to illustrate each structural point in context.

  Práctica exercises to practice and reinforce each structural concept. Exercise formats include word substitution, multiple choice, matching, and translation.

  En el laboratorio exercises to do in conjunction with the audiocassette program. Laboratory exercises include *Vocabulario* and *Práctica* (grammar) sections, as well as a *Para escuchar y entender* (listening comprehension) section, expanded in response to reviewers' requests.

- *¿Cuánto sabe usted ahora?* self-tests after every five lessons to allow students to check their understanding of key grammar and vocabulary from each lesson. An answer key is provided as an appendix in the Student Edition.
- Appendixes:
  Spanish pronunciation
  Verb paradigms
  Careers and occupations
  Answer key for *¿Cuánto sabe usted ahora?* self-tests
  Spanish-English / English-Spanish vocabulary

Audiocassette program

The revised laboratory program to accompany *Basic Spanish Grammar*, Fourth Edition, is available on audiocassettes. This program is a helpful resource for students who desire more opportunities to hear and practice Spanish outside of class.

Other components of the Basic Spanish Grammar program

Basic Spanish Grammar, Fourth Edition, continues to be the nucleus of a complete Spanish program consisting of seven manuals, each accompanied by its own audiocassette program.

Manuals

Two manuals develop practical communication skills for general use:

- *Getting Along in Spanish*, Third Edition
- *Spanish for Communication*, Fourth Edition

Each lesson in the communication manuals parallels the grammar and vocabulary focus of the corresponding lesson in the *Basic Spanish Grammar* text. Additionally, each lesson in *Getting Along in Spanish* is now thematically tied to the corresponding *Basic Spanish Grammar* lesson. *Spanish for Communication*, Fourth Edition, covers virtually the same themes as *Getting Along in Spanish*, Third Edition, but at a more advanced level. Realistic dialogues and situational exercises emphasize normal daily interactions and now include realia-based activities.

Five manuals develop communication skills in specific professional areas:

- *Spanish for Business and Finance*, Fourth Edition
- *Spanish for Law Enforcement*, Fourth Edition
- *Spanish for Medical Personnel*, Fourth Edition
- *Spanish for Social Services*, Fourth Edition
- *Spanish for Teachers*, Third Edition

Each career manual presents specific vocabulary needed for a given profession. Each lesson parallels the corresponding lesson in *Basic Spanish Grammar*, Fourth Edition. As a result, students are simultaneously exposed to the grammatical structure explained in the principal text and to the practical application of that structure in the corresponding manual. *Lección 11* of each career manual has been revised to reflect the earlier introduction of the familiar (*tú*) command in the core text.

Students studying Spanish for professional reasons have specific needs and limited study time. As we are aware of the unique situation of these students, we have endeavored to present the material of the entire *Basic Spanish Grammar* program in a way that facilitates its used for individualized instruction.

Career and communication manual lessons contain the following features:

- Dialogues that present practical topics or situations characteristic of each specific profession. For example, *"Un examen físico"* and *"En la sala de emergencia"* are two dialogues in the manual for medical personnel.
- New vocabulary used in the lesson, with cognates listed separately for easy reference. Vocabulary reviews are presented after every five lessons.
- Cultural information that broadens students' awareness of the Hispanic world.
- Dialogue recall practice (in some manuals).
- Grammatical exercises that recycle the vocabulary and theme of the lesson.
- Question-answer exercises, progressing from dialogue-based comprehension to personalized and / or professionally-oriented exchanges.
- Dialogue completion exercises, encouraging students to use their own experiences and imaginations while practicing new vocabulary and grammar.
- Situational activities, including roleplays, that provide open-ended practice in typical professional contexts.
- Realia-based exercises (in some manuals).
- Supplementary readings on professional topics (in some manuals).
- Vocabulary expansion (optional) related to the lesson theme.
- Appendixes containing pronunciation reference materials and a Spanish-English / English-Spanish vocabulary.

Audiocassette programs

Each career and communication manual continues to have its own audiocassette program based on the dialogues and vocabulary for each lesson. This taped material provides important listening comprehension and pronunciation practice.

Acknowledgments

We wish to thank our colleagues who have used previous editions of *Basic Spanish Grammar* for their many constructive comments and recommendations. We especially appreciate the valuable suggestions of the following reviewers of *Basic Spanish Grammar*, Third Edition:

Kim Bowman, *McNeese State University*
Aristeo Brito, *Pima County Community College*

Donald B. Gibbs, *Creighton University*
Carmen Velásquez, *Santa Fe Community College*
John Zahner, *Montclair State College*

We also thank Ruth Eisele, who prepared the comprehensive end vocabulary.

Finally, we would like to express our appreciation to the editorial and production staff of D. C. Heath and Company. José Blanco, Nicole Cormen, Katherine McCann, Gina Russo, and Denise St. Jean provided us with their assistance and expertise throughout the preparation of the manuscript.

Ana C. Jarvis
Raquel Lebredo
Francisco Mena-Ayllón

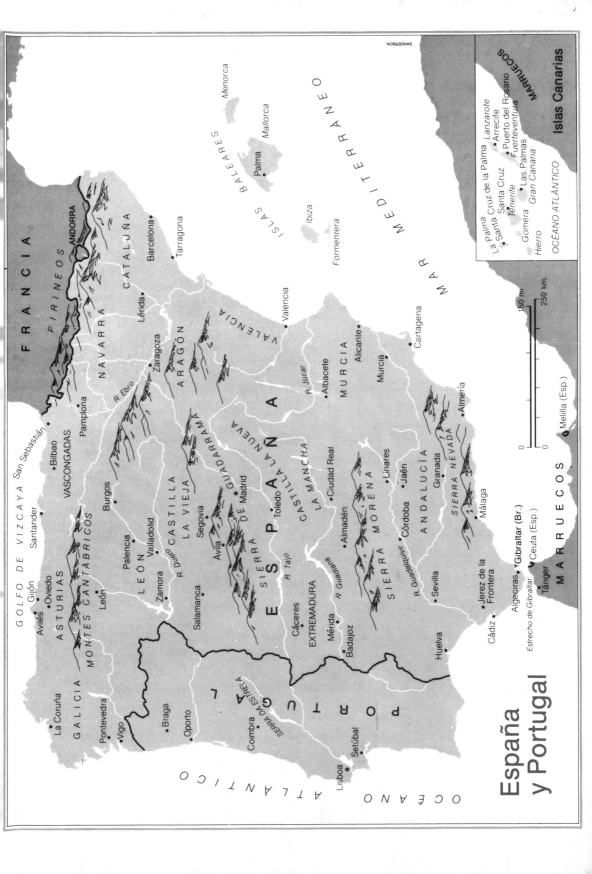

España y Portugal

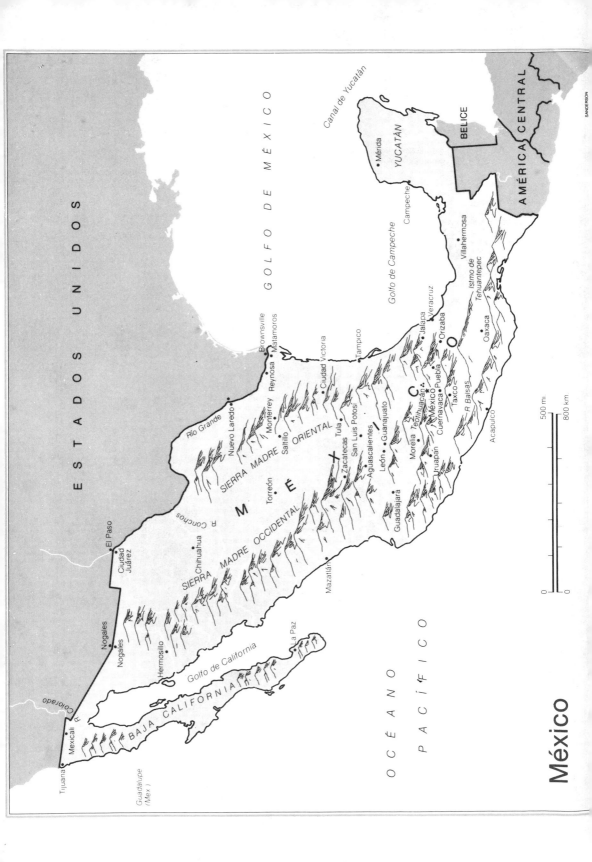

México

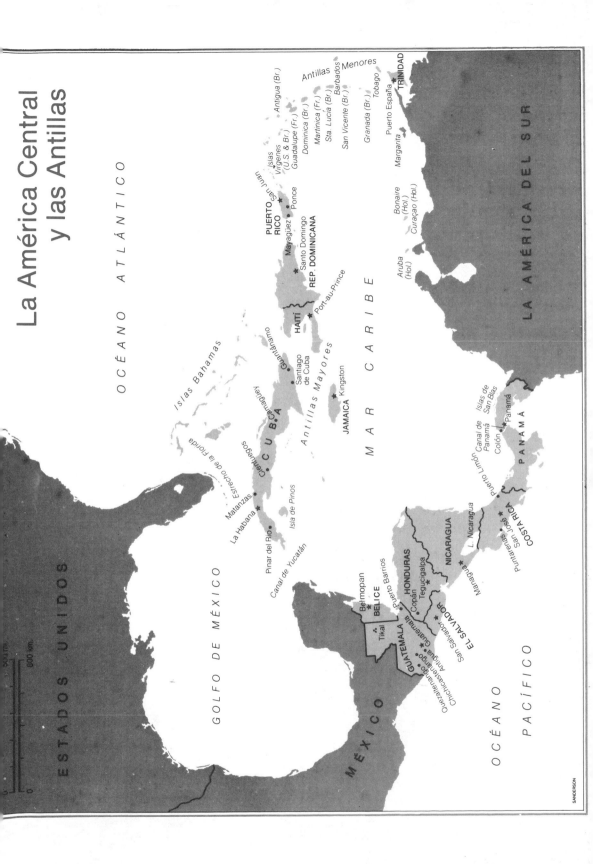

La América Central y las Antillas

ESTADOS UNIDOS

OCÉANO ATLÁNTICO

GOLFO DE MÉXICO

Islas Bahamas

Estrecho de la Florida

Pinar del Río
La Habana
Matanzas
Cienfuegos
Isla de Pinos
C U B A
Camagüey
Santiago de Cuba
Guantánamo

Antillas Mayores

JAMAICA Kingston

HAITÍ
Port-au-Prince

REP. DOMINICANA
Santo Domingo

PUERTO RICO
Mayagüez
Ponce
San Juan

Islas Vírgenes (U.S. & Br.)
Antigua (Br.)
Guadalupe (Fr.)
Dominica (Br.)
Martinica (Fr.)
Sta. Lucía (Br.)
Barbados
San Vicente (Br.)
Granada (Br.)
Puerto España
Margarita

Antillas Menores
Tobago
TRINIDAD

MAR CARIBE

Aruba (Hol.)
Bonaire (Hol.)
Curaçao (Hol.)

LA AMÉRICA DEL SUR

MÉXICO

Canal de Yucatán

Belmopan
BELICE
Tikal
Puerto Barrios
GUATEMALA
Guatemala
Quetzaltenango
Chichicastenango
Antigua
San Salvador
EL SALVADOR
Copán
HONDURAS
Tegucigalpa
NICARAGUA
Managua
L. Nicaragua
COSTA RICA
Puntarenas
San José
Puerto Limón
Canal de Panamá
Colón
Panamá
PANAMÁ
Islas de San Blas

OCÉANO PACÍFICO

0   600 km.

SANDERSON

La América del Sur

Contents

Lección 2

Lección 3

Lección 4

Lección 5

Lección 6

Lección 7

Lección 8

Lección 9

Lección 10

Lección 11

Lección 12

Lección 13

Lección 14

Lección 15

Lección 16

Lección 17

Lección 18

Lección 19

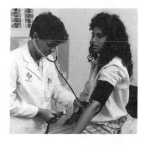

Lección 20

Appendixes/Vocabularies

Basic Spanish Grammar

Lección preliminar

I

1. Gender

> **Gender**   the classification of nouns, pronouns, and adjectives as masculine or feminine

In Spanish, all nouns, including abstract nouns and those denoting nonliving things, are either masculine or feminine.

masculine	*feminine*
hombre	mujer WOMAN
señor	señora
teléfono	lámpara LAMP
progreso	idea

Here are some practical rules to use to determine the gender of Spanish nouns.

♦ Most nouns ending in **-a** or denoting female beings are feminine; most nouns ending in **-o** or referring to male beings are masculine:

masculine	*feminine*
teléfono	silla CHAIR
dinero	casa
libro	mesa

ATENCIÓN: Two important exceptions to this rule are día (*day*), which is masculine, and mano (*hand*), which is feminine.

♦ Some words that end in **-a** are masculine. These nouns are of Greek origin and have kept the gender they had in that language:

problema	sistema
programa	telegrama
idioma (*language*)	clima (*climate*)

♦ Nouns ending in **-sión, -ción, -tad,** and **-dad** are feminine:

televisión	lección
decisión	conversación
libertad	universidad
amistad (*friendship*)	calamidad

♦ The gender of some nouns must be learned:

masculine	*feminine*
español (*Spanish language*)	calle (*street*)

◆ Many masculine nouns ending in **-o** have a corresponding feminine form ending in **-a**:

masculine	*feminine*
enfermer**o** (*nurse*)	enfermer**a**
secretari**o**	secretari**a**

◆ Certain masculine nouns ending in a consonant add **-a** to form the corresponding feminine noun:

masculine	*feminine*
profesor	profesor**a**
doctor	doctor**a**

Práctica

Are the following nouns feminine or masculine?

1. teléfono
2. día ᴍ
3. televisión ꜰ
4. enfermera
5. problema ᴍ
6. calle
7. mesa
8. universidad
9. dinero
10. idioma ᴍ
11. silla
12. amistad
13. mano ꜰ
14. ciudad
15. lección
16. progreso
17. señor
18. profesora
19. programa ᴍ
20. clima ᴍ

◆ 2. Number

> **Number**   a term that identifies words as singular and plural: chair, chairs

Nouns are made plural in Spanish by adding an **-s** to those ending in a vowel and an **-es** to those ending in a consonant. Nouns ending in **-z** are made plural by changing the **z** to **c** and adding **-es**:

teléfono	teléfonos
mesa	mesas
profesor	profesores
lápiz ᴘᴇɴᴄɪʟ	lápices
luz ʟɪɢʜᴛ	luces
lección	lecciones

ATENCIÓN: Accent marks that fall on the last syllable of singular words are omitted in the plural form.

Práctica

What are the plural forms of the following nouns?

1. silla*s*
2. libro*s*
3. lápiz *ces*
4. universidad*es*
5. telegrama*s*
6. ciudad*es*
7. lección*es*
8. señor*es*

9. clima*s*
10. conversación*es*
11. profesor*es*
12. luz *ces*
13. decisión*es*
14. doctor*es*
15. amistad*es* *FRIENDSHIPS*
16. lámpara*s*

3. The definite article el artículo definido

> **Definite article**   a word used before a noun to indicate a definite person or thing: **the** woman, **the** money

There are four forms in Spanish equivalent to the English definite article *the:*

	Masculine	*Feminine*
Singular	el	la
Plural	los	las

el profesor
los profesores
el lápiz
los lápices *PENCILS*

la profesora
las profesoras
la lámpara
las lámparas *LAMPS*

ATENCIÓN: Learning each noun's definite article will help you to remember the noun's gender.

Práctica

What are the definite articles for the following nouns?

1. universidades
2. problema
3. profesor
4. doctor
5. señora
6. señores
7. día
8. televisión

9. silla
10. mujeres
11. dinero
12. profesores
13. idea
14. telegrama
15. libertad

4. The indefinite article

> **Indefinite article**   a word used before a noun to indicate an indefinite person or object: **a** child, **an** apple, **some** students

The indefinite article in Spanish has four forms; they are equivalent to *a*, *an*, and *some.*

	Masculine	*Feminine*
Singular	un	una
Plural	unos	unas

un profesor
unos profesores
un lápiz
unos lápices

una profesora
unas profesoras
una pluma
unas plumas

Práctica

How would you say the following in Spanish?

1. a pen
2. a man
3. some days
4. some chairs
5. a problem
6. a house
7. a light
8. a program
9. some pencils
10. a lesson
11. a friendship
12. a decision

5. Cardinal numbers (0–21)

0	cero	11	once
1	uno	12	doce
2	dos	13	trece
3	tres	14	catorce
4	cuatro	15	quince
5	cinco	16	dieciséis
6	seis	17	diecisiete
7	siete	18	dieciocho
8	ocho	19	diecinueve
9	nueve	20	veinte
10	diez	21	veintiuno

Numbers are masculine in Spanish: **el cero, el veinte,** and so on.

◆ **Uno** becomes **un** in front of a masculine singular noun: *un* **libro** (*one book*). **Una** is used before a feminine noun: *una* **silla** (*one chair*). All other numbers ending in **-uno** or **-una** follow the same pattern: *veintiún* **libros** (*twenty-one books*), *veintiuna* **sillas** (*twenty-one chairs*).

Práctica

A. Read the following numbers aloud in Spanish:

0	28	7	9	13	11	5	4	20
15	10	14	16	1	8	21	19	12

B. Read the following telephone numbers in Spanish. Say each number one by one:

383–5079	254–2675	792–5136	689–0275
985–0746	765–1032	985–7340	872–0695

Vocabulario

COGNADOS[1]

la **calamidad**   calamity, disaster
la **ciudad**   city
la **conversación**   conversation
la **decisión**   decision
el, la **doctor(a)**   doctor
la **idea**   idea
la **lección**   lesson
la **libertad**   liberty
el **problema**   problem
el, la **profesor(a)**   professor
el **programa**   program
el **progreso**   progress
el, la **secretario(a)**   secretary
el **sistema**   system
el **teléfono**   telephone
el **telegrama**   telegram
la **televisión**   television
la **universidad**   university

NOMBRES

la **amistad**   friendship
la **calle**   street
la **casa**   house
el **clima**   climate
el **día**   day
el **dinero**   money
el (la) **enfermero(a)**   nurse
el **español**   Spanish (*language*)
el **hombre**   man
el **idioma**, la **lengua**   language
la **lámpara**   lamp
el **lápiz**   pencil
el **libro**   book
la **luz**   light
la **mano**   hand
el (la) **médico(a)**,
    doctor(a)   M.D., doctor
la **mesa**   table
la **mujer**   woman
la **pluma**   pen
el **señor**   gentleman, sir, Mr.
la **señora**   lady, madam, Mrs.
la **silla**   chair

---

[1] Cognates are words that resemble one another and have similar meanings in Spanish and English. Note that English cognates often have different spellings and always have different pronunciations than their Spanish counterparts.

Lección preliminar

II

1. **Personal information**
2. **Greetings and farewells**
3. **Days of the week**
4. **Cardinal numbers (30–200)**
5. **Months and seasons of the year**

◄ 1. Personal information

—¿Nombre y apellido?	*Name and surname?*
—María Valdés.	*Maria Valdes.*
—¿Estado civil?	*Marital status?*
—Casada.	*Married.*
—¿Apellido de soltera?[1]	*Maiden name?*
—Rivas.	*Rivas.*
—¿Nacionalidad?	*Nationality? (citizenship)*
—Norteamericana.[2]	*North American (U.S.).*
—¿Lugar de nacimiento?	*Place of birth?*
—La Habana, Cuba.	*Havana, Cuba.*
—¿Edad?	*Age?*
—Veintinueve años.	*Twenty-nine years (old).*
—¿Ocupación?[3]	*Occupation?*
—Enfermera.	*Nurse.*
—¿Dirección?	*Address?*
—Calle Magnolia,[4] número ciento ocho.	*Number one hundred eight Magnolia Street.*
—¿Ciudad?	*City?*
—Riverside.	*Riverside.*
—¿Número de teléfono?[1]	*Phone number?*
—682–7530.	*682–7530.*
—¿Número de seguro social?	*Social Security number?*
—566–14–9023.	*566–14–9023.*

Vocabulario: Información personal

los **años**   years
el **apellido**   surname
—**de soltera**   maiden name
casado(a)   married
la **dirección**, el **domicilio**   address

divorciado(a)   divorced
la **edad**   age
el **estado civil**   marital status
la **fecha de nacimiento**   date of birth
femenino   feminine

---

[1] The preposition **de** + *noun* in Spanish is the equivalent of two nouns used together in English. Notice that the first noun functions as an adjective in English.

[2] Native Spanish speakers use *norteamericano / a* or *americano / a* to refer to people from the United States.

[3] See Appendix C for a list of occupations.

[4] In Spanish, the name of the street is placed before the number.

el **lugar de nacimiento**
place of birth
el **lugar donde trabaja**
place of work
masculino masculine
la **nacionalidad** nationality
el **nombre** name
norteamericano(a) North
American (from the U.S.)
el **número** number
el **número de la licencia**
para conducir license
number

—**de seguro social** social
security number
—**de teléfono** telephone
number
la **ocupación** occupation
separado(a) separated
el **sexo** sex
soltero(a) single
viudo(a) widower (widow)

Práctica

Conduct an interview with another student. Ask your partner the following questions:

1. ¿Nombre y apellido?
2. ¿Estado civil?
3. ¿Apellido de soltera? (*If you are talking to a married woman.*)
4. ¿Nacionalidad?
5. ¿Lugar de nacimiento?
6. ¿Ocupación?
7. ¿Dirección? (¿Domicilio?)
8. ¿Ciudad?
9. ¿Número de teléfono?
10. ¿Número de seguro social?

Now reverse roles; you are the person being interviewed.

2. Greetings and farewells

—**Buenos días, doctor
Rivas. ¿Cómo está usted?**

*Good morning, Doctor
Rivas. How are you?*

—**Muy bien, gracias. ¿Y
usted?**

*Very well, thank you. And
you?*

—**Bien, gracias. Hasta
luego.**

*Fine, thank you. See you
later.*

—**Adiós.**

Goodbye.

—**Mucho gusto, profesor
Vera.**

*Pleased to meet you,
Professor Vera.*

—**El gusto es mío,
señorita Reyes.**

*The pleasure is mine, Miss
Reyes.*

—**Buenas tardes, señora.**

Good afternoon, madam.

—**Buenas tardes, señor.**

Good afternoon, sir.

—Pase y tome asiento, por favor.	*Come in and sit down, please.*
—Gracias.	*Thank you.*
—Buenas noches, señorita. ¿Cómo está usted?	*Good evening, miss. How are you?*
—No muy bien.	*Not very well.*
—Lo siento. Hasta mañana.	*I'm sorry. I'll see you tomorrow.*
—Muchas gracias, señor.	*Thank you very much, sir.*
—De nada, señora. Adiós.	*You're welcome, madam. Goodbye.*

Vocabulario: *Saludos y despedidas*

SALUDOS Y DESPEDIDAS

Adiós.	*Goodbye.*
Buenas noches.	*Good evening. (Good night.)*
Buenas tardes.	*Good afternoon.*
Buenos días.	*Good morning. (Good day.)*
¿Cómo está usted?	*How are you?*
Mucho gusto.	*It's a pleasure to meet you. (lit., much pleasure)*
El gusto es mío.	*The pleasure is mine.*
Hasta luego.	*I'll see you later. (lit., until later)*
Hasta mañana.	*I'll see you tomorrow.*

TÍTULOS

doctor[1] (abbrev. **Dr.**)	*doctor*
profesor	*professor*
señor (abbrev. **Sr.**)	*Mr., sir, gentleman*
señora (abbrev. **Sra.**)	*Mrs., madam, lady*
señorita (abbrev. **Srta.**)	*Miss, young lady*

EXPRESIONES ÚTILES

Bien.	*Well, fine.* (GOOD)
De nada.	*You're welcome.*
Lo siento.	*I'm sorry.*
Muchas gracias.	*Thank you very much.*
Muy bien, ¿y usted?	*Very well, and you?*
No.	*No (not).*
Pase.	*Come in.*

---

[1] Notice that in Spanish, titles are not capitalized except when they are abbreviated.

Por favor.	*Please.*
Tome asiento.	*Sit down.* or *Take a seat.*

Práctica

A. Familiarize yourself with each of the above dialogues, then act them out with another student.

B. What would you say in the following situations?

1. You meet Mr. García in the morning and ask him how he is.
2. You thank Miss Vera for a favor and tell her you will see her tomorrow.
3. You greet Mrs. Nieto in the afternoon and ask her to come in and sit down.
4. Professor Maria Rivas says **mucho gusto** to you. You reply.
5. Someone thanks you for a favor. You reply.
6. Mr. Ortiz says he is not feeling well. You reply.

3. Days of the week

—¿**Qué día es hoy?**	*What day is it today?*
—**Hoy es lunes.**	*Today is Monday.*
—**Hoy es martes, ¿no?**	*Today is Tuesday, isn't it?*
—**No, hoy es miércoles.**	*No, today is Wednesday.*
—¿**Qué día es hoy?**	*What day is it today?*
¿**Jueves?**	*Thursday?*
—**No, hoy es viernes.**	*No, today is Friday.*
—**Hoy es... sábado... ¡no!**	*Today is . . . Saturday . . .*
domingo...	*no! Sunday . . .*
—**Sí, hoy es domingo.**	*Yes, today is Sunday.*

Los días de la semana (*The days of the week*)

lunes[1]	*Monday*	**viernes**	*Friday*
martes	*Tuesday*	**sábado**	*Saturday*
miércoles	*Wednesday*	**domingo**	*Sunday*
jueves	*Thursday*		

ATENCIÓN: In Spanish, the days of the week are masculine: *el viernes, los sábados.* They are not capitalized.

---

[1] In Spanish calendars, the week starts with Monday.

Práctica

The people asking the following questions are always a day ahead. Tell them the correct day.

Modelo: —Hoy es lunes, ¿no?
      —**No, hoy es domingo.**

1. Hoy es miércoles, ¿no?
2. Hoy es domingo, ¿no?
3. Hoy es viernes, ¿no?
4. Hoy es martes, ¿no?
5. Hoy es sábado, ¿no?
6. Hoy es jueves, ¿no?

4. Cardinal numbers (30–200)

30 treinta	80 ochenta
31 treinta y uno	90 noventa
32 treinta y dos...	100 cien (ciento)
40 cuarenta	101 ciento uno...
50 cincuenta	150 ciento cincuenta...
60 sesenta	200 doscientos
70 setenta	

ATENCIÓN: **Ciento** becomes **cien** before a noun.

cien telegramas
cien casas

Remember that **uno** becomes **un** before a masculine noun and **una** before a feminine noun, even in compound numbers:

ciento **un** telegramas
ciento **una** sillas

Práctica

Read the following numbers aloud in Spanish:

33	48	57	123	30	69	74
80	91	100	65	111	123	200
197	136	115	175	169	185	101

5. Months and seasons of the year

Los meses del año (*The months of the year*)

enero	*January*	**mayo**	*May*
febrero	*February*	**junio**	*June*
marzo	*March*	**julio**	*July*
abril	*April*	**agosto**	*August*

septiembre	*September*	**noviembre**	*November*
octubre	*October*	**diciembre**	*December*

ATENCIÓN: The names of the months are not capitalized in Spanish.

◆ When asking the date, say:

—¿**Qué fecha es hoy?**	*What's the date today?*
—**Hoy es el quince de enero.**	*Today is January fifteenth.*
—¿**Hoy es el primero de mayo?**	*Is today May first?*
—**No, hoy es el dos de mayo.**	*No, today is May second.*

ATENCIÓN: Spanish uses cardinal numbers to refer to dates. The only exception is **primero** (*first*).

◆ When telling the date, always begin with the expression **Hoy es el...** :

Hoy es el veinte de mayo.   *Today is May twentieth.*

◆ Complete the expression by saying the number followed by the preposition **de** (*of*), and then the month:

el **quince de mayo**   *May 15th*
el **diez de septiembre**   *September 10th*
el **doce de octubre**   *October 12th*

ATENCIÓN: Notice that the number precedes the month. Thus, 3–6–92 means June 3rd, 1992. In Spanish, the article is usually included when giving the date orally, although it is sometimes omitted in writing.

Las estaciones del año (*The seasons of the year*)

la **primavera**	*spring*	el **verano**	*summer*
el **otoño**	*fall*	el **invierno**	*winter*

Práctica

A. The following are important dates to remember. Say them in Spanish:

1. the 4th of July
2. the 31st of October
3. March 21st
4. April 1st
5. the first of January
6. February 14th

7. December 25th
8. June 20th
9. your birthday
10. today's date

B. In which season are the following months?

1. febrero *invierno*
2. agosto *verano*
3. mayo *primavera*
4. enero *invierno*
5. octubre *otoño*
6. julio *verano*
7. abril *primavera*
8. noviembre *invierno*

Información personal

Provide the information requested.

Apellido y nombres	Fecha de nacimiento		
BOYD MARIA	DÍA	MES	AÑO

Dirección

P.O. Box 5748, SNOWMASS VILLAGE CO 8165

Teléfono

303 923 2719

Estado civil — Sexo — Edad

1. ____ soltero(a)   Masculino ____   ____
2. _X_ casado(a)   Femenino _X_
3. ____ divorciado(a)
4. ____ viudo(a)
5. ____ separado(a)

Nacionalidad CANADIANA

Ocupación CONSULTAR

Lugar donde trabaja en mi casa

Número de seguro social 009 36 8768

Número de la licencia para conducir license #

Lección

1

Vocabulario

COGNADOS

la **cafetería** cafeteria	el **restaurante** restaurant
el **italiano** Italian (*language*)	

NOMBRES

la **cerveza** beer	el **mantel** tablecloth
la **cuchara** spoon	el **refresco** soft drink, soda
el **francés** French (*language*)	la **servilleta** napkin
el **inglés** English (*language*)	el **tenedor** fork

VERBOS

desear to want, to desire	**necesitar** to need
estudiar to study	**tomar** to drink
hablar to speak, to talk	**trabajar** to work

querer- to want, to desire

OTRAS PALABRAS Y EXPRESIONES

en in, at	**sí** yes
pero but	

1. Subject pronouns

> **Subject**   a noun or noun substitute about which something is said in a sentence or phrase: **Mary** works. **The car** is new.
> **Pronoun**   a word that replaces a noun: **she, them, us, it**
> **Subject pronoun**   a personal pronoun that is used as a subject: **They** work.

Singular		*Plural*	
yo	I	{ **nosotros** we (*masculine*)	
		{ **nosotras** we (*feminine*)	
tú	you (*familiar*)	**ustedes**[2] you	
usted[1]	you (*formal*)		
él	he	**ellos**	they (*masculine*)
ella	she	**ellas**	they (*feminine*)

[1] Abbreviated **Ud.**
[2] Abbreviated **Uds.**

◆ The masculine plural pronoun may refer to the masculine gender alone or to both genders together:

Juan y Roberto: **ellos**	*John and Robert:* ***they***
Juan y María: **ellos**	*John and Mary:* ***they***

◆ Use the **tú** form as the equivalent of *you* when addressing a close friend, a relative, or a child. Use the **usted** form in all other instances. Notice that **ustedes** is used for both familiar and polite plural.

Práctica

Complete the following sentences with the appropriate subject pronoun:

Modelo: You refer to *Mr. Smith* as . . . **él**

1. You point to yourself and say . *yo*
2. You refer to Mrs. Smith as . *ella*
3. You are talking to a little boy and you call him . *tu*
4. You are talking to a woman you've just met and you call her . *Usted or tu.   TU is more commonly used.*
5. Your mother refers to herself and her sister as *nosotras*
6. Your father refers to himself and his sister as *nosotros*
7. You are talking to a few people and you call them *ellos*
8. You refer to Mr. Smith and his daughter as *ellos*
9. You refer to Mrs. Smith and her daughter as *ellas*
10. You refer to Mr. and Mrs. Smith as . *ellos*
11. You are talking with one of your professors and you call him . *usted*
12. You are talking with one of your friends and you call her . *tu*

2. The present indicative of regular -ar verbs

> **Verb**   a word that expresses an action or a state: We **sleep.** The baby **is** sick.
> **Infinitive**   the form of a verb showing no subject or number, generally preceded in English by the word *to*: **to do, to bring**

The infinitive of all Spanish verbs consists of a stem (such as **habl-**) and an ending (such as **-ar**). When looking up a verb in the dictionary, you will always find it listed under the infinitive (*e.g.,* **hablar:**

to speak). Spanish verbs are classified according to their endings. There are three conjugations: **-ar**, **-er**, and **-ir**. The stem does not change; the endings change with the subjects. Regular verbs ending in **-ar** are conjugated like **hablar**.

Hablar (to speak)

	Singular	
	Stem	*Ending*
yo	habl- **o**	Yo **hablo** español.[1]
tú	habl- **as**	Tú **hablas** español.
Ud.	habl- **a**	Ud. **habla** español.
él	habl- **a**	Juan **habla** español. Él **habla** español.
ella	habl- **a**	Ana **habla** español. Ella **habla** español.
	Plural	
nosotros	habl- **amos**	Nosotros **hablamos** español.
Uds.	habl- **an**	Uds. **hablan** español.
ellos	habl- **an**	Ellos **hablan** español.
ellas	habl- **an**	Ellas **hablan** español.

♦ The present tense in Spanish is equivalent to three forms in English:

Yo **hablo** italiano.
$$\begin{cases} \textit{I speak Italian.} \\ \textit{I do speak Italian.} \\ \textit{I am speaking Italian.} \end{cases}$$

♦ Since the verb endings indicate who the speaker is, the subject pronouns are frequently omitted:

—**Hablas** inglés, ¿no?   *You (familiar) speak English, don't you?*

—Sí, **hablo** inglés.   *Yes, I speak English.*

However, subject pronouns may be used for emphasis or clarification:

—**Ellos hablan** inglés, ¿no?   *They speak English, don't they?*

—**Ella habla** inglés.   *She speaks English.*
Él habla español.   *He speaks Spanish.*

---

[1] Names of languages and nationalities are not capitalized in Spanish.

◆ Some common verbs that follow the regular **-ar** pattern are:

desear   to want, to wish   **tomar**   to drink
estudiar   to study   **trabajar**   to work
necesitar   to need

—El señor Paz **trabaja** en
 una cafetería, ¿no?
—No, él **trabaja** en un
 restaurante.

*Mr. Paz works at a cafete-
 ria, doesn't he?*
*No, he works at a restau-
 rant.*

—Ud. **desea** una cerveza,
 ¿no?
—Sí, y ella **desea** tomar[1]
 un refresco.

*You want a beer, don't
 you?*
*Yes, and she wants to drink
 a soda.*

—Ud. **necesita** el mantel,
 ¿no?
—Sí, **necesito** el mantel y
 las servilletas.

*You need the tablecloth,
 don't you?*
*Yes, I need the tablecloth
 and the napkins.*

—Uds. **estudian** francés
 en la universidad, ¿no?
—No, pero **estudiamos**
 inglés.

*You study French at the
 university, don't you?*
No, but we study English.

ATENCIÓN: When speaking about a third person (indirect address)
and using a title with the last name, the definite article is
placed before the title (***El señor Paz habla español.***) It is not
used when speaking directly to someone (**Buenos días, *señor
Paz*.**).

Práctica

A. Form sentences that tell where these people work, what they
study and what they need:

trabajar: yo / un restaurante
        Anita / la cafetería
        tú / Los Ángeles
        nosotros / la universidad
estudiar: Uds. / francés
        Carlos / italiano
        Ud. / la lección dos
        él y yo / español
necesitar: Ana y Rosa / dinero
        nosotras / una mesa
        yo / los lápices
        tú / una servilleta

[1] When two verbs are used together, the second verb is in the infinitive.

> **desear:** ellos / una cerveza
> nosotros / un refresco
> yo / tomar una Coca Cola
> Elsa / estudiar inglés

B. Provide the missing information about yourself and other people:

1. Ella trabaja en Los Ángeles y yo...
2. Carlos estudia italiano y nosotros...
3. Yo necesito una pluma y tú...
4. Nosotros hablamos inglés y el profesor...
5. Tú y yo trabajamos en la cafetería y ellos...
6. Tú tomas refrescos y yo...
7. María necesita sillas y nosotros...
8. Ellos hablan francés y yo...
9. Ella toma cerveza y Uds...
10. Yo deseo estudiar francés y ellos...

3. Interrogative sentences

There are three ways of asking a question in Spanish to elicit a *yes /
no* answer. These three questions ask for the same information and
have the same meaning.

1. ¿**Ustedes** necesitan dinero?
2. ¿Necesitan **ustedes** dinero?   Sí, nosotros necesitamos
3. ¿Necesitan dinero **ustedes**?   dinero.

♦ Example 1 is a declarative sentence that is made interrogative
by a change in intonation:

Ustedes necesitan dinero.   ¿Ustedes necesitan dinero?

♦ Example 2 is an interrogative sentence formed by placing the
subject (**ustedes**) after the verb.

♦ Example 3, another interrogative sentence, is formed by
placing the subject (**ustedes**) at the end of the sentence.

ATENCIÓN: An auxiliary verb such as *do* or *does* is not used in
Spanish to form an interrogative sentence:

¿Ustedes necesitan dinero?
(Do)   you   need   money?

Notice that in Spanish interrogative sentences have a
question mark at the end and an inverted question mark at
the beginning.

Práctica

Using the model as an example, ask the following questions in two other ways:

Modelo: ¿**Elena** trabaja en Buenos Aires?
¿Trabaja **Elena** en Buenos Aires?
¿Trabaja en Buenos Aires **Elena?**

1. ¿Tú tomas cerveza?
2. ¿Ella estudia inglés?
3. ¿Uds. hablan español?
4. ¿Pedro necesita el mantel?
5. ¿Tú trabajas en California?
6. ¿Ud. desea tomar un refresco?

4. Negative sentences

To make a sentence negative, simply place the word **no** in front of the verb.

Ella	habla inglés.	*She*		*speaks English.*
Ella **no**	habla inglés.	*She doesn't speak English.*		

ATENCIÓN: Spanish does not use an auxiliary verb such as the English *do* or *does* in a negative sentence.

♦   If the answer to a question is negative, the word **no** appears twice: at the beginning of the sentence, as in English, and also in front of the verb.

¿Necesitas las cucharas?   *Do you need the spoons?*
No, (yo) **no** necesito las   *No, I don't need the spoons;*
cucharas; necesito los   *I need the forks.*
tenedores.

ATENCIÓN: The subject pronoun need not appear in the answer because the verb ending identifies the speaker.

Práctica

Using the information provided in parentheses, answer the following questions in the negative:

Modelo: —¿Ud. trabaja en un restaurante? (cafetería)
—**No,** (yo) **no trabajo en un restaurante; trabajo en una cafetería.**

1. ¿Uds. necesitan los tenedores?   (cucharas)
2. ¿Tú estudias francés?   (español)

3. ¿Hablan italiano en París?   (francés)
4. ¿Trabaja en la cafetería el profesor?   (la universidad)
5. ¿Estudian la lección dos?   (lección tres)
6. ¿Ellas toman cerveza?   (refresco)

5. Cardinal numbers (300–1000)

300 trescientos	700 setecientos
400 cuatrocientos	800 ochocientos
500 quinientos *Keenee-evdos*	900 novecientos
600 seiscientos	1,000 mil[1]

When counting in Spanish beyond a thousand, do not count in hundreds. After a thousand, the numbers are represented thus: **dos mil, tres mil, catorce mil,** etc. Notice that a period is used instead of a comma:

1.987   **mil novecientos ochenta y siete**

Práctica

Read the following numbers aloud in Spanish:

896	380	519	937	722
1.305	451	978	643	504
1.000	15.893	11.906	27.567	565.736

---

[1] Notice that the indefinite article is not used before the word **mil.**

En el laboratorio

LECCIÓN 1

The following material is to be used with the tape in the language laboratory.

I. Vocabulario

Repeat each word after the speaker. When repeating words that are cognates, notice the difference in pronunciation between English and Spanish.

COGNADOS:	la cafetería el italiano el restaurante
NOMBRES:	la cerveza la cuchara el francés el inglés el mantel el refresco la servilleta el tenedor
VERBOS:	estudiar desear hablar necesitar trabajar tomar
OTRAS PALABRAS Y EXPRESIONES:	en pero sí

Read the following numbers in Spanish. Repeat the correct answer after the speaker's confirmation. Listen to the model:

Modelo: 1581
      Mil quinientos ochenta y uno.

1. 322	6. 878	11. 5.873
2. 430	7. 985	12. 9.108
3. 547	8. 1.000	13. 12.920
4. 659	9. 543	14. 15.008
5. 761	10. 2.715	15. 23.192

II. Práctica

A. Repeat each sentence, then substitute the new subject given by the speaker.

Be sure the verbs agree with the new subject. Repeat the correct answer after the speaker's confirmation.

Modelo: Yo estudio español.
      Nosotros estudiamos español.

1. Yo estudio español. (nosotros / Ud. / ellos)
2. Ella trabaja en la cafetería. (Yo / Uds. / tú)

3. Tú necesitas dinero. (Él / nosotros / ellas)
4. Nosotros tomamos refrescos. (Tú / Elsa / yo)

B. Change each sentence to the interrogative form by placing the subject at the end of the sentence. Repeat the correct answer after the speaker's confirmation. Listen to the model.

Modelo: —Teresa necesita dinero.
            —**¿Necesita dinero Teresa?**

1. La señora López estudia inglés.
2. El señor Vega habla francés.
3. La señorita Díaz necesita los tenedores.
4. Uds. trabajan en el restaurante.
5. Tú deseas estudiar francés.

C. Change each of the following sentences to the negative. Repeat the correct answer after the speaker's confirmation. Listen to the model.

Modelo: —Yo hablo inglés.
            —Yo **no hablo** inglés.

1. Eva y Luis hablan español.
2. Nosotros estudiamos en la universidad.
3. Ella trabaja en un restaurante.
4. Yo necesito una cuchara.
5. Tú tomas cerveza.
6. Uds. desean trabajar en un restaurante.

III. Para escuchar y entender

1. Listen carefully to the dialogue. It will be read twice.

   (*Diálogo 1*)

   Now the speaker will make statements about the dialogue you just heard. Tell whether each statement is true (**verdadero**) or false (**falso**). The speaker will confirm the correct answer.

2. Listen carefully to the dialogue. It will be read twice.

   (*Diálogo 2*)

   Now the speaker will ask some questions about the dialogue you just heard. Answer each question, omitting the subject. The speaker will confirm the correct answer. Repeat the correct answer.

Capítulo

Lección

2

Vocabulario

COGNADOS

la **compañía** company	el **museo** museum
el **cheque** check	el **taxi** taxi
el, la **estudiante** student	el **té** tea
inteligente intelligent	el **teatro** theater

NOMBRES

la leña - firewood

el **café** coffee	el **muchacho** young man,
la **carpeta** folder	boy
la **muchacha** young woman,	el **ómnibus, autobús** bus
girl	*el camión*

VERBOS

leer
leo
lees
lee
leemos
leen

when to use which? no rule

Tomar —

entender (simple terms)

entiendo
entiendes
entiende
entendemos
entienden
(See page 94) for other stem verbs)

abrir to open	**esperar** to wait for, *hope*
aprender to learn	**leer** to read
beber to drink	**llamar** to call
comer to eat *more complicated*	**recibir** to receive
comprender to understand	**tomar** to take (*e.g.*, a bus)
decidir to decide	**visitar** to visit
escribir to write	**vivir** to live

ADJETIVOS

alemán (alemana) German	**grande** big
alto(a) tall	**guapo(a)** handsome
azul blue	**negro(a)** black
blanco(a) white	**rojo(a)** red
español(a) Spanish	**verde** green
feliz happy	

OTRAS PALABRAS Y EXPRESIONES

pronunciation?   Kee-en

¿dónde? where	**siempre** always
o or	**tarde** late
¿qué? what	**temprano** early
¿quién? who?, whom?	

1. Position of adjectives

Adjective   a word that modifies a noun or a pronoun: **tall** girl, **difficult** lesson

♦ Descriptive adjectives (such as adjectives of color, size, etc.) generally follow the noun in Spanish:

el libro **rojo**   *the red book*
la casa **grande**   *the big house*

la carpeta **azul**   *the blue folder*
el muchacho **guapo**   *the handsome young man*
el hombre **alto**   *the tall man*

♦ Adjectives denoting nationality always follow the noun:

el profesor **norteamericano**   *the North American professor*

♦ Other kinds of adjectives (possessive, demonstrative, numerical, etc.) precede the noun, as in English:

cinco lápices   *five pencils*
mi cheque   *my check*

—¿Necesitan Uds. los   *Do you need the red pen-*
    lápices **rojos**?   *cils?*
—No, necesitamos los **tres**   *No, we need the three black*
    lápices **negros**.   *pencils.*

Práctica

How would you say the following phrases in Spanish?

1. the blue pencil
2. the big city
3. the American doctor
4. fifteen chairs
5. the red book
6. the handsome man
7. my table
8. the tall young woman

2. Forms of adjectives

Adjectives whose masculine singular form ends in **-o** have four
forms, ending in **-o, -a, -os, -as**. Most other adjectives have only two
forms, a singular and a plural. Like nouns, adjectives are made
plural by adding **-s, -es**, or by changing **z** to **c** and adding **-es**.

Singular		Plural	
Masculine	*Feminine*	*Masculine*	*Feminine*
negro (*black*)	negra	negros	negras
inteligente	inteligente	inteligentes	inteligentes
feliz (*happy*)	feliz	felices	felices
verde (*green*)	verde	verdes	verdes

♦ Adjectives of ⟨nationality⟩ that end in a consonant are made feminine by adding -a to the masculine singular form:

español   española
alemán   alemana
inglés   inglesa

(neutral)   canadiense

—¿Dónde trabaja Elsa?   *Where does Elsa work?*
—Trabaja en una   *She works at a German*
    compañía **alemana**.   *company.*

Práctica

Match the items in column A with those in column B.

A		B
1. señor _c_		a. rojos
2. mesa _d_		b. inteligentes ·
3. señoritas _b_		c. español
4. libros _a_		d. negra
5. hombres _f_		e. alta
6. señora _e_		f. guapos

◢3. Agreement of articles, adjectives, and nouns

Agreement the correspondence in number and gender between an adjective and the noun that it modifies

In Spanish the article, the noun, and the adjective agree in number and gender:

la silla blanca   *the white chair*
el libro blanco   *the white book*
las sillas blancas   *the white chairs*
los libros blancos   *the white books*

Práctica

Make the adjectives agree with the nouns in the list and add the corresponding definite article:

1. _la_ mesa   negra   2. _el_ muchacho inteligente
   _el_ libro   _negro_   _los_ muchachos _es_
   las sillas   _negras_   _la_ muchacha _"_
   les lápices   _negros_   _las_ muchachas _"_

3. _el_ señor español 4. _la_ mujer feliz
   los señores _es_   _el_ hombre _'_
   las señoras _as_   _las_ mujeres _'ces_
   _la_ señora _a_   _los_ hombres _'' ces_

4. The present indicative of regular -er and -ir verbs

Regular verbs ending in **-er** are conjugated like **comer**. Regular verbs ending in **-ir** are conjugated like **vivir**.

comer (to eat)		*vivir* (to live)	
yo	com- **o**	yo	viv- **o**
tú	com- **es**	tú	viv- **es**
Ud. él ella	com- **e**	Ud. él ella	viv- **e**
nosotros	com- **emos**	nosotros	viv- **imos**
Uds. ellos ellas	com- **en**	Uds. ellos ellas	viv- **en**

◆ Some other common verbs that follow the same **-er** and **-ir** patterns are: **beber** (*to drink*), **aprender** (*to learn*), **leer** (*to read*), **comprender** (*to understand*), **escribir** (*to write*), **abrir** (*to open*), **recibir** (*to receive*), and **decidir** (*to decide*).

—¿Tú **bebes** café o té? Do you drink coffee or tea?
—**Bebo** café. I drink coffee.

—¿**Comen** Uds. temprano? Do you eat early?
—No, **comemos** tarde. No, we eat late.

—¿Dónde **vive** Ud.? Where do you live?
—**Vivo** en la calle Unión. I live on Union Street.

—¿**Escribe** el profesor en español? Does the professor write in Spanish?
—Sí, **escribe** en español. Yes, he writes in Spanish.

Práctica

A. Conjugate the verbs using the subjects provided:

    1. Yo no como temprano. (nosotros, Uds., Ana, tú, Ud.)
    2. Eva escribe un cheque. (Ud., ellos, yo, nosotros, tú)

B. I will tell you what *I* do; tell me what everyone else does:

Modelo: Yo bebo café. (Elsa)
          Elsa bebe té.

    1. Yo no comprendo la lección dos. (nosotros)
    2. Yo vivo en la calle Magnolia. (Alberto)
    3. Yo como temprano. (Adela)
    4. Yo escribo con una pluma verde. (Marta y Rosa)
    5. Yo bebo refrescos. (nosotras)
    6. Yo leo en español. (Alina)
    7. Yo recibo veinte pesos. (ellos) *reciban*
    8. Yo decido estudiar inglés. (Ana y yo)
    9. Yo abro la carpeta. (él)
   10. Yo aprendo inglés. (los estudiantes)

5. The personal a

In Spanish, as in English, a verb has a subject and may have one or more objects. The function of the object is to complete the idea expressed by the verb.

    In English, the direct object cannot be separated from the verb by a preposition: *She killed **the burglar**. He sees **the nurse**.* In the preceding sentences, *the burglar* and *the nurse* are direct objects.

    In Spanish, the preposition "**a**" must be used before a direct object that refers to a definite person. This preposition is called "the personal **a**" and has no equivalent in English:

Yo visito **a** Carmen.
I visit   Carmen.

◆ The personal **a** is not used when the direct object is not a person.

—¿Visitan Uds. **a** Rafael?	*Are you visiting Rafael?*
—No, visitamos **a** Pedro.	*No, we are visiting Pedro.*
—¿Visitan los estudiantes el museo o el teatro?	*Are the students visiting the museum or the theater?*
—Visitan el museo.	*They are visiting the museum.*

—¿A quién llama Ud.?   *Whom are you calling?*
—Llamo **a** la profesora.   *I'm calling the professor.*

—¿Desea llamar un taxi?   *Do you want to take a taxi?*
—No, siempre tomo el   *No, I always take the bus.*
   ómnibus. autobús o
            camión

Práctica

A Spanish-speaking friend needs you as an interpreter. How would you say the following in Spanish?

1. We wish to call the professor. (*fem.*)
2. What are the students visiting? The theater?
3. They want to call a taxi.
4. Who visits Mary?
5. We always take the bus.

1. Queremos llamar a la profesora.
2. ¿Visitan los estudiantes el teatro? ¿Qué visitan los estudiantes? ¿El teatro?
3. Quieren llamar un taxi.
4. ¿Quién visita a María? ¿Quiénes visitan a María?
5. Siempre tomamos el camión.

En el laboratorio

LECCIÓN 2

The following material is to be used with the tape in the language laboratory.

I. Vocabulario

Repeat each word after the speaker. When repeating words that are cognates, notice the difference in pronunciation between English and Spanish.

COGNADOS:	la compañía el cheque el estudiante inteligente el museo el taxi el té el teatro
NOMBRES:	el café la carpeta el muchacho el ómnibus el autobús
VERBOS:	abrir aprender beber comer comprender decidir escribir esperar leer llamar recibir tomar visitar vivir
ADJETIVOS:	alemán alto azul blanco español feliz grande guapo negro rojo verde
OTRAS PALABRAS Y EXPRESIONES:	¿dónde? o ¿qué? ¿quién? siempre tarde temprano

II. Práctica

A. Change each of the following phrases according to the new clue. Repeat the correct answer after the speaker's confirmation. Listen to the model:

Modelo: un señor español   (señorita)
una señorita española

1. (libros)	6. (estudiantes)
2. (sillas)	7. (profesora)
3. (señora)	8. (ciudad)
4. (lápiz)	9. (muchacho)
5. (libro)	10. (hombres)

B. Answer the questions, always using the second choice. Omit the subject. Repeat the correct answer after the speaker's confirmation. Listen to the model:

Modelo: —¿Ana vive en la calle Cinco o en la calle Siete?
          —**Vive en la calle Siete.**

C. Answer the questions, using the cues provided. Remember to use the personal **a,** when needed. Repeat the correct answer after the speaker's confirmation. Listen to the model.

Modelo: —¿A quién visitas? (Rosa)
          —**Visito a Rosa.**

  1. (el museo)
  2. (la señora Vega)
  3. (el ómnibus)
  4. (dinero)
  5. (la profesora)

III. Para escuchar y entender

1. Listen carefully to the dialogue. It will be read twice.

(*Diálogo 1*)

Now the speaker will make statements about the dialogue you just heard. Tell whether each statement is true (**verdadero**) or false (**falso**). The speaker will confirm the correct answer.

2. Listen carefully to the dialogue. It will be read twice.

(*Diálogo 2*)

Now the speaker will make statements about the dialogue you just heard. Tell whether each statement is true (**verdadero**) or false (**falso**). The speaker will confirm the correct answer.

3. Listen carefully to the dialogue. It will be read twice.

(*Diálogo 3*)

Now the speaker will ask some questions about the dialogue you just heard. Answer each question, omitting the subject. The speaker will confirm the correct answer. Repeat the correct answer.

Lección

3

Vocabulario

COGNADOS

argentino(a) Argentinian
el **auto, automóvil** car, automobile
el **hospital** hospital
el **hotel** hotel

el, la **ingeniero(a)** engineer
el **metal** metal
la **profesión** profession
el, la **recepcionista**[1] receptionist

NOMBRES
la **abuela** grandmother
el **abuelo** grandfather
el (la) **amigo(a)** friend
la **biblioteca** library
el **cuaderno** notebook
los **Estados Unidos** United States
la **fiesta** party
la **hija** daughter
el **hijo** son
la **madera** wood
la **mamá (madre)** mom, mother
la **novia** girlfriend
el **novio** boyfriend
el **papá (padre)**[2] dad, father
el (la) **primo(a)** cousin
la **sobrina** niece
el **sobrino** nephew

VERBOS
dar to give
deber must, should

estar to be
ir to go
ser to be

ADJETIVOS
bonito(a) pretty
difícil difficult
enfermo(a) sick
fácil easy

OTRAS PALABRAS Y EXPRESIONES
a to
¿a dónde? where to?
ahora now
¿cómo? how?
¿cómo es? what is he (she) like?
¿con quién? with whom?
¿cuál? what, which (one)?
de of, from
¿de dónde? where from?
¿de quién? whose?
muy very

[1] For nouns ending in **-ista,** change only the article to indicate gender.
[2] **padres** parents

1. The present indicative of ser

The verb **ser** (*to be*) is an irregular verb. Its forms are not like the forms of regular -er verbs.

The Verb SER		
yo	**soy**	I am
tú	**eres**	you are (*familiar*)
Ud.		you are (*formal*)
él	**es**	he is
ella		she is
nosotros	**somos**	we are
Uds.		you are
ellos	**son**	they are (*masculine*)
ellas		they are (*feminine*)

—¿De dónde **son** tus abuelos?	*Where are your grandparents from?*
—Mi abuelo **es** de México y mi abuela **es** de Cuba.	*My grandfather is from Mexico and my grandmother is from Cuba.*
—¿**Es** difícil la lección?	*Is the lesson difficult?*
—No, **es** fácil.	*No, it's easy.*
—¿De dónde **eres** tú?	*Where are you from?*
—Yo **soy** de Buenos Aires.	*I'm from Buenos Aires.*
—¿**Son** Uds. norteamericanos?	*Are you North American?*
—Sí, **somos** norteamericanos.	*Yes, we are North American.*

Práctica

A. Using the verb **ser**, complete the following conversations.

1. —¿De dónde _eres_ tú, Anita?
   —_Soy_ de Buenos Aires. ¿De dónde _es_ Ud., señora?
   —Yo _soy_ de Montevideo.
2. —¿Uds. _son_ norteamericanos?
   —Sí, _somos_ de California.
3. —¿_Son_ muy difíciles las lecciones?
   —La lección dos _es_ fácil...
4. —¿Qué día _es_ hoy?
   —Hoy _es_ miércoles.

B. Answer the following questions using complete sentences.

1. ¿Qué fecha es hoy?
2. ¿De dónde es Ud.?
3. ¿Es fácil o difícil la clase de español?
4. ¿Uds. son norteamericanos?
5. ¿De dónde es el profesor (la profesora) de español?

2. Possession with de

De + *noun* is used to express possession or relationship in Spanish; the apostrophe is not used:

Alberto's son
el hijo **de** Alberto
(*the son of Alberto*)

ATENCIÓN: Notice the use of the definite article before the word **hijo**.

—¿Con quién estudias?   *With whom do you study?*

—Estudio con **el** primo **de** Ana.   *I study with Ana's cousin.*

—¿De quién es la carpeta azul?   *To whom does the blue folder belong?*

—Es **la** carpeta **de** María.   *It's Maria's folder.*

Práctica

How would you say the following in Spanish?

1. He is Isabel's son.
2. Mary's house is white.
3. Carmen's cousin is from Mexico.
4. The students' books are blue.
5. Ana's cousin is very handsome.
6. Mrs. Vega's phone number is 732–4651.
7. The boy's last name is Sánchez.
8. I need Miss Soto's address.

3. Possessive adjectives

Possessive   a word that denotes ownership or possession: **our** house, **their** mother

Forms of the Possessive Adjectives

Singular	Plural	
mi	mis	my
tu	tus	your (*familiar*)
su	sus	his her its your their
nuestro(a)	nuestros(as)	our

Possessive adjectives agree in number with the nouns they modify:

—¿Necesita Ud. **mi** cuaderno?   *Do you need my notebook?*

—No, no necesito **su** cuaderno.   *No, I don't need your notebook.*

—¿Necesita Ud. **mis** cuadernos?   *Do you need my notebooks?*

—No, no necesito **sus** cuadernos.   *No, I don't need your notebooks.*

ATENCIÓN: These forms of the possessive adjectives always precede the nouns they introduce and are never stressed.

[handwritten: Necesito sus llaves. ¿De quién? De ustedes.]

♦ Since both **su** and **sus** may have different meanings, the form **de él (de ella, de ellos, de ellas, de Ud., de Uds.)** may be substituted to avoid confusion:

—¿Con quién hablan Uds.?   *With whom are you talking?*

—Hablamos con **su** amigo.   *We are talking with his (or her, your, their) friend.*

[handwritten: con amigo de usted]

—Hablamos con el amigo **de Ud.**   *We are talking with your friend.*

—¿Estudia con **mi** libro?   *Are you studying with my book?*

[handwritten: con]

—No, estudio con el libro **de ella.**   *No, I'm studying with her book.*

♦ **Nuestro** is the only possessive adjective that has the feminine endings **-a, -as.** The others use the same endings for both the masculine and feminine genders:

—¿Con quién debemos hablar?   *With whom should we speak?*

—Debemos hablar con **nuestras** sobrinas.   *We should speak with our nieces.*

Práctica

Fill in the blanks with the appropriate form of the possessive adjective in Spanish. Whenever **su** (**sus**) is required, give the alternate form with **de**:

Modelo: (his) _su_ silla   o la silla de él
su silla / la silla de él

1. (my) _mis_ carpetas
2. (his) _su_ abuela / _la_ abuela _de él_
3. (our) _nuestra_ casa
4. (her) _su_ idioma / _el_ idioma _de ella_
5. (your—Ud.) _su_ dinero /
_el_ dinero _de usted_
6. (my) _mi_ cuaderno
7. (our) _nuestro_ mantel
8. (your—tú) _tu_ profesión
9. (your—Uds.) _sus_ sobrinos /
los sobrinos _de ustedes_.
10. (their—fem.) _sus_ lecciones /
las lecciones _de ellas_.

4. The irregular verbs ir, dar, and estar

	ir (to go)	dar (to give)	estar (to be)
yo	Voy (a el) centro **voy**	doy	estoy
tú	vas	das	estás
Ud.	Va a la casa de Jorge		
él	va	da	está
ella	Van a la fiesta		
nosotros / Uds.	**vamos** Vamos (a el) museo	damos	estamos
ellos	van a	dan	están
ellas			

A dónde vas?
A dónde va?
A dónde van?
A dónde vamos?

—¿A dónde va Ud.?   *Where are you going?*
—**Voy** a la biblioteca.   *I'm going to the library.*

—¿**Dan** Uds. dinero para   *Do you give money for the*
  las fiestas?   *parties?*
—Sí, **damos** dinero.   *Yes, we give money.*

—¿Dónde **está** tu novia?   *Where is your girlfriend?*
—**Está** en el hotel.   *She is at the hotel.*

Práctica

give

A. Use the present indicative of **ir, dar,** and **estar** to complete the following sentences:

1. Él __da__ su nombre y dirección.
2. Yo __voy__ a la biblioteca. Debo estudiar.
3. ¿Dónde __están__ mis libros?
4. Ud. __va__ a Los Ángeles con los hijos de él.
5. Ellos siempre __dan__ dinero.
6. Uds. __están__ en México.
7. Yo no __doy__ mi número de teléfono.
8. Nosotras __vamos__ a la casa de nuestros primos. *our cousins' house*
9. ¿__Está__ Ud. en el hotel?
10. Yo __estoy__ en el hospital.

B. Tell something about yourself by answering the following questions:

1. ¿Ud. está en la universidad?
2. ¿Dónde está su profesor(a)? *whose professor? el profesor de ella, de él, de usted*
3. ¿Dónde están sus libros? *(de quién?) de ud.*
4. ¿A dónde va Ud. los viernes?
5. ¿Con quién va?
6. ¿Ud. va a la biblioteca los sábados?
7. ¿Van Uds. a la universidad los domingos?
8. ¿Ud. da su número de teléfono?

5. Uses of the verbs ser and estar

Although both **ser** and **estar** are equivalent to the English verb *to be*, they are not interchangeable. They are used to indicate the following:

Permanent ser	*estar Temporary*
1. Possession	1. Current condition (usually the product of a change)
2. Profession	2. Location
3. Nationality	
4. Origin	
5. Basic characteristics (color, shape, size, etc.)	
6. Marital status	
7. Expressions of time and dates	
8. Material (metal, wood, glass, etc.)	

possession —El auto **es** de Pedro, ¿no?   The car is Pedro's, isn't it?
—No, **es** de Juan.   No, it's Juan's.

profession —¿Cuál **es** la profesión de   What is your father's pro-
tu padre?   fession?
—**Es** ingeniero.   He is an engineer.

Basic characteristics —Elena **es** muy inteligente.   Elena is very intelligent.

origin —Ella **es** de la Argentina,   She's from Argentina, isn't
¿no?   she?

nationality —Sí, **es** argentina, pero   Yes, she's an Argentinian,
location ahora **está** en los   but now she's in the
Estados Unidos.   United States.

characteristics —¿Cómo **es** tu mamá?   What is your Mom like?
—**Es** muy bonita.   She's very pretty.

marital status —¿**Es** Ud. casada?   Are you married?
—No, **soy** soltera.   No, I am single.

time —¿Qué día **es** hoy?   What day is today?
—Hoy **es** martes.   Today is Tuesday.

material —¿**Es** de madera la mesa?   Is the table made of wood?
—No, **es** de metal.   No, it is made of metal.

Temp. cond. —¿Cómo **está** Ud.?   How are you?
—**Estoy** bien, gracias.   I am fine, thanks.

—¿Dónde **está** tu abuelo?   Where is your grandfather?
location —**Está** en el hospital.   He is in the hospital.
Temp. cond. **Está** enfermo.   He is sick.

Práctica

A. ¿**Ser** or **estar**? Which will it be?

1. —¿Cómo _es_ Amelia?
   —_Es_ muy inteligente y muy bonita.
   —¿De dónde _es_ ella?
   —_Es_ española, pero ahora _está_ en los Estados
   Unidos.
   —¿_Es_ soltera?
   —No, _es_ casada.
   —¿Hoy no trabaja?
   —No... , _está_ enferma.
2. —¿Las sillas _son_ de metal?
   —No, _son_ de madera.
   —¿_Son_ de Ernesto?
   —No, _son_ de Raquel.

3. —¿Cuál __es__ su profesión, señor Paz?
   —__Soy__ ingeniero.
4. —¿Cómo __son__ sus hijos?   ¿Como es tu abuelita?
   —__Son__ altos y guapos.   Es muy bonita y
5. —¿Qué fecha __es__ hoy?   muy vieja.
   —Hoy __es__ el veinte de mayo.
   —¿__es__ lunes?
   —No, hoy __es__ martes.

B. How would you say the following in Spanish?

Alberto is a very handsome young man. He's not an American; he's from Buenos Aires, but now he's in California. His father is an engineer and his mother is a doctor. He's single. Alberto studies at the University of California. Today he's at home (*en casa*); he is very sick.

C. Using **ser** or **estar**, provide the following information about yourself:

1. nationality and origin   Soy de Canada y soy canadiense.
2. profession (student)   Soy una consultora.
3. marital status   Soy casada
4. basic characteristics (*i.e.*: appearance, qualities)   Soy   mediana, soy
5. state of health   Estoy bien, no estoy enferma.   delgado o
6. location   Ahora, estoy en Colorado, en   no gordo.
        la cuidad   Estoy a gusto.
        pueblo de S.V.

de origin francés y irlandés

también rubia bondadosa

En el laboratorio

LECCIÓN 3

The following material is to be used with the tape in the language laboratory.

I. Vocabulario

Repeat each word after the speaker. When repeating words that are cognates, notice the difference in pronunciation between English and Spanish.

COGNADOS:	argentino el auto el automóvil el hospital el hotel el ingeniero el metal la profesión el recepcionista
NOMBRES:	la abuela el abuelo el amigo la biblioteca el cuaderno los Estados Unidos la fiesta la hija el hijo la madera la mamá la madre la novia el novio el papá el padre el primo la sobrina el sobrino
VERBOS:	dar deber estar ir ser
ADJETIVOS:	bonito difícil enfermo fácil
OTRAS PALABRAS Y EXPRESIONES:	a ¿a dónde? ahora ¿cómo? ¿cómo es? ¿con quién? ¿cuál? de ¿de dónde? ¿de quién? muy

II. Práctica

A. Using the cues provided, say to whom the following items belong. Repeat the correct answer after the speaker's confirmation. Listen to the model.

Modelo: —el libro (Susana)
        —Es el libro de Susana.

1. (Antonio) auto
2. (los estudiantes)
3. (Juan) amigo
4. (la profesora) cuadernos
5. (Estela) hija

B. Answer the questions, always selecting the second choice. Repeat the correct answer after the speaker. Listen to the model.

44

Modelo: —¿Tú eres de la Argentina o de los Estados Unidos?
—Soy de los Estados Unidos.

III. Para escuchar y entender

1. Listen carefully to the narration. It will be read twice.

   (*Narración 1*)

   Now the speaker will make statements about the narration you just heard. Tell whether each statement is true (**verdadero**) or false (**falso**). The speaker will confirm the correct answer.

2. Listen carefully to the narration. It will be read twice.

   (*Narración 2*)

   Now the speaker will make statements about the narration you just heard. Tell whether each statement is true (**verdadero**) or false (**falso**). The speaker will confirm the correct answer.

3. Listen carefully to the dialogue. It will be read twice.

   (*Diálogo*)

   Now the speaker will ask you some questions about the dialogue you just heard. Answer each question, omitting the subject. The speaker will confirm the correct answer. Repeat the correct answer.

Lección

4

Vocabulario

for physical / manual work

COGNADOS

la **clase** class	el, la **instructor(a)** instructor
el **diccionario** dictionary	el, la **supervisor(a)** supervisor

NOMBRES *not very commonly used*

la **chica** girl, young woman
el **chico** boy, young man
la **esposa** wife
el **esposo** husband
el (la) **gerente** manager
el **gimnasio** gym
la **habitación**, el **cuarto** room
el **mercado** market
la **pensión** boarding house
la **piscina** swimming pool *la alberca*
la **tienda** store

VERBOS
llegar to arrive *"j" sound*
tener to have
venir to come

ADJETIVOS
barato(a) cheap *, inexpensive*
bueno(a) good
cansado(a) tired

caro(a) expensive
malo(a) bad
mayor older, bigger
mejor better
menor younger, smaller
mucho(a) much
pequeño(a) small, little (*size*) *peke*
peor worse
poco(a) little (*quantity*)
solo(a) alone

OTRAS PALABRAS Y EXPRESIONES
¿a quién? to whom?
con with
¿cuándo? when?
¿cuántos(as) how many?
mal badly
más more
menos less
que than
también also, too

la muchacha
el muchacho

"y"

Contracciones

1. Contractions

> **Contraction** the combination of two or more words into one, with certain sounds or letters missing: **isn't, don't, can't, I'm**

In Spanish there are only two contractions: **al** and **del**.

♦ The preposition **de** (*of, from*) plus the article **el** is contracted to form **del**:

Leen los libros **de + el** profesor.   Leen los libros **del** profeso

♦ The preposition **a** (*to, toward*) or the personal **a** plus the article **el** is contracted to form **al**:

Esperamos **a + el** profesor.   Esperamos **al** profesor.

ATENCIÓN: None of the other combinations of preposition and definite article (**de la, de los, de las, a la, a los, a las**) is contracted.

—¿Llaman Uds. **al** gerente **del** hotel?

Are you calling the hotel manager?

—No, llamamos **a la** supervisora.

No, we're calling the supervisor.

—¿Vas **a la** tienda?

Are you going to the store?

—No, voy **al** mercado.

No, I'm going to the market.

—El diccionario es **del** profesor, ¿no?

The dictionary is the teacher's, isn't it?

—No, el diccionario es **de los** estudiantes.

No, the dictionary belongs to the students.

Práctica

Complete the sentences using one of the following: **de la, de las, del, de los, a la, a las, al, a los.**

1. Necesito los cuadernos _de los_ estudiantes.
2. El diccionario es _del_ profesor. *de la profesora (wrd "for").*
3. La casa es _de la_ señora Pérez.
4. Esperamos _al_ gerente y _a la_ supervisora.
5. ¿Cuándo vamos _al_ mercado?
6. Recibimos dinero _de la_ universidad.
7. ¿Llamas _a las_ profesoras _de los_ hijos _del_ señor Soto?
8. El gerente llama _a los_ chicos.

2. Comparison of adjectives and adverbs

♦ In Spanish, the comparative of most adjectives and adverbs is formed by placing **más** (*more*) or **menos** (*less*) before the adjective or the adverb and **que** after:

Ella es **más bonita** que Rosa.

*She is **prettier**[1] than Rosa.*

	más	*adjective*		
		or	+	**que**
	menos	*adverb*		

---

[1] The English comparative suffix *-er* is equivalent to **más**, which also means *more*.

In the above construction, **que** is equivalent to *than*.

—El hotel Azteca es **barato.**	*The Azteca hotel is inexpensive.*
—Sí, pero es **más caro que** el hotel Torres.	*Yes, but it is more expensive than the Torres hotel.*
—¿Quién llega **más tarde?** ¿Tú o ella?	*Who arrives later? You or she?*
—Ella llega **más tarde que** yo.	*She arrives later than I.*

Su coche es mas elegante que (el tuya) yours.
Soy mas inteligente que tú.

◆ In an equal comparison, **tan... como** is used:

$$\textbf{tan} + \begin{matrix} adjective \\ \text{or} \\ adverb \end{matrix} + \textbf{como}$$

Tan... como is equivalent to *as . . . as:*

—¿Está Ud. **tan** cansada **como** ellos?	*Are you as tired as they?*
—No, yo estoy menos cansada que ellos.	*No, I am less tired than they.*

◆ The superlative construction is similar to the comparative. It is formed by placing the definite article before the person or thing being compared; and substituting **de** for **que**:

Mas-de

$$\begin{matrix} definite \\ article \end{matrix} + noun + \textbf{más} + adjective + \textbf{de}$$

—¿Cuál es **la habitación más grande de** la pensión?	*Which one is the biggest room in the boarding house?*
—La habitación número 15.	*Room number 15.*

ATENCIÓN: After a superlative construction, *in* is expressed by **de** in Spanish. In many instances, the noun may not be expressed in a superlative.

—La habitación número 15 es **la más grande.**	*Room number 15 is the biggest (one).*

la verdura mas caro
la mujer es mas simpatico

Práctica

A. Complete the following sentences with the Spanish equivalent
of the words in parentheses:

1. El hotel Azteca es _____ la ciudad. (*the largest in*)
2. Rosa es _____ Marta. (*prettier than*)
3. El supervisor llega _____ ellos. (*as early as*)
4. Mis estudiantes son _____ Uds. (*less intelligent than*)
5. Mi hijo es _____ yo. (*as tall as*)
6. El gerente llega _____ Uds. (*later than*)
7. Es _____ libro. (*the most difficult lesson in the*)
8. Ella es _____ la universidad. (*the least intelligent
   student in*)
9. Ud. está _____ Rafael. (*less tired than*)
10. El hotel es _____ la pensión. (*more expensive than*)
11. Mi auto es _____ el auto de Juan. (*cheaper than*)
12. Elena es _____ (*the prettiest*)

B. Compare these people, places or things to each other.

Modelo: Vermont / California (pequeño)
    Vermont es **más pequeño que** California.

1. Texas / Rhode Island (grande)
2. tu amigo / tú (alto)
3. Tom Cruise (Kim Basinger) / yo (guapo / bonita)
4. Chile / Brasil (pequeño)
5. un Rolls Royce / un Ford (caro)

3. Irregular comparison of adjectives and adverbs

Adjectives		Adverbs		Comparative		Superlative	
bueno	good	**bien**	well	**mejor**	better	**el mejor**	the best
malo	bad	**mal**	badly	**peor**	worse	**el peor**	the worst
mucho	much	**mucho**	much	**más**	more	**el más**	the most
poco	little	**poco**	little	**menos**	less	**el menos**	the least
grande	big			**mayor**	bigger, older	**el mayor**	the biggest, oldest
pequeño	small			**menor**	smaller, younger	**el menor**	the smallest, youngest

ATENCIÓN: When the adjectives **grande** and **pequeño** refer to
size, the regular forms are generally used: **más grande** (*bigger*)
and **más pequeño** (*smaller*). When referring to age, the
irregular forms are used: **mayor** (*older*) and **menor** (*younger*).

—¿Quién estudia **más?** ¿Ud. o Marta?   *Who studies more? You or Marta?*

—Yo estudio **mucho,** pero Marta estudia **más.**   *I study a great deal, but Marta studies more.*

—¿Quién es **mayor?** ¿Ud. o Elsa?   *Who is older? You or Elsa?*

—Elsa. Ella es **la mayor** de la clase.   *Elsa. She is the oldest in the class.*

—¿Su esposo habla español tan **bien** como Ud.?   *Does your husband speak Spanish as well as you do?*

—No, él habla español mucho **mejor** que yo.   *No, he speaks Spanish much better than I.*

—La casa de Ana es **más grande** que la casa de Eva, ¿no?   *Ana's house is bigger than Eva's house, isn't it?*

—No, la casa de Ana es **más pequeña** que la casa de Eva.   *No, Ana's house is smaller than Eva's house.*

Práctica

A. Compare these people to one another using comparative adjectives.

Marisa

Antonio *flaco*

José

Olga *fea*

Anita

Anita es mas pequeña que Marisa
Marisa es más mayor que Anita

José es mas gordo que Antonio
Antonio es mas delgado que José
Olga es menor bonita que Marisa

Modelo: Olga es _____ Anita.
Olga es **más alta que** Anita.

1. Marisa es ~~más alta que~~ Olga.
2. José es ~~más gordo~~ Antonio.
3. Olga es ~~más baja que~~ Antonio.
4. Antonio es _____ todos. *el más grande de todos, más alto que todos.*
5. José es ~~el gordo de~~ todos.
6. Anita es ~~menor que~~ Marisa. *mas chica, mucho menor*
7. Olga es ~~menor que~~ Marisa. *menos altas que*
8. Anita es ~~el menor de~~ todos.

o es mas grande

B. You are an interpreter. How would you say the following in Spanish?

1. I read many books, but he reads more. *Leo muchos libros pero él lee más.*
2. Cuba is bigger than Puerto Rico. *Cuba es más grande que P.R.*
3. My son is older than your daughter. *Mi hijo es mayor que su hija.*
4. My professors are better than Robert's professors. *Mis profesoras son mejores que los profesores de Robert.*
5. He speaks English worse than I. *El habla inglés peor que yo.*
6. Are you the youngest in the class, Ann? *¿Eres la menor de la clase, Ann?* *la mas chica*
7. The store is smaller than the market. *La tienda es mas pequeña que el mercado.* *la mas joven*
8. I write well, but you write better, Miss Soto. *Escribo bien pero escribe mejor, Sra. Soto.*
9. You drink little coffee, but I drink less. *bebes café pero bebo menos.*
10. Our books are bad, but your book is the worst. *Nuestros libros son malos pero tu libro es el peor.*

4. The irregular verbs tener and venir

Tomas poco cafe pero Tomo menos.

tener *(to have)*		venir *(to come)*	
yo	**tengo**	yo	**vengo**
tú	**tienes**	tú	**vienes**
Ud.		Ud.	
él	**tiene**	él	**viene**
ella		ella	
nosotros	**tenemos**	nosotros	**venimos**
Uds.		Uds.	
ellos	**tienen**	ellos	**vienen**
ellas		ellas	

—¿El hotel **tiene** piscina?   *Does the hotel have a pool?*
—Sí y también **tiene**   *Yes, and it also has a gym.*
    gimnasio.

—¿Con quién **viene** Ud.?   *With whom are you*
  ¿Con su hijo?   *coming? With your son?*
—No, **vengo** sola.   *No, I am coming alone.*

—¿Cuántas hijas **tiene**   *How many daughters do*
  Ud.?   *you have?*
—**Tengo** tres hijas.   *I have three daughters.*

ATENCIÓN: The personal **a** is not used with the verb **tener**.

—Ana, ¿**tienes** novio?   *Ana, do you have a*
                        boyfriend?
—No, no **tengo** novio.   *No, I don't have a*
                        boyfriend.

ATENCIÓN: With the verb **tener**, the indefinite article is not used in Spanish when the numerical concept is not emphasized: **No, no *tengo* novio.**

Práctica

Complete the following, using **tener** or **venir**.

1. Yo no _tengo_ novia.
2. ¿Con quién _vienen_ Uds. a la clase?
3. ¿David _viene_ tarde o temprano?
4. Ellos no _tienen_ la dirección de Pedro, pero nosotros _tenemos_ su número de teléfono.
5. ¿Cuándo _vienen_ ellos? Yo _vengo_ temprano.
6. El hotel _tiene_ piscina y también gimnasio.
7. Yo _vengo_ sola, pero Marisa _viene_ con Oscar.
8. ¿Cuántos muchachos _tienen_ Uds. en la clase?
9. ¿Cuál es el mejor profesor que Uds. _tienen_?
10. La pensión _tiene_ habitaciones muy grandes.

5. **Expressions with** tener

In Spanish, many useful idiomatic expressions are formed with the verb **tener** and a noun, while English uses *to be* and an adjective.

tener calor *to be hot*	**tener hambre** *to be hungry*
tener frío *to be cold*	**tener sed** *to be thirsty*
tener cuidado *to be careful*	**tener prisa** *to be in a hurry*
tener sueño *to be sleepy*	**tener razón** *to be right*
tener miedo *to be afraid*	
tener... años (de edad) *to be . . . years old*	

(handwritten annotations: (el) preceding tener calor, frío, cuidado, sueño, miedo; los preceding tener... años; el preceding tener hambre with "mucha (f.)"; la preceding tener sed, prisa, razón)

(handwritten at bottom:) (la) tener flojera → to be lazy.
tener éxito → to succeed

♦ The equivalent of *I am very hungry*, for example is **Tengo mucha hambre** (literally, *I have much hunger*).

—¿**Tienes hambre,** María?	*Are you hungry, María?*
—No, pero **tengo** mucha **sed**.	*No, but I am very thirsty.*
—¿**Tienes calor,** Carlos?	*Are you hot, Carlos?*
—Sí, **tengo** mucho **calor.**	*Yes, I'm very hot.*
—¿Cuántos **años tiene** su hija?	*How old is your daughter?*
—Mi hija **tiene** seis **años.**	*My daughter is six years old.*
—Deseo hablar con el instructor, por favor.	*I wish to speak with the instructor, please.*
—Ahora no. Lo siento. Él **tiene** mucha **prisa.**	*Not now, I'm sorry. He's in a big hurry.*
—**Tiene razón.** Es tarde.	*You're right. It's late.*

Práctica

A. Tell what is happening in each of the pictures. Follow the model.

Modelo:

Ella...
Ella tiene hambre.

1. Carlos...*tiene miedo.*

tiene frío

2. Él…

tengo prisa

3. Yo…

tienen calor

4. Ellas…

5. ¿Ud….? *tiene sueño?*

6. Tú... *tienes sed*

7. Nélida... *tiene quatro años de edad*

B. Answer the following questions, first in the affirmative and then in the negative.

1. ¿Tiene Ud. hambre?
2. ¿Tienen Uds. miedo? *tenemos*
3. ¿Tienes sueño? *Yo*
4. ¿Tiene mucha sed el profesor (la profesora)?
5. ¿Tú tienes diez años?
6. ¿Tengo yo razón?
7. ¿Tienen Uds. prisa? *Tenemos.*
8. ¿Tiene Ud. calor?
9. ¿Tienen Uds. frío?

C. How would you say the following in Spanish?

1. I'm hungry and I'm also very thirsty. *Tengo hambre y también tengo mucha sed.*
   Me too.
2. Aren't you cold, Paquito? *No tiene frío, P.?*
   No, I'm hot. *No, no tengo frío.*
3. How old are you, Anita? *Cuantos años tienes anita?*
   I'm six years old. *Tengo seis años de edad.*
4. Are you in a hurry, Miss Vega? *Tiene ud. prisa, Sta.*
   Yes, it's very late.
5. You **must be** careful, Mrs. Lopez. *Debe ud. tener cuidado, Sra. Lopez.*
   You are right.

En el laboratorio

LECCIÓN 4

The following material is to be used with the tape in the language laboratory.

I. Vocabulario

Repeat each word after the speaker. When repeating words that are cognates, notice the difference in pronunciation between English and Spanish.

COGNADOS:	la clase el diccionario el instructor el supervisor
NOMBRES:	la chica el chico la esposa el esposo el gerente el gimnasio la habitación el cuarto el mercado la pensión la piscina la tienda
VERBOS:	llegar tener venir
ADJETIVOS:	barato bueno cansado caro malo mayor mejor menor mucho pequeño peor poco solo
OTRAS PALABRAS Y EXPRESIONES:	¿a quién? con ¿cuándo? ¿cuántos? mal más menos que también

II. Práctica

A. Answer the questions, using the cues provided. Repeat the correct answer after the speaker's confirmation. Listen to the model.

Modelo: —¿A dónde vas?   (hotel)
            —**Voy al hotel.**

1. (hospital)
2. (biblioteca)
3. (profesor)
4. (médico)
5. (señor Díaz)
6. (cafetería)
7. (señorita Vera)

B. Answer the questions, always selecting the second choice. Repeat the correct answer after the speaker's confirmation. Listen to the model.

Modelo: —¿Quién es más alto, Alberto o Mario?
          —Mario es más alto que Alberto.

C. Answer the questions in the affirmative, always using **mucho** or **mucha**. Repeat the correct answer after the speaker's confirmation. Listen to the model:

Modelo: —¿Tienes hambre?
          —Sí, tengo mucha hambre.

III. Para escuchar y entender

1. Listen carefully to the dialogue. It will be read twice.

    (*Diálogo 1*)

    Now the speaker will make statements about the dialogue you just heard. Tell whether each statement is true (**verdadero**) or false (**falso**). The speaker will confirm the correct answer.

2. Listen carefully to the dialogue. It will be read twice.

    (*Diálogo 2*)

    Now the speaker will make statements about the dialogue you just heard. Tell whether each statement is true (**verdadero**) or false (**falso**). The speaker will confirm the correct answer.

3. Listen carefully to the dialogue. It will be read twice.

    (*Diálogo 3*)

    Now the speaker will ask you some questions about the dialogue you just heard. Answer each question, omitting the subject. The speaker will confirm the correct answer. Repeat the correct answer.

Lección

5

1. **Telling time**
2. **Stem-changing verbs** (e:ie)
3. *Ir a* + **infinitive**
4. **Uses of** hay
5. **Ordinal numbers and their uses**

Vocabulario

el **concierto** concert
el **dólar** dollar
la **oficina** office

NOMBRES
la **cena** dinner
el **cine** movie theater
el **jabón** soap
la **mañana** morning
la **noche** (*late*) evening,
  night
el **piso** floor, story
la **reunión, junta** meeting
la **revista** magazine
la **tarde** afternoon
la **toalla** towel
el **vuelo** flight

VERBOS
  cerrar (e:ie) to close
  comenzar (e:ie) to begin,
    to start

comprar to buy
desayunar to have
  breakfast
empezar (e:ie) to begin,
  to start
entender (e:ie) to
  understand
perder (e:ie) to lose
preferir (e:ie) to prefer
querer (e:ie) to want
viajar to travel

**OTRAS PALABRAS Y
EXPRESIONES**
¿cuánto(a)? how much?
para to, in order to
¿por qué? why?
porque because

Resumen de palabras interrogativas

¿a dónde? where to?
¿a quién? to whom?
¿cuál(es)? which?
¿cuándo? when?
¿cuánto(a)? how much?
¿cuántos(as)? how many?
¿de dónde? from where?
¿de quién(es)? whose?
¿dónde? where?
¿por qué? why?
¿qué? what?
¿quién(es)? who?

¿A dónde vas?
¿A quién llamas?
¿Cuál prefieres?
¿Cuándo vienen ellos?
¿Cuánto dinero necesitas?
¿Cuántas toallas quieres?
¿De dónde es Ud.?
¿De quién es la revista?
¿Dónde está el cine Rex?
¿Por qué no van al concierto?
¿Qué desea comprar, señora?
¿Quiénes van a venir a la
  reunión?

cómo —how

porque –because

◀1. Telling time

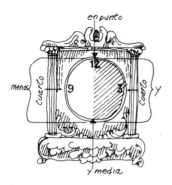

♦   Here are some important points to remember when telling time in Spanish.

1. **Es** is used with **una:**

> **Es** la una y cuarto.   *It is a quarter after one.*

Son is used with all the other hours:

> **Son** las dos y cuarto.   *It is a quarter after two.*
> **Son** las cinco y diez.   *It is ten after five.*

2. The definite article is always used before the hour:

> Es **la** una y veinte.   *It is twenty after one.*
> Son **las** cuatro y media.   *It is four thirty.*

3. The hour is given first, then the minutes:

> Son las **cuatro** y **diez.**   *It is ten after four* (literally: *"four and ten"*).

4. The equivalent of *past or after* is **y:**

> Son las doce y cinco.   *It is five after twelve.*

5. The equivalent of *to* or *till* is **menos.** It is used with fractions of time up to a half hour:

> Son las ocho **menos** veinte.   *It is twenty to eight.* 20 para las 8.

6. When telling time, follow this order:

> **a. Es** or **Son**
> **b. la** or **las**
> **c.** the hour
> **d. y** or **menos**   para (before, to)
> **e.** the minutes

Son las cuatro cincuenta

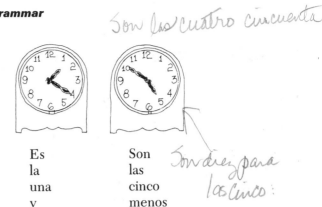

Es	Son	*Son diez para las cinco*
la	las	
una	cinco	
y	menos	
veinte.	diez.	

7:00 Sharp
~~Son las~~ A las
~~Siete en punto~~

◆ The equivalent of *at + time* is **a + la(s) +** *time*:

A la una. *At one o'clock.*
A las cinco y media. *At five thirty.*

◆ There is a difference between **de la** and **por la** when used with time.

When a specific time is mentioned, **de la (mañana, tarde, noche)** should be used:

Mi clase de inglés es a las seis **de** la tarde.	*My English class is at six in the evening.*

When a specific time is *not* mentioned, **por la (mañana, tarde, noche)** should be used:

Nosotros trabajamos **por la** mañana.	*We work in the morning.*
Juan estudia **por la** tarde.	*Juan studies in the afternoon.*
—¿A qué hora desayunan Uds.?	*(At) What time do you have breakfast?*
—Desayunamos a las siete.	*We have breakfast at seven.*
—¿Y a qué hora es la[1] cena?	*And (at) what time is dinner?*
—A las nueve de la noche.	*At nine P.M.*

¿A qué hora es la classe?
¿A qué horas " " " " ?
¿Qué hora es?
¿Qué horas son?

[1] In Spanish the definite article is used before the words for *breakfast*, *lunch* and *dinner*.

Práctica

A. ¿Qué hora es?

[handwritten: Que hora su; Son las ocho en punto; medio día en punto o media noche en punto; media]

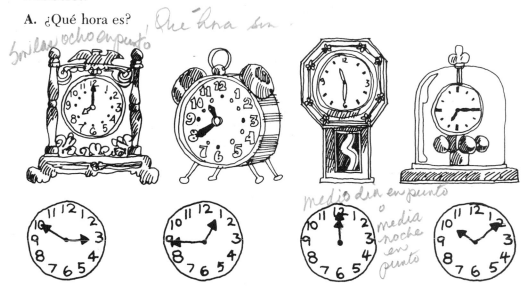

B. You are an interpreter. How would you say the following in Spanish?

1. We are coming at two-thirty in the afternoon. *[handwritten: Venimos a dos y media de la tarde]*
2. He is going to the library in the morning. *[handwritten: El va a la biblioteca por la tarde]*
3. They don't work in the evening. *[handwritten: No trabajen por la noche]*
4. It's three o'clock in the morning. *[handwritten: Son las tres de la mañana]*
5. I am arriving at nine o'clock in the evening. *[handwritten: Llego a las nueve de la noche]*
6. Dinner is at eight P.M. *[handwritten: La cena es las ocho de la noche]*
7. Pedro has breakfast at seven-thirty. *[handwritten: Pedro desayuna a las siete medio]*
8. We go to our Spanish class at eight o'clock in the morning. *[handwritten: Vamos a nuestra clase de Español a las ocho de la mañana]*
9. He reads in the evening. *[handwritten: Lee por la noche]*
10. They go to the hospital at six o'clock. *[handwritten: Vamos al hospital a las seis.]*
11. I visit the museum at three-thirty. *[handwritten: Visito al museo a las tres medio.]*
12. She calls the supervisor at nine o'clock. *[handwritten: Ella llama la supervisora a las nueve,]*

2. Stem-changing verbs (e:ie)

In Spanish, some verbs undergo a stem change in the present indicative. For these verbs, when **e** is the last stem vowel and it is stressed, it changes to **ie** as follows:

preferir (to prefer)	
prefiero	preferimos
prefieres	
prefiere	prefieren

◆ Notice that the stem vowel is not stressed in the verb form corresponding to **nosotros**, and therefore the **e** does not change to **ie**.

◆ Stem-changing verbs have regular endings like other **-ar**, **-er**, and **-ir** verbs.

◆ Some other verbs that undergo the same change are: **cerrar** (*to close*), **perder** (*to lose*), **comenzar**[1] (*to begin*), **querer** (*to want*), **entender** (*to understand*), and **empezar**[1] (*to begin*).

—¿**Quieres** ir al cine?	*Do you want to go to the movies?*
—No, no **quiero** ir al cine.	*No, I don't want to go to the movies.*
—¿Por qué no?	*Why not?*
—Porque **prefiero** ir al concierto.	*Because I prefer to go to the concert.*
—¿A qué hora **cierran** Uds.?	*What time do you close?*
—**Cerramos** a las nueve.	*We close at nine.*
—¿Cuándo **comienzan** las clases?	*When do classes start?*
—**Comienzan** en septiembre.	*They start in September.*
—Pedro **entiende** el francés y el alemán, ¿no?	*Pedro understands French and German, doesn't he?*
—**Entiende** el francés, pero no **entiende** el alemán.	*He understands French, but he doesn't understand German.*

Práctica

A. Complete the following sentences with the present indicative of **preferir, cerrar, empezar, comenzar, querer, perder,** and **entender,** as needed. Use each verb once:

1. Nosotros no *queremos* beber té; *preferimos* beber café.
2. El concierto *comienza* a las ocho de la noche.
3. Yo no *entiendo* la lección.
4. ¿Por qué *pierdes* (tú) la revista?
5. Los conciertos *empiezan* en marzo.
6. Roberto *pierde* su dinero en Las Vegas.

[1] When **comenzar** and **empezar** are followed by an infinitive, the preposition **a** is used: **Yo comienzo (empiezo) a trabajar a las seis.** Notice that these two verbs are synonymous.

B. Finish the following in an original manner, matching the verbs to the new subjects:

1. Luis comienza a trabajar a las siete y nosotros. *comenzamos a las ocho.*
2. Tú prefieres ir al cine y yo.. *prefiero ir al teatro.*
3. Nosotros cerramos a las nueve y ellos.. *cierren a medianoche en*
4. Yo empiezo a trabajar el lunes y Uds.. *empiezan el miércoles. punto.*
5. Rafael quiere aprender francés y nosotros.. *queremos aprender español.*
6. Yo no entiendo inglés y ustedes.. *no entienden español. nosotros* *no entendemos el uno al otro.*

3. Ir a + infinitive

The construction **ir a** + *infinitive* is used to express future time. It is equivalent to the English expression *to be going to*. The formula is:

ir	+ **a** +	*infinitive*	
Yo voy	**a**	**viajar**	solo.
I'm going		*to travel*	*alone.*

—¿Qué **vas a comprar**?　　What are you going to buy? *Qué vas a comprar*

—**Voy a comprar** jabón y una toalla.　　I'm going to buy soap and a towel.

—Nosotros **vamos a comprar** una revista.　　We are going to buy a magazine.

—¿A qué hora **va a empezar** la clase?　　What time is the class going to start?

—**Va a empezar** a las siete.　　It's going to start at seven.

Práctica

A. Make new sentences using the subjects provided.

1. Tú vas a viajar.　(Nosotros, Mi hermana, Yo, Ud., Ellos)
2. El gerente va a hablar con ella.　(Yo, Uds., Nosotras, Tú)

B. Change the following to tell what these people are going to do instead of what they are doing.

Modelo: Teresa lee una revista.
　　　Teresa va a leer una revista.

1. Yo voy al cine solo. *Yo voy a ir al cine solo.*
2. ¿Tú compras jabón? *Tú vas a comprar jabón?*
3. La clase comienza a las siete. *La clase va a comenzar —*
4. Mis primos hablan español. *Mis primos van a hablar esp.*
5. Ella da su nombre y apellido. *Ella va a dar su n. y a.*
6. Nosotros viajamos a Lima. *Nosotros vamos a viajar a L.*

C. Use your imagination to describe what these people are going to do.

Modelo: Yo / mañana
          Yo voy a estudiar mañana.

1. Carlos / por la noche *Carlos va a ir al cine por la noche*
2. Nosotros / el lunes *Nosotros vamos a esquiar el lunes*
3. Tú / mañana por la tarde *Tu vas a visitar su familia*
4. Los muchachos / el sábado *Los much. van a mañana jugar football por la tarde. el sábado.*
5. Ud. / el viernes *Ud va a ir a la reunión el viernes*

4. Uses of hay

The form **hay**[1] means *there is* or *there are*. It has no subject and must not be confused with **es** (*it is*) and **son** (*they are*).

—¿**Hay** reunión hoy?   *Is there a meeting today?*
—No, no **hay** reunión.   *No, there isn't a meeting.*

—¿**Hay** vuelos para Lima   *Are there flights to Lima to-*
   hoy?   *day?*
—Sí, **hay** un vuelo a las   *Yes, there is one flight at*
   ocho de la noche.   *eight P.M.*

Qué hay? Hay un teléfono
Práctica *Hay mesas.*

Answer the following questions:

1. ¿Cuántos estudiantes hay en la clase? *Hay seis estud.*
2. ¿Hay reunión de estudiantes hoy? *no, no hay reunión hoy.*
3. ¿Hay un vuelo para Madrid a las ocho? ¿Quieres ir? *Hay mañana*
4. Hoy es domingo. ¿Hay clase? *no, no hay clase*
5. ¿Cuántos teatros hay en su ciudad? *Hay muchos teatros en su ciudad*
6. ¿Hay muchos muchachos guapos en la clase? *Hay nada. Pero, hay mucho hombres guapos en la clase.*

5. Ordinal numbers and their uses

primero(a)	*first*
segundo(a)	*second*
tercero(a)	*third*
cuarto(a)	*fourth*
quinto(a)	*fifth*
sexto(a)	*sixth*
séptimo(a)	*seventh*
octavo(a)	*eighth*
noveno(a)	*ninth*
décimo(a)	*tenth*

[1] **Hay** is the impersonal form of **haber** (*to have*).

Ordinal numbers agree in gender and number with the nouns they modify:

—¿Qué oficina prefiere?   *Which office do you prefer?*
—Prefiero **la quinta** oficina.   *I prefer the fifth (one).*

♦ The ordinal numbers **primero** and **tercero** drop the final **-o**
before masculine singular nouns:

el primer diamento

—¿Qué día llegan Uds.?   *What day are you arriving?*
—Llegamos el **primer** día   *We are arriving the first*
  del mes.   *day of the month.*

♦ Ordinal numbers are seldom used after *the tenth:*

—¿En qué piso viven Uds.?   *On which floor do you live?*
—Vivimos en el piso **doce.**   *We live on the twelfth floor.*

♦ Remember that cardinal numbers are used in Spanish for dates
except for *the first:*

—¿Qué día es hoy?   *What day is it today?*
—Hoy es el **treinta** de   *Today is April 30th.*
  abril. Mañana es el   *Tomorrow is the first*
  primero de mayo.   *day of May.*

Práctica

Complete the following sentences with the correct ordinal number.

1. Él es el ___primer___ supervisor.   (*first*)
2. Yo vivo en el ___quinto___ piso.   (*fifth*)
3. Ella prefiere la ___secundo___ mesa.   (*second*)
4. La oficina de mi esposo está en el ___tercer___ piso.   (*third*)
5. Llegamos el ___primero___ de mayo.   (*first*)
6. Los chicos llegan en los ___primeros___ días del mes.   (*first*)
7. Yo quiero la ___cuarta___, la ___sexta___, y la ___septima___
   sillas.   (*fourth / sixth / seventh*)
8. No tenemos clases la ___novena___ semana. Tenemos clases la
   ___décima___ semana.   (*ninth / tenth*)

En el laboratorio

LECCIÓN 5

The following material is to be used with the tape in the language laboratory.

I. Vocabulario

Repeat each word after the speaker. When repeating words that are cognates, notice the difference in pronunciation between English and Spanish.

COGNADOS: el concierto   el dólar   la oficina

NOMBRES: la cena   el cine   el jabón   la junta
la mañana   la noche   el piso
la reunión   la revista   la tarde
la toalla   el vuelo

VERBOS: cerrar   comenzar   comprar   desayunar
empezar   entender   perder   preferir
querer   viajar

OTRAS PALABRAS Y
EXPRESIONES: ¿cuánto?   para   ¿por qué?   porque

II. Práctica

A. Change the verb in each sentence according to the new subject. Repeat the correct answer after the speaker's confirmation.

1. (Uds.)
2. (tú)
3. (ella)
4. (yo)

5. (ellos)
6. (Ud.)
7. (él)

B. Answer the questions, using the cues provided. Repeat the correct answer after the speaker's confirmation. Listen to the model.

Modelo: —¿Cuándo vas a venir tú? (el viernes)
—**Voy a venir el viernes.**

1. (al cine)
2. (una revista)
3. (a las nueve)

4. (el quinto)
5. (con mi primo)
6. (el gerente)

7. (con mi sobrino)
8. (al concierto)

C. Say the ordinal number that corresponds to each cardinal number. Repeat the correct answer after the speaker's confirmation. Listen to the model.

Modelo: cuatro   *cuarto*

1. nueve	4. uno	7. diez
2. tres	5. ocho	8. dos
3. cinco	6. seis	9. siete

III. Para escuchar y entender

1. Listen carefully to the dialogue. It will be read twice.

    (Diálogo 1)

    Now the speaker will make statements about the dialogue you just heard. Tell whether each statement is true (**verdadero**) or false (**falso**). The speaker will confirm the correct answer.

2. Listen carefully to the narration. It will be read twice.

    (Narración)

    Now the speaker will make statements about the narration you just heard. Tell whether each statement is true (**verdadero**) or false (**falso**). The speaker will confirm the correct answer.

3. Listen carefully to the dialogue. It will be read twice.

    (Diálogo 2)

    Now the speaker will ask you some questions about the dialogue you just heard. Answer each question, omitting the subject. The speaker will confirm the correct answer. Repeat the correct answer.

¿Cuánto sabe usted ahora?

LECCIONES 1–5

Lección 1   **A.** Subject pronouns

Replace the subjects below with the appropriate subject pronouns.

1. tú y yo *nosotros*
2. los estudiantes *ellos*
3. Ana y Rosa *ellas*
4. usted, usted, usted y usted *ustedes*
5. Teresa y Roberto *ellos*
6. la profesora y yo *nosotros*

B. The present indicative of regular **-ar** verbs

Complete the sentences below with the Spanish equivalent of the verbs provided.

1. Ellos *quieren* una cerveza.   (*want*)
2. Nosotros *queremos* el mantel y las servilletas.   (*need*)
3. ¿Tú *estudias* francés?   (*study*)
4. Yo *tomo* refresco.   (*drink*)
5. Carlos *trabaja* en un restaurante.   (*works*)

C. Interrogative and negative sentences

How would you say the following in Spanish?

1. Does she need the spoons?
   No, she doesn't need the spoons; she needs the forks.
2. Do you (*pl.*) speak Italian?
   No, we don't speak Italian; we speak Spanish.
3. Does Mr. Vega work in Lima?
   No, he doesn't work in Lima; he works in Santiago.

D. Cardinal numbers (300–1000)

Write the following numbers in Spanish:

1. 341
2. 783
3. 1000
4. 575
5. 467
6. 896

E. Vocabulary

Complete the following sentences, using words learned in Lección 1.

1. Necesito el mantel y las _____.

2. En California hablan _____, en Roma hablan _____ y en París hablan _____.
3. Necesito una cuchara y un _____.
4. ¿Trabaja en una cafetería o en un _____?
5. Jorge _____ cerveza y _____.
6. Ellos _____ francés en la _____.

A. Position and forms of adjectives; agreement of articles, adjectives and nouns   **Lección 2**

How would you say the following in Spanish?

1. We need the white chairs and the black table.
2. I need two red pencils.
3. I study with two very intelligent girls.
4. Do you need the blue folders, Miss Vega?

B. The present indicative of regular **-er** and **-ir** verbs

Complete the following sentences using the present indicative of the verbs provided:

beber   vivir   recibir   comer   leer   escribir

1. Yo _bebo_ Coca-Cola y ellos _beben_ Pepsi.
2. Nosotros _leemos_ y _escribimos_ en español.
3. ¿Tú _comes_ en la cafetería?
4. Ellos _reciben_ veinte pesos.
5. Yo _vivo_ en la calle Magnolia y Ana _vive_ en la calle Universidad.

C. The personal **a**

How would you say the following in Spanish?

1. I wish to visit Miss Arévalo.
2. Do you call Mary?
3. The students visit the museum.

D. Vocabulary

Complete the following sentences, using words learned in Lección 2.

1. ¿Tú _bebes_ café o _té_?
2. Nosotros _comemos_ en la cafetería.
3. Yo _vivo_ en la calle Magnolia.
4. Ella escribe con una _pluma_ negra.
5. Yo no _estudio_ la lección tres.
6. ¿A _quién_ llama ella? ¿A María?
7. Los estudiantes _visitan_ el museo.

8. ¿Ud. toma un taxi o toma el *autobus*/*camión*

9. Yo escribo con un *lápiz* rojo.

Lección 3   **A.** The present indicative of the verb **ser**

Use the present indicative of the verb **ser** to complete the following sentences.

1. ¿Qué fecha __*es*__ hoy?
2. ¿Tú __*eres*__ de California?
3. Nosotros __*somos*__ estudiantes y ella __*es*__ profesora.
4. Mis padres __*son*__ de Buenos Aires.
5. Yo __*soy*__ de Venezuela. ¿De dónde __*es*__ Ud.?

B. Possession with **de**

How would you say the following in Spanish?

1. Carlos is Maria Iriarte's son.
2. Ana's cousin is from Colombia.
3. The girl's last name is Torres.
4. She needs Mrs. Madera's phone number.
5. David's house is green.

C. Possessive adjectives

How would you say the following in Spanish?

1. Do you need his address or her address?
2. Miss Vega is our friend.
3. I need my notebook.
4. Do you need to speak with your sons, Mr. Varela?
5. Do you want your black pencils, Paquito?

D. The irregular verbs **ir**, **dar**, and **estar**

Use the present indicative of **ir**, **dar**, or **estar** to complete the following sentences.

1. Ella no __*da*__ su número de teléfono y nosotros no __*damos*__ nuestra dirección.
2. ¿Adónde __*vas*__ tú los sábados? ¿Adónde __*van*__ ellos?
3. Yo __*estoy*__ en el hotel Acapulco. ¿En qué hotel __*están*__ ustedes?
4. Nosotros __*vamos*__ a la universidad los martes y jueves.
5. ¿Dónde __*estás*__ tú?

E. The verbs **ser** and **estar** (summary of uses)

Use the present indicative of **ser** or **estar** to complete the following sentences.

1. Ella __*es*__ de Buenos Aires, pero ahora __*está*__ en California.

2. Nosotros _somos_ norteamericanos.   *(n os)*
3. Ella _es_ muy bonita, pero _está_ casada.
4. Hoy _es_ jueves.
5. Yo _estoy_ muy bien, gracias.
6. ¿Las sillas _son_ de madera o de metal?
7. Teresa _es_ profesora; _es_ la hija de Carlos Montoya.
8. ¿Tú _estás_ enfermo, Luis?

F. Vocabulary

Complete the following sentences, using words learned in Lección 3.

1. Es de Buenos Aires; es _Argentina_
2. Es el papá de mi mamá; es mi _padres_
3. David es de los _Estados_ Unidos.
4. ¿Su _padre_? Es ingeniero.
5. No es mi novia; es mi _sobrina_
6. Necesito el libro y el _lápiz_ .
7. ¿De _dónde_ es ella? ¿De Venezuela?
8. ¿De _quién_ es el libro? ¿De Teresa?
9. ¿_Quién_ es ella? ¿Es bonita?
10. ¿Es fácil o _difícil_?

A. Contractions   **Lección 4**

How would you say the following in Spanish?

1. I need Mr. Soto's phone number.
2. She goes to the university on Fridays.
3. I call the manager on Tuesdays.
4. She is Mr. Miranda's daughter.
5. We go to the market on Saturdays.

B. Comparison of adjectives and adverbs; irregular comparison

How would you say the following in Spanish?

1. She is as tall as my son.
2. The Azteca Hotel is the most expensive in the city. It's the best.   *menor   mayor*
3. Is she younger or older than David?
4. Colombia is smaller than the United States.
5. I have little money, but he has less money than I.
6. We are as tired as you (*are*), Anita.

poco
o
poquito

C. The irregular verbs **tener** and **venir**

Use the present indicative of **tener** or **venir** to complete the following sentences.

1. Aníbal no _tiene_ novia. ¿Tú _tienes_ novia, Ariel?
2. Yo _vengo_ a la fiesta con mi sobrina porque no _tengo_ carro.
3. Mi prima y yo _tenemos_ doscientos pesos.
4. ¿Uds. _tienen_ la dirección de Ana? Nosotros _venimos_ a California el sábado.
5. ¿Tú _vienes_ al gimnasio mañana?

D. Expressions with **tener**

How would you say the following in Spanish?

1. I'm not hungry, but I'm very thristy. _Que edad tienes?_
2. Darío is nineteen years old. How old are you, Paco?
3. Are you in a hurry, Miss Perales? _Cuantos años tienes?_
4. Are you cold, Dad? I'm hot!
5. We are very sleepy. _mucho sueño._
6. You're right, Mrs. Vega! Paquito is very scared. _miedo_

E. Vocabulary _muchísimo_

Complete the following sentences, using words learned in Lección 4.

1. ¿El hotel es más caro o más _barato_?
2. ¿Es un hotel o una _pensión_?
3. ¿Es grande o _pequeño_? _mas chica_
4. Alicia es mayor que yo. Yo soy _menor_ que ella.
5. Yo no hablo muy bien el inglés. Ella habla inglés muy bien. Ella habla inglés _mejor_ que yo.
6. El hotel tiene _piscina_ y gimnasio.
7. ¿_Cuántos_ años tiene Roberto? ¿Siete?
8. ¿Tienes _hambre_? ¿Deseas comer?
9. ¿Tiene Ud. _sed_? ¿Desea beber?
10. ¿Tienes calor o _frío_?

Lección 5   A. Telling time

Give the Spanish equivalent of the words in parentheses.

1. La clase de español es _las siete y media de la mañana_. (at seven-thirty in the morning)
2. Nosotros trabajamos _de la tarde_. (in the afternoon)
3. La cena es _las nueve y cuarto de la noche_. (at a quarter after nine in the evening)
4. Son _veinte y cinco para las siete_. (twenty-five to seven)
5. Es _la una_. (one o'clock)

B. Stem-changing verbs (**e:ie**)

Complete the following sentences using the present indicative of the verbs provided.

1. —¿Tú _quieres_ ir hoy?   (querer)
   —No, _prefiero_ ir mañana.   (preferir)
2. —¿A qué hora _cierra_ la cafetería?   (cerrar)
   —A las nueve. ¿A qué hora _empieza_ el concierto?   (empezar)
   —A las diez y media.
3. —¿Uds. _entienden_ (entender)
   —No _entenemos_ mucho…   (entender)

C. Ir a + infinitive

Using the subjects and the cues provided, describe what everyone is going to do.

1. tú / el libro _tu vas a leer el libro_
2. nosotros / los sándwiches _nosotros vamos a comer los sand._
3. ellos / la lección dos _Ella va a estudiar la lección dos._
4. yo / café _Yo voy a beber café_
5. ella / francés _Eela va a hablar francés_

D. Uses of **hay**

How would you say the following in Spanish?

1. How many students are there in the classroom?
2. There isn't a meeting tomorrow.
3. There is a flight to Caracas at seven-thirty.
4. There are five theatres in the city.

E. Ordinal numbers and their uses

Complete the following sentences using the corresponding ordinal numbers.

1. Ella vive en el _tercer_ piso.   (3er)
2. Llegan el _primer_ de mayo.   (1°)
3. ¿Tú quieres la _quinta_ o la _sexto_ mesa?   (5ª / 6ª)
4. Ellos viven en el _octavo_ piso.   (8°)
5. No tenemos clases la _séptima_ semana.   (7ª)

F. Vocabulary

Complete the following sentences using words learned in Lección 5.

1. Nosotros _desayunamos_ a las siete de la mañana. La cena es a las ocho de la noche.
2. Ella tiene la _periódica_ Time.
3. ¿_Cuánto_ dinero necesitas tú?

4. Estudia por la mañana y por la tarde, pero no estudia por la _noche_

5. ¿Quieres ir al cine o _prefieres_ ir al concierto?

6. ¿Tú _entiendes_ una conversación en francés?

7. ¿Hay _vuelos_ para Lima los sábados?

8. La oficina está en el tercer _piso_.

9. El director tiene una _reunión_ en su oficina.

10. ¿Por _que_ no quieres ir al cine? ¿Estás cansado?

Lección

6

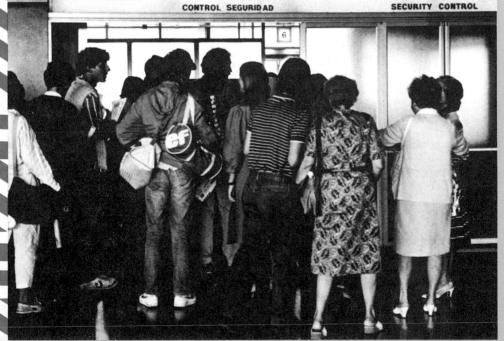

1. **Some uses of the definite article**
2. **Stem-changing verbs** (o:ue)
3. **Affirmative and negative expressions**
4. **Uses of** tener que **and** hay que
5. **Pronouns as object of a preposition**

Vocabulario

COGNADOS

la **agencia** agency	la **igualdad** equality
el, la **director(a)** director	**importante** important
la **educación** education	

NOMBRES
la **agencia de viajes** travel agency
la **cárcel** jail, prison
la **escuela** school
la **hermana** sister
el **hermano** brother
la **iglesia** church
el **mes** month
el **pasaje, billete** ticket (*for transportation*)
el **regalo** present, gift
el éxito success, outcome.
VERBOS
dormir **(o:ue)** to sleep
hacer **(yo hago)** to do, to make
poder **(o:ue)** to be able, can
recordar **(o:ue)** to remember

volar (o:ue) to fly
volver (o:ue) to return, to come (go) back

ADJETIVOS
pasado(a) last
próximo(a) next

OTRAS PALABRAS Y EXPRESIONES
a casa (toward) home
aquí here
de about
de ida one-way
de ida y vuelta round-trip
en on
mañana tomorrow
que viene next, coming
tener éxito to succeed

viaje redondo

◀ 1. Some uses of the definite article

♦ The definite article is used in Spanish with expressions of time, the seasons, and the days of the week:

—¿Cuándo es su clase de español?

When is your Spanish class?

—Tengo clase de español los[1] lunes, miércoles y viernes, a **las** nueve.

I have Spanish class on Mondays, Wednesdays, and Fridays at nine.

---

[1] Notice that the definite article is used here as the equivalent of **on**.

ATENCIÓN: The definite article is omitted with the seasons and days of the week when used after the verb **ser:**

—¿Es primavera ahora en Chile?	*Is it spring in Chile now?*
—Sí, es primavera.	*Yes, it is spring.*
—¿Qué día es hoy?	*What day is today?*
—Hoy es domingo.	*Today is Sunday.*

♦ The definite article precedes nouns used in a general sense:

—¿Qué quieren **las** mujeres y **los** hombres de hoy?	*What do today's women and men want?*
—Quieren **la** igualdad.	*They want equality.*

♦ The definite article is used with abstract nouns:

—¿Es importante **la** educación?	*Is education important?*
—Sí, **la** educación es muy importante.	*Yes, education is very important.*

♦ The definite article is used before **próximo** (*next*) and **pasado** (*last*) with expressions of time:

—¿Las clases comienzan **la** semana **próxima?**	*Do classes start next week?*
—Sí, comienzan **la** semana que viene.	*Yes, they start next week.*

♦ The definite article is used with the nouns **iglesia, escuela** and **cárcel** when they are preceded by a preposition:

—¿Vas a **la iglesia** los viernes?	*Do you go to church on Fridays?*
—No, los viernes voy a **la escuela.**	*No, I go to school.*

Práctica

A. Is the definite article needed or not? Decide as you complete the dialogues.

1. —¿Tú vas a __la__ iglesia hoy?
   —No, hoy es _____ sábado, y yo voy a __la__ iglesia __los__ domingos.
   —¿Vas a __la__ escuela __los__ lunes?
   —No, __los__ lunes no tengo clases.

2. —¿Uds. van a viajar a la Argentina en julio?
—No, porque cuando en los Estados Unidos es _____ verano, en la Argentina es _____ invierno y nosotros preferimos _el_ verano.

[handwritten: nouns used in general a general sense]

3. —_los_ hombres son más inteligentes que _las_ mujeres.
—¡No! _las_ mujeres somos tan inteligentes como _los_ hombres.

[handwritten: definite article is used]

4. —¿A dónde vas a ir _el_ domingo próximo?
—Voy a ir a visitar a Julio, que está en _la_ cárcel.

B. You are an interpreter. How would you say the following in Spanish?

[handwritten: definite article general sense / no article]

1. Are you going to school or to church, Miss Vera?
2. Equality is very important.
3. Do you prefer fall or spring?
4. I don't have classes on Wednesdays.
5. Is today Sunday?

[handwritten: la semana próxima]

6. The class starts next week.

◄ 2. Stem-changing verbs (o:ue)

As you learned in Lesson 5, certain verbs undergo a change in the stem in the present indicative. When the last stem vowel is a stressed **o**, it changes to **ue**.

volver (to return)		
vuelvo	volvemos	
vuelves		
vuelve	vuelven	

◆ Notice that the stem vowel is not stressed in the verb form corresponding to **nosotros**; therefore, the **o** does not change to **ue**.

—¿Cuándo **vuelven** Uds.?   *When are you coming back?*
—**Volvemos** a las siete.   *We are coming back at seven.*

◆ Some other common verbs that undergo the same change in the stem are:

costar	*to cost*	**poder**	*to be able*
recordar	*to remember*	**dormir**	*to sleep*
volar	*to fly*		

—¿Cuánto **cuesta** el billete de ida y vuelta?	*How much does the round trip ticket cost?*
—Quinientos dólares.	*Five hundred dollars.*
—¿**Puede** Ud. comprar el pasaje mañana?	*Can you buy the ticket tomorrow?*
—Sí. ¡Ah!, no, porque ahora **recuerdo** que no tengo dinero.	*Yes. Oh! No, because now I remember that I have no money.*
—¿Cuándo **vuela** Ud.?	*When are you flying?*
—**Vuelo** la semana que viene.	*I'm flying next week.*
—¿Cuándo **pueden** Uds. ir a la agencia de viajes?	*When can you go to the travel agency?*
—**Podemos** ir mañana.	*We can go tomorrow.*
—¿Cuántas horas **duerme** tu hermano?	*How many hours does your brother sleep?*
—**Duerme** diez horas.	*He sleeps ten hours.*

Práctica

A. Complete the following sentences with the correct form of the verb in parentheses.

1. ¿Cuándo _vuelve_ (volver) Ud. de México? vuelve
2. Yo no _____ (recordar) su número de teléfono. recuerdo
3. Nosotras _____ (volar) la semana que viene. volamos
4. Ellos no _____ (poder) comprar el billete hoy. pueden
5. Tú no _____ (volver) en el verano porque no _____ vuelves (poder). puedes
6. Uds. _____ (volar) en mayo. vuelan
7. Yo _____ (poder) venir mañana. puedo
8. ¿_____ (recordar) Ud. a la hermana de Juan? recuerda
9. Nosotros _dormimos_ (dormir) mucho, pero él _____ (dormir) duerme más.
10. Nosotras no _____ (poder) ir a la agencia de viajes hoy. podemos

B. Tell about yourself by answering the following questions.

1. Cuando Ud. viaja, ¿vuela o va en ómnibus?
2. ¿Cuánto cuesta un billete de ida y vuelta a Acapulco?
3. ¿A qué hora vuelve Ud. a su casa?
4. ¿Cuántas horas duerme Ud.?
5. ¿Puede Ud. venir a clase mañana?
6. ¿Recuerda Ud. el número de teléfono de la universidad?

3. Affirmative and negative expressions

Study the expressions in the following tables.

Affirmative		Negative	
algo	something, anything	**nada**	nothing
alguien	someone, anyone	**nadie**	nobody, no one
alguno(a)		**ninguno(a)**	
algún	any, some	**ningún**	none, not any
algunos(as)			
siempre	always	**nunca**	
alguna vez	ever *once*	**jamás**	never
algunas veces	sometimes		
también	also, too	**tampoco**	neither
o... o	either . . . or	**ni... ni**	neither . . . nor

(handwritten notes: unique (use when occurrence is a one time deal) — *next to* alguna vez; ninguna vez – no time; algee-en*)*

—¿Hay **algo** en la mesa? *Is there anything on the table?*

—No, no hay **nada**. *No, there is nothing. (No, there isn't anything.)*

—¿Hay **alguien** con el director? *Is there anyone with the director?*

—No, no hay **nadie**. *No, there is no one. (No, there isn't anyone.)*

—¿Van Uds. **siempre** a Los Ángeles? *Do you always go to Los Angeles?*

—No, no vamos **nunca**. *No, we never go.*

—¿Quieren venir Uds. **también?** *Do you want to come too?*

—No, Juan no quiere ir, **ni** yo tampoco. *No, Juan doesn't want to go and neither do I.*

—¿Qué quiere Ud., té **o** café? *What do you want, tea or coffee?*

—Yo no bebo **ni** té **ni** café. *I don't drink either tea or coffee.*

◆ **Alguno** and **ninguno** drop the **-o** before a masculine singular noun, but **alguna** and **ninguna** keep the final **-a**.

—¿Hay **algún** libro o **alguna** pluma en la mesa? *Is there any book or pen on the table?*

—No, no hay **ningún** libro ni **ninguna** pluma. *No, there isn't any book or pen.*

◆ **Alguno(a)** is used in the plural form to agree with a plural noun, but **ninguno(a)** must be used in the singular form.

—¿Desea comprar **algunos** regalos?

—No, no deseo comprar **ningún** regalo.

Do you want to buy any presents?

No, I don't want to buy any presents (not one present).

—¿Vienen **algunas** chicas a la reunión?

—No, no viene **ninguna** chica.

Are some girls coming to the meeting?

No, no girls are coming (not one girl).

◆ A double negative is frequently used in Spanish. In this construction, the adverb **no** is placed immediately before the verb. The second negative word may either precede the verb, follow the verb, or come at the end of the sentence. If the negative word precedes the verb, **no** is not used:

—¿Habla Ud. alemán **siempre?**

—No, yo **no** hablo alemán **nunca.**
(Yo **nunca** hablo alemán.)

Do you always speak German?

No, I never speak German.

—¿Compra Ud. **algo** aquí?

—No, aquí **no** compro **nada nunca.**
(**Nunca** compro **nada** aquí.)

Do you buy anything here?

No, I never buy anything here.

Práctica

A. Answer the following questions in the negative.

1. ¿Necesita Ud. algo? *No necesito nada*
2. ¿Hay alguien aquí? *No hay nadie aquí*
3. ¿Estudia Ud. siempre por la noche? *No, no estudio nunca por la noche.*
4. ¿Quiere té o café? *No, no quiero té ni café* *(Ninguno de los dos)*
5. ¿Va a comprar Ud. algunos regalos? *ningún regalo / nada*
6. Juan no va a la reunión. ¿Va Ud.? *No voy tampoco*
7. ¿Va Ud. a Los Ángeles algunas veces? *No, yo jamás voy*

B. How would you say the following in Spanish?

1. I never buy tickets at the travel agency. *Yo nunca compro*
2. We don't need round-trip tickets either. *tampoco.*
3. I never buy any presents for anybody. *Nunca – para nadie*
4. I don't want (either) beer or soda.
5. Is there anybody at the office? *Hay alguien en la oficina.*
6. I never remember anything either. *Jamás recuerdo nada tampoco.*

Usos de

4. Uses of tener que and hay que

♦ The Spanish equivalent of *to have to* is **tener que:**

Yo	**tengo**	**que**	estudiar.
I	*have*		*to study.*

—¿Qué **tiene que** hacer hoy?

What *do you have to* do today?

—**Tengo que** trabajar.

I have to work.

♦ The Spanish equivalent of *one must* is **hay que:**

Hay que comenzar temprano.　　*One must* start early.

—¿Qué **hay que** hacer para tener éxito?

What *must one* do to succeed?

—**Hay que** trabajar.

One must work.

ATENCIÓN: Note that **tener que** and **hay que** are followed by the infinitive. Note also that no subject is used with **hay que;** it is an invariable expression.

Práctica

A. Complete the following sentences with **hay que** or the correct form of **tener que** as needed:

1. Para tener éxito, _hay que_ trabajar.
2. Yo _tengo que_ estudiar mucho.
3. Nosotros _tenemos que_ volar a Chicago la semana que viene.
4. _Hay que_ dormir ocho horas.
5. Mi hermano _tiene que_ volver a las diez de la noche.
6. _Hay que_ comenzar más tarde.
7. Uds. no _tienen que_ venir hoy.
8. Para aprender, _hay que_ estudiar.

B. Use your imagination to explain what these people have to do.

Modelo: José / mañana
José tiene que trabajar mañana.

1. yo / por la noche
2. mi papá / el sábado
3. nosotros / el domingo
4. el director / el lunes
5. tú / mañana por la tarde

5. Pronouns as object of a preposition

> **Preposition**   a word that introduces a noun, pronoun, adverb, or verb and indicates its function in the sentence: They were **with** us. She is **from** Lima.

Prepositional Pronouns

Singular		*Plural*	
mí	me	**nosotros**	us
ti	you (*familiar*)		
Ud.	you (*formal*)	**Uds.**	you (*formal, plural*)
él	him	**ellos**	them (*masc.*)
ella	her	**ellas**	them (*fem.*)

◆ Notice that only the first and second persons singular (**mí, ti**) have special forms. The other persons use the forms of the subject pronouns.

◆ When used with the preposition **con**, the first and second person singular forms become **conmigo** and **contigo**:

—¿Vas a casa **conmigo?**   *Are you going home with me?*

—No, no voy **contigo.** Voy **con** ellos.   *No, I'm not going with you. I'm going with them.*

—¿Es **para nosotros** el regalo?   *Is the present for us?*

—Sí, es **para Uds.**   *Yes, it's for you.*

—¿Hablan **de ti?**   *Are they talking about you?*
—No, no hablan **de mí.**   *No, they're not talking about me.*

Práctica

Complete the following sentences with the correct form of the pronoun.

1. Mi hermana va a la agencia con *nosotros*. (*us*)
2. El regalo es para *él*.   (*him*)

3. Ellos siempre hablan de _ti_____, no de _mí_. (*you, fam. / me*)
4. El billete es para _ella_. (*her*)
5. Ellos vienen con _tigo_____; no vienen con _migo_____. (*you, fam. / me*)

En el laboratorio

LECCIÓN 6

The following material is to be used with the tape in the language laboratory.

I. Vocabulario

Repeat each word after the speaker. When repeating words that are cognates, notice the difference in pronunciation between English and Spanish.

COGNADOS:	la agencia el director la educación la igualdad importante
NOMBRES:	la agencia de viajes la cárcel la escuela el éxito la hermana el hermano la iglesia el mes el pasaje, el billete el regalo
VERBOS:	dormir hacer poder recordar volar volver
ADJETIVOS:	pasado próximo
OTRAS PALABRAS Y **EXPRESIONES:**	a casa aquí de de ida de ida y vuelta en mañana que viene tener éxito

II. Práctica

A. Answer the questions, always selecting the first choice. Repeat the correct answer after the speaker's confirmation. Listen to the model.

Modelo: —¿Tú vas a la iglesia los sábados o los domingos?
    —Yo voy a la iglesia los sábados.

B. Answer the questions, using the cues provided. Repeat the correct answer after the speaker's confirmation. Listen to the model.

Modelo: —¿Cuándo puede volver usted? (mañana)
    —Puedo volver mañana.

1. (a las dos y cuarto)
2. (el lunes)
3. (ocho horas)
4. (los sábados)
5. (con el señor Álvarez)

C. Change the following negative statements to the affirmative. Repeat the correct answer after the speaker's confirmation. Listen to the model.

Modelo: Ellos nunca van.
      Ellos siempre van.

D. Say what these people *have to do,* instead of what they are doing. Repeat the correct answer after the speaker's confirmation. Listen to the model.

Modelo: Ellos van conmigo.
      Ellos tienen que ir conmigo.

III. Para escuchar y entender

1. Listen carefully to the narration. It will be read twice.

(*Narración*)

Now the speaker will make statements about the narration you just heard. Tell whether each statement is true (**verdadero**) or false (**falso**). The speaker will confirm the correct answer.

2. Listen carefully to the dialogue. It will be read twice.

(*Diálogo*)

Now the speaker will ask some questions about the dialogue you just heard. Answer each question, omitting the subject. The speaker will confirm the correct answer. Repeat the correct answer.

Lección

7

1. **Stem-changing verbs** (*e:i*)
2. **Irregular first-person forms**
3. *Saber* **contrasted with** *conocer*
4. **The impersonal** *se*
5. **Direct object pronouns**

Vocabulario

COGNADOS

el **banco** bank	la **novela** novel
excelente excellent	el **pasaporte** passport
favorito(a) favorite	el **poema** poem

NOMBRES
la **cama** bed
la **carne** meat
la **carta** letter
el **coche, carro** car
la **ensalada** salad
la **frazada, manta,**
  cobija blanket
la **librería** bookstore
el (la) **maestro(a)** teacher
  (elementary school) *any level*
el **postre** dessert
la **sábana** sheet
la **sopa** soup
el (la) **vecino(a)** neighbor
la **verdad** truth

el diario- diary

VERBOS
  cambiar to change
  conducir to conduct, to
  drive
  conocer to know, to be
  acquainted with
  conseguir (e:i) to obtain,
  to get
  decir (e:i) to say, to tell

llevar to take (*something
  or someone to someplace*)
nadar to swim
pedir (e:i) to request, to
  ask for, to order
poner to put, to place
repetir (e:i) to repeat
saber to know how, to
  know a fact
salir to go out, to leave
seguir (e:i) to follow, to
  continue
servir (e:i) to serve
traducir to translate
traer to bring
ver to see

**OTRAS PALABRAS Y
EXPRESIONES** *muy seguido*
**a menudo, muchas
  veces** often
de memoria by heart
todos los días every day *diario*
una vez por semana once
  a week
ya already, now

*dos veces por semana
twice a week.*

not commonly used (margin note, pointing to **frazada, manta**)

manejar- to handle to drive (margin note)

◀ 1. Stem-changing verbs (e:i)

Some **-ir** verbs undergo a special stem change in the present indicative. For these verbs, when **e** is the last stem vowel and it is stressed, it changes to **i**.

servir (to serve)		
sirvo	servimos	
sirves		
sirve	sirven	

◆ Notice that the stem vowel is not stressed in the verb form corresponding to **nosotros;** therefore, the **e** does not change to **i.**

—¿Qué **sirven** Uds.?	*What do you serve?*
—**Servimos** café.	*We serve coffee.*
—¿Qué **sirven** en la cafetería de la universidad?	*What do they serve in the college cafeteria?*
—**Sirven** sopa, ensalada, carne y postre.	*They serve soup, salad, meat, and dessert.*

◆ Some other common verbs that undergo the same **e** to **i** change in the stem are **pedir** (*to ask for*), **seguir** (*to follow, to continue*), and **repetir** (*to repeat*). Verbs like **seguir** contain a **u** to preserve the hard *g* sound before an **e** or an **i.** Verbs that follow this pattern drop the **u** before an **a** or an **o: yo sigo, yo consigo** (from **conseguir** *to obtain*).

—¿Qué **pide** Enrique?	*What is Enrique ordering?*
—**Pide** un refresco.	*He's ordering a soda.*
—¿A quién **siguen** Uds.?	*Whom are you following?*
—**Seguimos** a nuestra maestra.	*We are following our teacher.*

◆ The verb **decir** (*to say, to tell*) undergoes the same **e** to **i** stem change, but in addition it is irregular in the first person singular: **yo digo.**

—¿**Dice** Ud. la verdad siempre?	*Do you always tell the truth?*
—Sí, yo siempre **digo** la verdad.	*Yes, I always tell the truth.*

Práctica

A. Complete these dialogues, using the verbs provided:

1. —En este (*this*) restaurante mexicano _sirven_ una sopa muy buena. (**servir**)
   —Cuando yo vengo aquí siempre _pido_ tacos. (**pedir**) order
   —Yo siempre _digo_ que los tacos de aquí son los mejores. (**decir**)
2. —Carlos, ¿dónde _consigues_ tú libros en español? (**conseguir**) get
   —Yo _consigo_ algunos en Los Ángeles y algunos en México. (**conseguir**)
   —¿Tú _sigues_ en la clase de la Dra. Peña? (**seguir**) continue
   —Sí, y ella siempre _dice_ que yo soy su estudiante favorito. (**decir**)

3. —Los chicos *dicen* que tú siempre *sirves* carne y
ensalada. (**decir / servir**)
—No es verdad; algunas veces *sirvo* sopa. (**servir**).

B. Tell about yourself by answering these questions.

Los consigo

1. ¿Dónde consigue Ud. libros de español? *get*
2. ¿Sigue Ud. en la clase de español?   *Si, si sigo*
3. En un restaurante mexicano, ¿qué pide Ud.?
4. ¿A qué hora sirven Uds. la cena?   *nosotros la servimos a las nueve*
5. ¿Dice Ud. siempre la verdad?   *Si, siempre digo la verdad.*

The three types of stem-changing verbs

Here is a list of stem-changing verbs studied up to now. Every
time you learn a new one, add it to the list.

e:ie	o:ue	e:i
cerrar	costar	conseguir
comenzar	dormir	decir
empezar	poder	pedir *ask for*
entender	recordar	repetir
perder	volar	seguir
preferir	volver	servir
querer		

2. Irregular first-person forms

Some common verbs are irregular in the present indicative only in
the first person singular. The other persons are regular:

Verb	First-person (yo) form	Regular forms
salir (*to go out*)	**salgo**	sales, sale, salimos, salen
hacer (*to do, make*)	**hago**	haces, hace, hacemos, hacen
poner (*to put, place*)	**pongo**	pones, pone, ponemos, ponen
traer (*to bring*)	**traigo**	traes, trae, traemos, traen
conducir (*to drive; to conduct*) *manejar*	**conduzco** *manejo*	conduces, conduce, conducimos, conducen
traducir (*to translate*)	**traduzco**	traduces, traduce, traducimos, traducen
conocer (*to know*)	**conozco**	conoces, conoce, concemos, conocen
ver (*to see*)	**veo**	ves, ve, vemos, ven
saber (*to know*)	**sé**	sabes, sabe, sabemos, saben

Ser   *soy*

—¿**Sale** Ud. a menudo?   *Do you go out often?*
—Sí, yo **salgo a menudo**.   *Yes, I go out often.*

—¿Cuántas frazadas **pone**   *How many blankets do you*
   Ud. en su cama?   *put on your bed?*
—Yo **pongo** dos.   *I put two.*

—¿**Sabe** Ud. conducir?   *Do you know how to drive?*
—Sí, yo **sé** conducir.   *Yes, I know how to drive. I*
Conduzco el coche de   *drive my brother's car.*
   mi hermano.

—¿**Conoce** Ud. una buena   *Do you know a good board-*
   pensión?   *ing house?*
—Sí, la pensión Carreras   *Yes, Carreras boarding*
   es excelente.   *house is excellent.*

Práctica

Tell about yourself by answering these questions.

1. ¿Sale Ud. a menudo?
2. ¿Ve Ud. a sus amigos los sábados?
3. ¿Hace Ud. algo los domingos?
4. ¿Conoce Ud. la ciudad de Nueva York?
5. ¿Conduce Ud. bien?
6. ¿Sabe Ud. francés?
7. ¿Traduce Ud. del español al inglés?
8. ¿Trae Ud. sus libros a clase?
9. ¿Dónde pone Ud. sus libros?
10. ¿Conoce Ud. a alguien de Venezuela?

◢ 3. Saber **contrasted with** conocer

There are two verbs in Spanish that mean *to know:* **saber** and
conocer. These verbs are not interchangeable.

♦ **Saber** means to know something by heart, to know how to do
something, or to know a fact:

—¿**Sabe** Ud. algunos   *Do you know any poems by*
   poemas de memoria?   *heart?*
—No, no **sé** ninguno.   *No, I don't know any.*

—¿**Saben** ellos nadar?   *Do they know how to swim?*
—Sí, ellos **saben** nadar.   *Yes, they know how to swim.*

—¿**Sabes** qué hora es?   *Do you know what time it is?*

—Sí, **son** las ocho.   *Yes, it's eight o'clock.*

◆ **Conocer** means to be familiar or acquainted with a person, a thing, or a place:

—¿**Conoces** a la hija del vecino?   *Do you know the neighbor's daughter?*

—¿A Marta? Sí.   *Marta? Yes.*

—**Conocen** Uds. las novelas de Cervantes?   *Are you familiar with Cervantes' novels?*

—Sí, **conocemos** algunas.   *Yes, we are familiar with some (of them).*

—¿**Conoces** Puerto Rico?   *Are you familiar with Puerto Rico?*

—No, yo no **conozco** Puerto Rico.   *No, I'm not familiar with Puerto Rico.*

Práctica

Tell what these people know or don't know, using **saber** or **conocer**.

1. Ellos / California *conocen*
2. Ud. / a mi vecino *conoce*
3. ¿Tú / el poema de memoria? *sabes*
4. Él ya / al supervisor *conoce*
5. Yo no / nadar *sé*
6. ¿Uds. / las novelas de Cervantes? *conocen*
7. Yo no / qué día es hoy *sé*
8. Yo no / la ciudad de México *conozco*
9. Nosotras no / francés ni alemán *Sabemos*
10. Ellas / al hijo del profesor *conocen*

◄ 4. The impersonal *se*

In Spanish, the pronoun **se** is used before the third person of the verb (either singular or plural, depending on the subject) when the person(s) performing the action is not mentioned or is not known:

La librería **se abre** a las ocho.   *The bookstore opens (is opened) at eight.*

Las oficinas **se cierran** a las cinco.   *The offices close (are closed) at five.*

Notice the use of **se** in the following impersonal constructions, announcements, and general directions:

—¿A qué hora **se abre** la   *What time does the*
   biblioteca?   *library open?*
—**Se abre** a las ocho.   *It opens at eight.*

—¿A qué hora **se cierran**   *What time do banks close?*
   los bancos?
—Los bancos **se cierran** a   *Banks close at 3 P.M.*
   las tres de la tarde.

—¿Aquí **se habla** inglés?   *Is English spoken here?*
—No, **se habla** sólo   *No, only Spanish is*
   español.   *spoken (here).*

◆ **Se** is also used with the third person singular of the verb as the equivalent of *one, they,* or *people,* when the subject of the verb is not definite:

—¿Cómo **se dice**   *How does one say*
   «always» en español?   *"always" in Spanish?*
—**Se dice** «siempre».   *One says "siempre".*

Práctica

Luis Otero, a student from Chile, is visiting your home town and needs some information. Can you answer his questions?

1. ¿A qué hora se abre la librería de la universidad?
2. ¿Se habla español aquí?
3. ¿Cómo se dice *dirección* en inglés?
4. ¿A qué hora se cierra la cafetería?
5. ¿Se abren las oficinas de la universidad los sábados?
6. ¿A qué hora se cierra el museo?
7. ¿Se abren los bancos los sábados?
8. ¿Cómo se escribe su apellido?

5. **Direct object pronouns**

> **Direct object**   generally a noun or a pronoun that is the receiver of a verb's action and answers the question *"what?"* or *"whom?"*: Take **it**. We know **her**.

what? whom?

The forms of the direct object pronouns are as follows:

seguir

Subject	Direct Object	
yo	**me** (me)	Ella **me** visita.
tú	**te** (you, *familiar*)	Yo **te** sigo. *to follow*
Ud.	{ **lo** (you, *masc., formal*)	*know* Yo **lo** conozco. (a Ud.)[1] *conocer*
	{ **la** (you, *fem., formal*)	Yo **la** conozco. (a Ud.)[1]
él	**lo** (him, it)	Él **lo** ve. (a él)[1] *see*
ella	**la** (her, it)	Él **la** ve. (a ella)[1]
nosotros } nosotras }	**nos** (us, *masc. and fem.*)	Tú **nos** comprendes.
Uds.	{ **los** (you, *masc., pl., formal*)	Nosotros **los** visitamos. (a Uds.)[1]
	{ **las** (you, *fem., pl., formal*)	Nosotros **las** visitamos. (a Uds.)[1]
ellos	**los** (them, *masc.*)	Él **los** ve. (a ellos)[1]
ellas	**las** (them, *fem.*)	Él **las** ve. (a ellas)[1]

la esperas – you wait for her

la espero

The direct object pronoun replaces the direct object noun and is placed *before* the conjugated verb:

Yo espero **al señor Lima.**
Yo　　　　　**lo**　　espero.

Ella escribe **la carta.**
Ella　　　　　**la**　　escribe.

Nosotros llevamos **a nuestros amigos.** *we take*
Nosotros　　　　　　**los**　　llevamos.

—¿**Me** ves ahora?	*Do you see me now?*
—Sí, ahora **te** veo.	*Yes, now I see you.*
—¿~~Conduce~~ *Maneja* Ud. el coche?	*Do you drive the car?*
—Sí, yo **lo** ~~conduzco~~ *manejo*.	*Yes, I drive it.*
—¿Pides los pasaportes?	*Are you asking for the passports?*
—Sí, **los** pido.	*Yes, I am asking for them.*

◆ In a negative sentence, the **no** must precede the object pronoun:

Yo traduzco **las lecciones.**
Yo　　　　　　**las**　　traduzco.
Yo　**no**　　**las**　　traduzco.

[1] Use for clarification to avoid confusion between **Ud.** and **él** or **ella,** or between **Uds.** and **ellos** or **ellas.**

—¿Cambia Ud. las sábanas
  todos los días?

*Do you change the sheets
  every day?*

—No, no **las** cambio todos
  los días. **Las** cambio
  una vez por semana.

*No, I don't change them ev-
  ery day. I change them
  once a week.*

♦ If a conjugated verb and an infinitive appear together, the direct
  object pronoun may be placed before the conjugated verb or
  attached to the infinitive:

Te quiero ver. ⎫
  Quiero ver**te**. ⎭ *I want to see you.*

¿Vas a traer las?

—¿**Vas** a traer **las cartas?**

*Are you going to bring the
  letters?*

—Sí, **las** voy a traer *or*
—Sí,   voy a traer**las**.

*Yes, I am going to bring
  them.*

No, las voy a traer

Práctica

A. Tell the person asking you these questions that you have to do
  everything.

Modelo: —¿Quién sirve **el café?**
         —Yo **lo** sirvo.

1. ¿Quién cambia las sábanas? *Yo las cambio*
2. ¿Quién hace la ensalada?
3. ¿Quién conduce el coche? *maneja*
4. ¿Quién abre la librería?
5. ¿Quién traduce las lecciones?
6. ¿Quién lee los libros?
7. ¿Quién pone la manta en la cama?
8. ¿Quién escribe las cartas?
9. ¿Quién compra la carne?
10. ¿Quién llama a las chicas?

B. You are planning a trip to Spain. How are you getting ready for
  it? What is going to happen there? Answer the following questions always using direct object pronouns.

1. ¿Tiene Ud. su pasaporte?
2. ¿Sabe Ud. hablar bien el español? *Sí, lo sé hablar*
3. ¿Sus amigos van a esperarlo (esperarla)? *Sí, me van a esperar*
4. ¿Va a ver a sus profesores allí?
5. ¿Va a visitar los museos?
6. ¿Va a conducir su coche? *manejar*

7. ¿Ud. va a llamarnos? _Sí, voy a llamarlos._

8. ¿Va a llevarme a España con Ud.? _Sí, voy a llevarlo._

C. You are an interpreter. How would you say the following in Spanish?

1. Do you call him every day? _Lo llamas todos los días? (diario)_
2. This poem is excellent. Do you want to read it? _Este poema está excelente. Lo quieres leer._
3. The books? I am going to bring them. (*both ways*)
4. She visits us once a week.
5. Now I see you, Ana.
6. You don't know me, Mr. Lima.
7. I'm going to take them (*fem.*) to the boarding house.
8. She is my favorite cousin. I'm going to take her to the party.

3. Los libros? Voy a traerlos

4. Nos visita una vez a la semana.
        una vez por semana.

5. Ahora, te veo, Ana.

6. No me conoce, Sr. Lima.

7. Voy a llevarlas a la pensión.

8. Ella es mi prima consentida. Te voy a llevar
   a la fiesta.   preferida

use with people

use "favorita" with things

En el laboratorio

LECCIÓN 7

The following material is to be used with the tape in the language laboratory.

I. Vocabulario

Repeat each word after the speaker. When repeating words that are cognates, notice the difference in pronunciation between English and Spanish.

COGNADOS:
el banco   excelente   favorito
la novela   el pasaporte   el poema

NOMBRES:
la cama   la carne   la carta   el coche
el carro   la ensalada   la frazada
la manta   la cobija   la librería
el maestro   el postre   la sábana
la sopa   el vecino   la verdad

VERBOS:
cambiar   conducir   conocer   conseguir
decir   llevar   nadar   pedir   poner
repetir   saber   salir   seguir   servir
traducir   traer   ver

OTRAS PALABRAS Y EXPRESIONES:
muy seguido.
a menudo   muchas veces   de memoria
todos los días   una vez por semana   ya

II. Práctica

A. Change each sentence, using the verb provided. Repeat the correct answer after the speaker's confirmation. Follow the model.

Modelo: Yo quiero carne.   (pedir)
Yo **pido** carne.

B. Answer the questions, always selecting the first choice. Repeat the correct answer after the speaker's confirmation. Follow the model.

Modelo: —¿Conduces un Ford o un Chevrolet?
—Conduzco **un Ford.**

C. Answer the questions using the cue provided. Repeat the correct answer after the speaker's confirmation. Follow the model.

Modelo: ¿A qué hora se abre el banco?   (a las diez)
    El banco se abre **a las diez.**

    1. (a las nueve)
    2. (español)
    3. (frazada) manta o cojida .
    4. (no)
    5. (a las doce)

D. Answer in the negative. Replace the direct objects with the appropriate pronouns. Repeat the correct answer after the speaker's confirmation. Follow the model.

Modelo: —¿Ud. conoce a **Carlos?**
    —No, no **lo** conozco.

    1. ¿Tú **me** llamas mañana?
    2. ¿Yo **los** visito a **Uds.?** No, no nos invitas .
    3. ¿Uds. ponen **el dinero** en el banco?
    4. ¿**Te** esperan tus amigos?
    5. ¿Quieres ver **a tu amiga?**

III. Para escuchar y entender

1. Listen carefully to the dialogue. It will be read twice.

   (*Diálogo 1*)

   Now the speaker will make statements about the dialogue you just heard. Tell whether each statement is true (**verdadero**) or false (**falso**). The speaker will confirm the correct answer.

2. Listen carefully to the narration. It will be read twice.

   (*Narración*)

   Now the speaker will ask some questions about the narration you just heard. Answer each question, omitting the subject. The speaker will confirm the correct answer. Repeat the correct answer.

3. Listen carefully to the dialogue. It will be read twice.

   (*Diálogo 2*)

   Now the speaker will ask some questions about the dialogue you just heard. Answer each question, omitting the subject. The speaker will confirm the correct answer. Repeat the correct answer.

Lección

8

Vocabulario

COGNADOS

generoso(a)   generous
la información   information
la medicina   medicine
el momento   moment
el parque   park

el (la) presidente(a)
   president
la raqueta   racket
el tenis   tennis

NOMBRES
la comida   food, dinner, meal
los hijos   children (sons and daughters)
la mochila   backpack
los niños   children, kids
los patines   skates
la pelota   ball
el periódico, diario   newspaper
la raqueta de tenis   tennis racket
la sección deportiva   sports section
la tía   aunt
el tío   uncle

VERBOS
creer   to believe, to think
esquiar   to ski
jugar[1]   to play (e.g.: a game)
pagar   to pay
preguntar   to ask (a question)
prestar   to lend, borrow from

OTRAS PALABRAS Y EXPRESIONES
allá   over there
ir a esquiar   to go skiing
¿para quién?   for whom?
que   that, which

Handwritten notes:
presentar — to introduce
cocinar — to cook
acostar — to go to bed
ahí
la bola (small balls)
la propina — tip
las pinturas —
no me aguanto de esquiar / de viajar — I can't wait.

1. Demonstrative adjectives and pronouns

> **Demonstrative**   a word that points out a definite person or object: this that these those

Demonstrative adjectives

Demonstrative adjectives point out persons or things. They agree in gender and number with the nouns they modify or point out.

---

[1] Present tense: juego, juegas, juega, jugamos, juegan

The forms of the demonstrative adjectives are as follows:

Masculine		Feminine		
Singular	*Plural*	*Singular*	*Plural*	
este	**estos**	**esta**	**estas**	this, these
ese	**esos**	**esa**	**esas**	that, those
aquel	**aquellos**	**aquella**	**aquellas**	that, those ~~(at a distance)~~

—¿Para quién es **esta** raqueta de tenis?

Who is this tennis racket for?

—**Esta** raqueta es para Marta y **esa** pelota es para Rita.

This racket is for Marta and that ball is for Rita.

—¿Podemos comer hoy en **este** restaurante?

Can we eat at this restaurant today?

—No, vamos a comer en **aquella** cafetería que está allá.

No, we are going to eat at that cafeteria (which is) over there.

Práctica

Change the demonstrative adjectives so that they agree with the new nouns.

1. Este cuaderno, _esta_ carpeta, _estas_ revistas, _estos_ programas.
2. Esas ciudades, _esos_ teatros, _esa_ biblioteca, _ese_ museo.
3. Aquella mesa, _aquellas_ sillas, _aquel_ tenedor, _aquellos_ restaurantes.
4. Esta lección, _este_ idioma, _estos_ problemas, _estas_ universidades.
5. Ese jabón, _esas_ sábanas, _esos_ cuartos, _esa_ toalla.

Demonstrative pronouns

The demonstrative pronouns are the same as the demonstrative adjectives, except that the pronouns have a written accent mark.

The forms of the demonstrative pronouns are as follows:

Masculine		Feminine		Neuter	
Singular	Plural	Singular	Plural		
éste	éstos	ésta	éstas	esto	this (one), these
ése	ésos	ésa	ésas	eso	that (one), those
aquél	aquéllos	aquélla	aquéllas	aquello	that (one), those (at a distance)

—¿Qué patines quiere Ud.? ¿**Éstos** o **aquéllos**?
Which skates do you want? These or those (over there)?

—Quiero **aquéllos**.
I want those (over there).

—¿Necesitan Uds. estos periódicos o **ésos**?
Do you need these newspapers or those (ones)?

—No, necesitamos **aquél** que está en la mesa.
No, we need that one (which is) on the table.

(handwritten note: Use accent mark when there is no subject.)

♦ Each demonstrative pronoun has a neuter form. The neuter pronoun has no accent, because there are no corresponding demonstrative adjectives.

♦ The neuter forms are used to refer to situations, ideas or things that are abstract, general or unidentified. The neuter pronouns are equivalent to the English *this* or *that* (*matter, business; thing, stuff*).

—¿Qué crees de **eso**?

What do you think about that (matter, issue)?

—Creo que **eso** es un problema para el presidente.

I think that is a problem for the president.

—¿Qué es **esto**?

What is this (thing, stuff)?

—No sé.

I don't know.

Práctica

Complete the following sentences with the Spanish equivalent of the pronouns in parentheses:

1. Quiero este coche y _ese_ aquel (that one). aquella
2. Necesitamos esa pelota y _esa_ (that one [over there]). aquella
3. Compramos esos patines y _estos_ (these). (or aquellos)
4. Recibimos este periódico y _esos_ (those). (or aquellos)
5. ¿Estudia Ud. esta lección o _esa_ (that one)?
6. ¿Habla Ud. con este niño o con _aquel_ (that one [over there])?
7. ¿Prefieren ellos estas mesas de madera o _aquellas_ (those [over there])?
8. ¿Va Ud. a leer este libro o _esos_ (those)? aquellos
9. Deseo aquellas revistas y _estas_ (these).
10. ¿Van Uds. a comprar esa raqueta o _esta_ (this one)?
11. Ellas no saben qué es _esto_ (this). neutral
12. ¿Quién dice _eso_ (that)? neutral

◢ 2. The present progressive

The present progressive describes an action that is in progress at the moment we are talking. In Spanish, it is formed with the present tense of **estar** and the Spanish equivalent of the *-ing* form[1] of the main verb.

-ing Form Endings *use w/ estar*		
-ar: **hablar**	-er: **comer**	-ir: **vivir**
habl- **ando**	com- **iendo**	viv- **iendo**

◆ Some irregular *-ing* forms:

pedir	**pidiendo**	servir	**sirviendo**
decir	**diciendo**	leer	**leyendo**[2]
dormir	**durmiendo**	traer	**trayendo**[2]

[1] The equivalent of the *-ing* form of the verb is called **el gerundio** in Spanish.
[2] Notice that the **-i** of **-iendo** becomes **y** between vowels.

—¿Qué están **haciendo** los niños en este momento?

What are the children doing right now (at this moment)?

—Están **jugando** en el parque.

They are playing in the park.

—¿Qué **estás comiendo?**

What are you eating?

—**Estoy comiendo** el postre.

I'm eating dessert.

—¿Qué **está leyendo** Ud.?

What are you reading?

—**Estoy leyendo** la sección deportiva.

I'm reading the sports section.

ATENCIÓN: Unlike in English, the present progressive is never used in Spanish to refer to a future action. Instead, the present indicative is used for actions that will occur in the near future: **Salgo mañana.** *I'm leaving tomorrow.*

Verbs such as **ser, estar, ir** (**yendo**), and **venir** (**viniendo**) are rarely used in the progressive construction.

Práctica

Tell us what these people are doing right now:

Modelo: Yo (tomar café)
Yo estoy tomando café.

1. Julia (leer la sección deportiva) está leyendo.
2. Ellos (pedir los patines) están pidiendo
3. Nosotros (decir la verdad) estamos diciendo
4. Ud. (comer carne) está comiendo carne
5. José (servir la sopa) está sirviendo.
6. Ella (dormir en el hotel) está durmiendo en el hot
7. Tú (hablar con el presidente) Tu estás hablando con el pres.
8. Yo (esperar a Rosa) estoy esperando a Rosa

3. Indirect object pronouns

Indirect object a word that tells *to whom* or *for whom* something is done. An indirect object pronoun can be used in place of the indirect object. In Spanish, the indirect object pronoun includes the meaning *to* or *for*: Yo **les** mando los libros (*a los estudiantes*). I send the books **to them** (*to the students*).

The forms of the indirect object pronouns are as follows:

Subject	Indirect Object	
yo	**me** (to / for me)	Él **me** da las revistas. *él me las da*
tú	**te** (to / for you, *familiar*)	Yo **te** doy el cuaderno. *Te lo doy*
Ud.	**le** (to / for you, *formal, masc. and fem.*)	Ella **le** compra una corbata. *a usted*
él ⎫ ella ⎭	**le** (to / for him / her)	Yo **le** hablo en inglés, *a usted, a él, a ella*
nosotros ⎫ nosotras ⎭	**nos** (to / for us, *masc. and fem.*)	Ella **nos** da la lección. *Nos la da*
Uds. ⎫ ellos ⎬ ellas ⎭	**les** (to / for you, *formal pl., masc. and fem.*) **les** (to / for them, *masc. and fem.*)	Yo **les** digo la verdad. El presidente **les** da el dinero.

Lucha nos da de comer – Lucha gives us food. (Feeds us)

The forms of the indirect object pronouns are the same as the forms of the direct object pronouns, except in the third person. Indirect object pronouns are usually placed *in front* of the verb. *Changed to plural*

—¿Quién **les** compra a   Who buys you the tickets?
   Uds. los pasajes?
—Mi padre **nos** compra   My father buys us the   *Mi padre nos los compra*
   los pasajes.   tickets.

—¿En qué idioma **le**   In which language do you
   hablas? *a él*   speak to him?
—**Le** hablo en español.   I speak to him in Spanish.

◆ When an infinitive follows the conjugated verb, the indirect object pronoun may be placed in front of the conjugated verb or attached to the infinitive:

Te voy a comprar   una mochila.
   Voy a comprar**te**   una mochila.

◆ With the present progressive forms, the indirect object pronoun can be placed in front of the conjugated verb or it can be attached to the end of the progressive construction.

Le estoy escribiendo   a mi esposa.
   Estoy escribiéndo**le** a mi esposa.

ATENCIÓN: The indirect object pronouns **le** and **les** require clarification when the person to whom they refer is not specified. Spanish provides clarification by using the preposition **a** + *personal (subject) pronoun.*

Le doy la información.	*I give the information . . . (to whom? to him? to her? to you?)*
but: **Le** doy la información **a ella**.	*I give the information to her.*

This prepositional form is also used to express emphasis.

Le doy el pasaje **a él**.   *I give the ticket to **him*** (and to nobody else).

Te doy el pasaje a ti

Although the prepositional form provides clarification, it is not a substitute for the indirect object pronoun. The prepositional form may be omitted, but the indirect object pronoun must always be used.

—¿Qué **le** vas a traer (a Roberto)?
—**Le** voy a traer un libro.

Práctica

A. Express the following, using indirect object pronouns:

Modelo: Ella trae el diario **para él**.
           Ella **le** trae el diario.

1. Yo compro la mochila **para ti**.
2. Nosotros vamos a traer los refrescos **para Uds**.   (*both ways*)
3. Ada hace la sopa **para mí**.
4. Ellos están escribiendo una carta **para ella**.   (*both ways*)
5. Yo voy a traer los pasajes **para Ud**.   (*both ways*)
6. Fernando compra los patines **para nosotros.**

B. Answer the following questions, using the information in parentheses:

1. ¿Qué vas a comprarle a tu hijo?   (un automóvil)
2. ¿Qué les da a Uds. el profesor?   (unos cuadernos)
3. ¿Quién te escribe?   (mi novio / mi novia)
4. ¿Qué vas a traerme?   (una pelota)
5. ¿Qué les vas a mandar a los niños?   (unas raquetas)
6. ¿Cuándo nos va a escribir Ud.?   (mañana)

C. Answer these questions:

1. ¿Tú le pides dinero a tu papá?
2. ¿El profesor te va a dar una «A» en español?

3. ¿Puedes darme el periódico? *Si, puedo darte lo.*
4. ¿Uds. pueden traernos unos refrescos?
5. ¿El profesor les trae a Uds. revistas en español?

D. You are an interpreter. How would you say the following in Spanish?

1. I always give you the tickets, Mr. Smith.
2. Are you writing to him at this moment? *(both ways)*
3. My wife always tells me the truth.
4. Are you going to buy us a magazine? *(both ways)*
5. I speak to them *(fem.)* in English.
6. I'm going to bring the coffee to my dad. *(both ways)* *Voy a traerle a mi papa.*
Le voy a traer el cafe a mi papa.

4. Direct and indirect object pronouns used together *juntos*

When both an indirect object pronoun and a direct object pronoun are used in the same sentence, the indirect object pronoun always appears first:

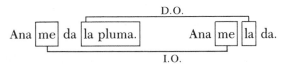

D.O.

Ana │me│ da │la pluma.│   Ana │me│ │la│ da.

I.O.

—¿Cuándo me pagas el dinero?
—**Te lo** pago[1] mañana.

When are you paying me the money?
I'll pay (it to) you tomorrow.

♦ With an infinitive, the pronouns may be placed either before the main verb or attached to the infinitive:

I.O.   D.O.

Ana │me│ │la│ va a dar.

Ana   va a │dármela.│[2]

I.O.   D.O.

—Necesito el diccionario. ¿Puedes prestár**melo**?
—Sí, **te lo** puedo prestar.

I need the dictionary. Can you lend it to me?

Yes, I can lend it to you.

---

[1] The present indicative is frequently used in Spanish to express future time.
[2] See Appendix A, part 7, number 3 (p. 280) for rules governing the use of accent marks in Spanish.

◆ With a gerund, the pronouns can be placed either before the conjugated verb or after the gerund.

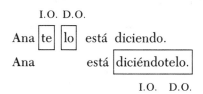

I.O. D.O.

Ana |te| |lo| está diciendo.

Ana   está |diciéndotelo.|

          I.O.   D.O.

◆ If both pronouns begin with l, the indirect object pronoun (**le** or **les**) is changed to **se**.

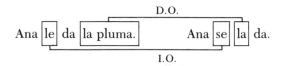

                      D.O.

Ana |le| da |la pluma.| Ana |se| |la| da.

              I.O.

◆ For clarification, it is sometimes necessary to specify the person(s) to whom the pronoun refers: **a él, a ella, a Ud., a Uds., a ellos, a ellas, a José,** etc.

—¿**Le** sirves la comida a   *Do you serve dinner to him*
  él o **a ella?**   *or to her?*
—**Se** la sirvo **a él.**   *I serve it to him.*

—¿**Les** dan Uds. la medi-   *Are you giving the medicine*
  cina a **ellas** o **a ellos?**   *to them (fem.) or to them*
                                    (masc.)?
—**Se** la damos **a ellos.**   *We are giving it to them*
                                    (masc.).

Práctica

A. Mom is always doing things for us. Explain what she does using the information provided:

Modelo: **Yo** quiero **una mochila.**   (comprar)
          Mamá **me la** compra.

1. **Papá** quiere **café.**   (servir)
2. **Nosotros** necesitamos **dinero.**   (dar)
3. **Tú** quieres **los periódicos.**   (traer)
4. **Yo** quiero **una raqueta.**   (prestar)
5. **Mis hijos** necesitan **toallas.**   (comprar)
6. **Papá** quiere **sopa.**   (traer)
7. **Uds.** necesitan **la medicina.**   (dar)
8. **Ud.** quiere comer **comida mexicana.**   (hacer)

B. You keep changing your mind. First you say "yes" and then you say "no". Substitute pronouns for the boldface nouns:

Modelo: —¿Me compra Ud. **el jabón?**
—Sí, se lo compro.
—No, no se lo compro.

1. ¿Me presta Ud. **sus patines?**
2. ¿Me compra Ud. **la manta?**
3. ¿Les paga Ud. **los pasajes** a ellos?
4. ¿Está Ud. leyéndole **el periódico** a Inés?
5. ¿Nos va a traer Ud. **las medicinas?** *Si, se las voy a traer*
6. ¿Va a servirme Ud. **la comida** ahora?

C. How would you say the following in Spanish?

1. The rackets? My cousin can bring them to us.
2. Do you need the sheet, Anita? I can give it to you.
3. I need soap. Can you buy it for me, Paquito?
4. Do you want to read this magazine, Miss Soto? I can lend it to you.
5. If the children want to play with the ball, I can give it to them.

Comparado con

5. Pedir **contrasted with** preguntar

♦ **Pedir** means *to ask for* or *to request (something):*

—¿Qué te **piden** los muchachos?	*What do the boys ask you for?*
—Me **piden** la medicina para su madre.	*They ask me for the medicine for their mother.*
—¿Vas a **pedirle** dinero a tu tío?	*Are you going to ask your uncle for money?*
—No, voy a **pedírselo** a mi tía. Ella es más generosa.	*No, I'm going to ask my aunt (for it). She's more generous.*
—¿Cuánto le vas a **pedir?**	*How much are you going to ask for?*
—Veinte dólares.	*Twenty dollars.*

♦ **Preguntar** means *to ask (a question):*

—¿Qué vas a **preguntarle** a René?	*What are you going to ask René?*
—Voy a **preguntarle** si quiere ir a esquiar.	*I'm going to ask him if he wants to go skiing.*

—¿Qué le vas a **preguntar** a Ana?

What are you going to ask Ana?

—Le voy a **preguntar** cuántos hijos tiene.

I'm going to ask her how many children she has.

Práctica

What are these people doing? Use **pedir** or **preguntar**, as needed:

1. Mis hijos *piden* dinero.
2. Yo le *pregunto* qué quiere. *a él, a ella*
3. Ella le va a *preguntar* si es el tío de Jorge.
4. Yo nunca le *pido* nada. Ella no es muy generosa.
5. Le voy a *preguntar* si quiere ir a esquiar allá.
6. ¿Qué le vas a *pedir* tú a Santa Claus?[1]
7. ¿Qué te *pide* Carlos? ¿Dinero?
8. Yo nunca les *pregunto* nada a mis primos, porque ellos no saben nada.

---

[1] In most Latin American countries and in Spain, it is the custom to expect presents from the Three Wise Men, *los Tres Reyes Magos*, on January 6.

En el laboratorio

The following material is to be used with the tape in the language laboratory.

I. Vocabulario

Repeat each word after the speaker. When repeating words that are cognates, notice the difference in pronunciation between English and Spanish.

COGNADOS:	generoso la información la medicina el momento el parque el presidente la raqueta el tenis
NOMBRES:	la comida los hijos la mochila los niños los patines la pelota el periódico el diario la raqueta de tenis la sección deportiva la tía el tío
VERBOS:	creer esquiar jugar pagar preguntar prestar
OTRAS PALABRAS Y EXPRESIONES:	allá ir a esquiar ¿para quién? que

II. Práctica

A. Give the Spanish equivalent of the demonstrative adjective that agrees with each noun mentioned by the speaker. Repeat the correct answer after the speaker's confirmation. Listen to the model.

Modelo: this / raqueta
esta raqueta

1. this / these
2. that / those
3. that (*over there*) / those (*over there*)

B. Change the verbs to the present progressive. Repeat the correct answer after the speaker's confirmation. Listen to the model.

Modelo: —Yo tomo café.
—Yo **estoy tomando** café.

C. Repeat each sentence, then substitute the new indirect object pronouns in the sentence. Repeat the correct answer after the speaker's confirmation. Listen to the model.

115

Modelo: —Carmen **me da** el dinero.   (les)
          —Carmen **les da** el dinero.

1. Pedro me trae los patines.   (nos / les / te / le)
2. Van a pedirte la mochila.   (me / nos / les / le)
3. Está escribiéndote una carta.   (nos / le / me / les)

D. Repeat each sentence, changing the direct object to the corresponding direct object pronouns. Make all the necessary changes in the sentence. Repeat the correct answer after the speaker's confirmation. Listen to the model.

Modelo: —**Le** traen **el periódico.**
          —**Se lo** traen.

E. Answer the questions, using the cue provided. Repeat the correct answer after the speaker's confirmation. Listen to the model.

Modelo: —¿Qué te pide Jorge?   (la pelota)
          —**Me pide la pelota.** bola)

1. (su dirección)
2. (500 dólares)
3. (no, a mi papá)
4. (si pueden ir al cine)
5. (la sección deportiva)

III. Para escuchar y entender

1. Listen carefully to the dialogue. It will be read twice.

(*Diálogo 1*)

Now the speaker will make statements about the dialogue you just heard. Tell whether each statement is true (**verdadero**) or false (**falso**). The speaker will confirm the correct answer.

2. Listen carefully to the dialogue. It will be read twice.

(*Diálogo 2*)

Now the speaker will ask some questions about the dialogue you just heard. Answer each question, omitting the subject. The speaker will confirm the correct answer. Repeat the correct answer.

9

1. Possessive pronouns
2. Reflexive constructions
3. Command forms (*Ud.* and *Uds.*)
4. Uses of object pronouns with command forms

Vocabulario

el **documento** document
generalmente generally
el **guía** guide

[handwritten: without waiting]
[handwritten: desesperado]
impaciente impatient
la **terraza** terrace
[handwritten: el deck]

[handwritten: la cintura – belt]

NOMBRES
la **bebida** drink
la **cinta** tape *[handwritten: casete]*
el **disco** record *[handwritten: C.D. compacto]*
el **dormitorio** bedroom
la **entrada** ticket (*for a show, for admission*)
el **escenario** stage
la **maleta, valija** suitcase
la **medianoche** midnight
el **pantalón**, los **pantalones** pants
el **parque de diversiones** amusement park
el **peine** comb, *[handwritten: brush]*
la **puerta** door
la **tarjeta** card
— **de crédito** credit card
la **tintorería** dry cleaners
la **ventana** window
el **vestido** dress
[handwritten: el cepillo – brush]

VERBOS
acordarse (o:ue) (de) to remember
acostar(se) (o:ue) to put to bed; to go to bed
[handwritten: rasurarse] **afeitar(se)** to shave (*oneself*)
bañar(se) to bathe (*oneself*)

despertar(se) (e:ie) to wake up
doblar to turn, *[handwritten: to fold]*
dormirse to fall asleep
irse to leave, to go away
lavar(se) to wash (*oneself*)
levantar(se) to lift, to raise; to get up
ponerse to put on
probar(se) (o:ue) to try, to taste; to try on
quejarse (de) to complain
quitar(se) to take away, to take off
sentar(se) (e:ie) to sit, to sit down
vestir(se) (e:i) to dress, to get dressed

[handwritten: presentarse – to show up, to present oneself, to introduce]

ADJETIVO
querido(a) dear

OTRAS PALABRAS Y EXPRESIONES
a la derecha to the right
a la izquierda to the left
antes de before
cerca de near
seguir (e:i) derecho to continue straight ahead
tan so
todavía yet

1. Possessive pronouns

Singular		Plural		
Masculine	*Feminine*	*Masculine*	*Feminine*	
el mío	la mía	los míos	las mías	mine
el tuyo	la tuya	los tuyos	las tuyas	yours (*familiar*)
el suyo	la suya	los suyos	las suyas	his, hers, yours (*formal*)
el nuestro	la nuestra	los nuestros	las nuestras	ours
el suyo	la suya	los suyos	las suyas	theirs, yours (*formal*)

The possessive pronouns in Spanish agree in gender and number with the thing possessed. They are generally used with the definite article:

—Aquí están las entradas de ellos. ¿Dónde están **las nuestras?**   *Here are their tickets. Where are ours?*

—**Las nuestras** están en el dormitorio.   *Ours are in the bedroom.*

—Tus pantalones están aquí. ¿Dónde están **los míos?**   *Your trousers are here. Where are mine?*

—**Los tuyos** están en la tintorería.   *Yours are at the cleaners.*

—Mi vestido está allá. ¿Dónde está **el suyo?**   *My dress is over there. Where is yours?*

—**El mío** está en la cama.   *Mine is on the bed.*

♦ After the verb **ser,** the definite article is frequently omitted:

—¿**Son tuyos** estos peines?   *Are these combs yours?*

—Sí, estos peines **son míos,** pero aquéllos **son tuyos.**   *Yes, these combs are mine, but those over there are yours.*

—¿Esta tarjeta de crédito **es suya,** Sr. Muñoz?   *Is this credit card yours, Mr. Muñoz?*

—Sí, **es mía.** Gracias.   *Yes, it's mine, thanks.*

♦ Since the third-person forms of the possessive pronouns (**el suyo, la suya, los suyos, las suyas**) could be ambiguous, they may be replaced for clarification by the following:

el de	Ud.
la de	él
los de	ella
las de	Uds.
	ellos
	ellas

—Estos discos y estas
~~cintas~~ son de Marta y *[handwritten: casetes]*
de Arturo, ¿no?
—Bueno, los discos son **de
ella,** pero las cintas son
de él. *[handwritten: casetes]*

*These records and these
tapes are Martha's and
Arturo's, right?
Well, the records are hers
but the tapes are his.*

Práctica

A. Supply the correct possessive pronouns and read aloud. Follow the models:

Modelos: Yo tengo una cinta. Es _____.
Yo tengo una cinta. Es mía.

Juan tiene un disco. Es _____ / (Es _____.)
Juan tiene un disco. Es suyo. (Es (de él.)) *[handwritten: belongs to him]*

1. Tú tienes un vestido. Es _tuyo_.
2. Juan tiene un diccionario. Es _suyo_. (Es _de él_.)
3. Nosotros tenemos una tarjeta de crédito. Es _nuestra_.
4. Ud. tiene unos peines. Son _suyos_ (Son _de ud._) *[handwritten: belongs to you]*
5. Yo tengo un coche. Es _mío_.
6. Uds. tienen dos lápices. Son _suyos_ (Son _de uds._)
7. Yo tengo unos pantalones. Son _míos_.
8. Lucía tiene tres hijos. Son _suyos_ (Son _de ella_.)

[handwritten left margin: aclarar — to clarify]

B. You are an interpreter. How would you say the following in Spanish?

1. This ticket is mine. Where is yours, Mr. Britos?
2. These records aren't ours.
3. His pants are at the cleaners. Where are yours, Anita?
4. The books are hers, but the pens are theirs.
5. Your tape is here, Mrs. Ortiz. Mine is in the bedroom.
6. Her dress is blue and mine is green.

[handwritten left margin: Sus pantalones / Los pantalones de él]

[handwritten bottom: Estar 1) current condition 2) location]

2. Reflexive constructions

Reflexive pronouns

A reflexive construction, such as *I introduce myself*, consists of a reflexive pronoun and a verb. Reflexive pronouns refer to the same person who is the subject of the sentence.

Subjects	Reflexive Pronouns	
yo	me	*myself, to / for myself*
tú	te	*yourself, to / for yourself* (tú form)
nosotros	nos	*ourselves, to / for ourselves*
Ud.		*yourself, to / for yourself*
Uds.		*yourselves, to / for yourselves*
él	se	*himself, to / for himself*
ella		*herself, to / for herself*
		itself, to / for itself
ellos, ellas		*themselves, to / for themselves*

♦ Note that, with the exception of **se**, reflexive pronouns have the same forms as the direct and indirect object pronouns.

♦ The third-person singular and plural **se** is invariable.

♦ Reflexive pronouns are positioned in the sentence in the same manner as object pronouns. They are placed in front of a conjugated verb: **Yo *me* levanto a las ocho.** *I get up at eight.* They may be attached to an infinitive or to a gerund: **Yo voy a levantar*me* a las ocho.** *I am going to get up at eight.* **Yo estoy levantándo*me*.** *I am getting up.*

♦ Most verbs can be made reflexive in Spanish if they act upon the subject with the aid of a reflexive pronoun.

Julia **le** prueba el vestido a su hija.	*Julia tries the dress **on her** daughter.*
Julia **se prueba** el vestido.	*Julia tries **on** the dress.*

Julia le prueba el
vestido a su hija.

Julia se prueba
el vestido.

Reflexive verbs

♦ Some commonly used reflexive verbs:

lavarse (*to wash oneself, to wash up*)	
Yo **me lavo**	*I wash (myself)*
Tú **te lavas**	*You wash (yourself*-fam.*)*
Ud. **se lava**	*You wash (yourself*-formal*)*
Él **se lava**	*He washes (himself)*
Ella **se lava**	*She washes (herself)*
Nosotros **nos lavamos**	*We wash (ourselves)*
Uds. **se lavan**	*You wash (yourselves)*
Ellos **se lavan**	*They* (masc.) *wash (themselves)*
Ellas **se lavan**	*They* (fem.) *wash (themselves)*

Other verbs frequently used in the reflexive are:

despertarse (e:ie)   *to wake up*
levantarse   *to get up*
vestirse (e:i)   *to get dressed*
afeitarse   *to shave*
bañarse   *to bathe*
sentarse (e:i)   *to sit down*
acostarse (o:ue)   *to go to bed, to lie down*

[handwritten: rasurse]

[handwritten: darse cuenta - to notice, to realize]

♦ Some verbs are *always* used with reflexive pronouns in Spanish:

acordarse (o:ue) (de)   *to remember,* *[handwritten: to think of]*
quejarse (de)   *to complain*

Notice that the use of a reflexive pronoun does not necessarily imply a reflexive action.

[handwritten: reco]

♦ Some verbs change their meaning when they are used with reflexive pronouns:

acostar (o:ue) *to put to bed*	**acostarse** *to go to bed*
dormir (o:ue) *to sleep*	**dormirse** *to fall asleep*
ir *to go*	**irse** *to leave, to go away*
levantar *to lift, to raise*	**levantarse** *to get up*
probar (o:ue) *to try, to taste*	**probarse** *to try on*
poner *to put*	**ponerse** *to put on (e.g. clothing)*
quitar *to take away, to remove*	**quitarse** *to take off (e.g., clothing)*

♦ Notice the use of the reflexive in the following sentences:

—¿A qué hora **se levanta** Ud., señorita López?	*What time do you get up, Miss Lopez?*
—Generalmente **me levanto** a las ocho, pero no **me acuesto** hasta la medianoche.	*I generally get up at eight o'clock, but I don't go to bed until midnight.*
—¿**Se acuerda** Ud. de Rosita?	*Do you remember Rosita?*
—Sí, **me acuerdo** de ella.	*Yes, I remember her.*
—¿Por qué no **te acuestas**, querido?	*Why don't you go to bed, dear?*
—Primero voy a **acostar** a los chicos.	*First I'm going to put the children to bed.*
—¿Qué vas a hacer antes de salir[1]?	*What are you going to do before leaving?*
—**Me voy a lavar** las manos y **me voy.**	*I'm going to wash my hands and I'm leaving.*

ATENCIÓN: Notice that in Spanish, the definite article is used in place of the possessive adjective with articles of clothing or parts of the body.

Práctica

A. Describe what these people do using the present indicative or the infinitive of the verbs in parentheses.

1. Elena _____ (probarse) el vestido.
2. Ella _____ (acostarse) y Ud. _____ (acostar) a los niños.
3. Carlos _____ (bañarse) y Luis _____ (vestirse).

[1] The infinitive, not the -*ing* form, is used after a preposition in Spanish.

4. Tú siempre _te duermas_ (dormirse) en la clase.
5. Nosotros nunca _quejamos_ (quejarse) de nada.
6. Yo _me quito_ (quitarse) los pantalones.
7. Debes _bañarte_ (bañarse) antes de _vestirte_ (vestirse).
8. Nosotros vamos a _sentarnos_ (sentarse) aquí.
9. ¿Por qué no _te afeitas_ (afeitarse), querido?
10. Pepito, debes _lavarte_ (lavarse) las manos ahora.

B. Tell about yourself by answering the following questions:

1. ¿A qué hora se acuesta Ud.?
2. ¿Se duerme Ud. en clase? _A veces_
3. ¿A qué hora se levanta Ud.?
4. ¿Siempre se despierta temprano?
5. ¿Qué se va a poner Ud. para salir mañana?
6. ¿Se acuerda Ud. de sus amigos?
7. ¿Ud. siempre prueba la comida antes de servirla?
8. ¿Se queja su profesor de los estudiantes?

C. Describe what you do during a typical day from the time you wake up to the time you go to bed.

Summary of Personal Pronouns

Subject	Direct object	Indirect object	Reflexive	Object of prepositions
yo	me	me	me	mí
tú	te	te	te	ti
usted (f.)	la			usted
usted (m.)	lo	le	-se	usted
él	lo			él
ella	la			ella
nosotros	nos	nos	nos	nosotros
ustedes (f.)	las			ustedes
ustedes (m.)	los	les	se	ustedes
ellos	los			ellos
ellas	las			ellas

3. Command forms (Ud. and Uds.)

Command form the form of a verb used to give an order or a direction: **Go! Come back! Turn to the right.**

To form the command for **Ud.** and **Uds.**,[1] drop the **-o** of the first person singular of the present indicative and add the following endings to the stem.

> **-ar** verbs: **-e** (Ud.) and **-en** (Uds.)
> **-er** verbs: **-a** (Ud.) and **-an** (Uds.)
> **-ir** verbs: **-a** (Ud.) and **-an** (Uds.)

ATENCIÓN: Notice that the endings for the **-er** and **-ir** verbs are the same.

Infinitive	First Person Present Ind.	Stem		Commands Ud.	Uds.
hablar	Yo hablo	habl-	habla	hable	hablen
comer	Yo como	com-	come	coma	coman
abrir	Yo abro	abr-	abre	abra	abran
cerrar	Yo cierro	cierr-	cierra	cierre	cierren
volver	Yo vuelvo	vuelv-	vuelve	vuelva	vuelvan
pedir	Yo pido	pid-	pide	pida	pidan
decir	Yo digo	dig-	dige	diga	digan
hacer	Yo hago	hag-	haz	haga	hagan
traducir	Yo traduzco	traduzc-	traduce	traduzca	traduzcan

—¿Con quién debo hablar? — *With whom must I speak?*
—**Hable** con el guía. — *Speak with the guide.*

—¿Vengo por la mañana o por la tarde? — *Shall I come in the morning or in the afternoon?*

—**Venga** por la mañana y **traiga** sus documentos. — *Come in the morning and bring your documents.*

—¿Cierro la puerta? — *Shall I close the door?*
—No, no **cierre** la puerta. **Cierre** la ventana, por favor. — *No, don't close the door. Close the window, please.*

—¿Sigo derecho o **doblo** a la derecha? — *Shall I continue straight ahead or shall I turn right?*

—**Doble** a la izquierda. — *Turn left.*

---

[1] The **tú** form will be studied in Lesson 11.

♦ The command forms of the following verbs are irregular:

	dar	estar	ser	ir
Ud.	dé	esté	sea	vaya
Uds.	den	estén	sean	vayan

(handwritten: Tu — da, estés)

—¿Podemos ir solas al   *Can we go to the amuse-*
  parque de diversiones?   *ment park alone?*
—No, no **vayan** solas.   *No, don't go alone. Go with*
  Vayan con sus padres.   *your parents.*

—¡Le digo que quiero ver   *I'm telling you I want to see*
  a mis hijos!   *my children.*
—Un momento, señora.   *One moment, madam.*
  ¡No **sea** tan impaciente!   *Don't be so impatient!*

Práctica

A. Tell these people what to do, using the cues provided:

Modelos: —¿Hablo con el recepcionista?   (director)
           —**No, hable con el director.**

           —¿Hablamos con el recepcionista?   (director)
           —**No, hablen con el director.**

1. ¿Hago la lección número uno?   (la lección número dos)
2. ¿Cerramos las ventanas?   (las puertas)
3. ¿Compramos toallas?   (sábanas)
4. ¿Damos nuestra dirección?   (nuestro número de teléfono)
5. ¿Duermo aquí?   (en el dormitorio)
6. ¿Estudiamos con Alberto?   (con Ana)
7. ¿Trabajamos hoy?   (mañana)
8. ¿Vuelvo el lunes?   (el martes)
9. ¿Sirvo café?   (té)
10. ¿Pedimos refrescos?   (sopa y postre)
11. ¿Doblo a la derecha?   (a la izquierda)
12. ¿Estoy aquí a las ocho?   (a las nueve)
13. ¿Salimos por la tarde?   (por la noche)
14. ¿Traducimos la lección ocho?   (la lección seis)
15. ¿Traigo la carne?   (la ensalada)
16. ¿Vamos al cine?   (al teatro)

B. You are an interpreter. How would you say the following in Spanish?

No vaya derecho. Vaya a la izquierdo.

1. Don't continue straight ahead. Turn left.

Sean 2. Don't be so *tan* impatient, ladies.

3. Wait one moment, Mr. Peña. *Espere*
4. Go with the guide. *Vaya*
5. Bring your documents, Miss Ruiz.
6. Be at the amusement park at seven P.M., girls.

Vayan a la feria

(feria — also means "money")

Tienen mucha feria

4. Uses of object pronouns with command forms

Affirmative commands

With all direct *affirmative* commands, the object pronouns are placed *after* the verb and are attached to it, thus forming only one word:

—¿Dónde pongo las bebidas?	*Where shall I put the drinks?*
—**Póngalas**¹ en la mesa.	*Put them on the table.*
—¿Dónde sirvo el café?	*Where shall I serve (the) coffee?*
—**Sírvalo** en la terraza.	*Serve it on the terrace.*
—¿Qué les doy a las chicas?	*What shall I give the girls?*
—**Deles** el postre.	*Give them dessert.*
—¿Abrimos la puerta?	*Shall we open the door?*
—Sí, **ábranla.**	*Yes, open it.*
—¿Se lo digo a Ana?	*Shall I tell (it to) Ana?*
—Sí, **dígaselo** a Ana.	*Yes, tell (it to) Ana.*
—¿Dónde me siento?	*Where shall I sit?*
—**Siéntese** aquí, cerca del escenario.	*Sit here, near the stage.*

Díselo (tú)

Díganselo (Uds.)

Siéntate (Informal)

---

¹ See Appendix A, part 7, number 3 (p. 280) for rules governing the use of accent marks in Spanish.

Práctica

Answer the following questions according to the appropriate model.

Modelos: —¿Traigo las sillas?
—**Sí, tráigalas, por favor.**

—¿Traemos las sillas?
—**Sí, tráiganlas, por favor.**

—¿Le traigo el dinero?
—**Sí, tráigamelo, por favor.**

—¿Le traemos el dinero?
—**Sí, tráiganmelo, por favor.**

1. ¿Traduzco la lección?
2. ¿Abrimos la puerta de la terraza? deck
3. ¿Cerramos las ventanas?
4. ¿Te servimos la sopa ahora?
5. ¿Me siento aquí?
6. ¿Hago el café?
7. ¿Le escribo la carta a Luis?
8. ¿Te compramos el vestido?
9. ¿Me baño?
10. ¿Nos acostamos ahora?
11. ¿Me visto?
12. ¿Nos vestimos ahora?
13. ¿Te traigo el té?
14. ¿Le doy el dinero a Marta?
15. ¿Le decimos tu número de teléfono a Pedro?

Negative commands

With all *negative* commands, the object pronouns are placed *in front of* the verb:

—¿Nos levantamos ahora?   *Shall we get up now?*
—No, **no se levanten**   *No, don't get up yet.*
todavía.

—Voy a traducir la lección   *I'm going to translate the*
al francés.   *lesson into French.*
—No, **no la traduzca** al   *No, don't translate it into*
francés. Tradúzcala al   *French. Translate it into*
español.   *Spanish.*

—¿Te traemos los   *Shall we bring you the*
vestidos?   *dresses?*

—No, **no me traigan** los
  vestidos. Tráiganme los
  pantalones.

*No, don't bring me the
  dresses. Bring me the
  pants.*

—¿Sirvo los refrescos?
—No, **no los sirva** todavía.

Shall I serve the sodas?
No, don't serve them yet.

—¿Te traemos las
  maletas?
—No, **no me las traigan.**

*Shall we bring you the
  suitcases?*
No, don't bring them to me.

Práctica

Someone gives the following commands. Tell people not to do
what this person asks:

Modelos: —Traiga el disco.
      —**¡No lo traiga!**

      —Tráigale el disco.
      —**¡No se lo traiga!**

1. Compre ese vestido.
2. Tráigale la maleta a Raúl.
3. Acuéstese.
4. Vístase.
5. Cierren las ventanas.
6. Quéjense.
7. Levántese.
8. Aféitense.
9. Tráigale el café al señor.
10. Dígaselo a María.
11. Pónganse los pantalones.
12. Dele la tarjeta de crédito a Elena.

En el laboratorio

LECCIÓN 9

The following material is to be used with the tape in the language laboratory.

I. Vocabulario

Repeat each word after the speaker. When repeating words that are cognates, notice the difference in pronunciation between English and Spanish.

COGNADOS:	el documento generalmente el guía impaciente la terraza
NOMBRES:	la bebida la cinta el disco el dormitorio la entrada el escenario la maleta la valija la medianoche el parque de diversiones los pantalones el peine la puerta la tarjeta la tarjeta de crédito la tintorería la ventana el vestido
VERBOS:	acordarse acostarse afeitarse bañarse despertarse doblar dormirse irse lavarse levantarse ponerse probarse quejarse quitarse sentarse vestirse
ADJETIVO:	querido
OTRAS PALABRAS Y EXPRESIONES:	a la derecha a la izquierda antes de cerca de seguir derecho tan todavía

II. Práctica

A. Answer the questions, using the cue provided. Repeat the correct answer after the speaker's confirmation. Listen to the model.

Modelo: —Mi maleta es verde. ¿Y la de Eva?   (blanca)
   —**La suya es blanca.**

   1. (grande)   4. (también)
   2. (aquí)   5. (en Honduras) _padres_
   3. (rojos)   6. (de Guatemala)

B. Answer the questions, using the cue provided. Repeat the correct answer after the speaker's confirmation. Listen to the model.

Modelo: —¿A qué hora te levantas tú?   (a las seis)
        —**Me levanto a las seis.**

1. (no, tarde) *desp*   4. (aquí) *no te*
2. (en el dormitorio) *vestir* 5. (no, de nada) *te quejas*
3. (no, por la noche)   6. (sí)

C. Change the following statements to commands. Repeat the correct answer after the speaker's confirmation. Listen to the model.

Modelo: —**Debe hablar** con la recepcionista.
        —**Hable** con la recepcionista.

III. Para escuchar y entender

1. Listen carefully to the narration. It will be read twice.

(*Narración*)

Now the speaker will make some statements about the narration you just heard. Tell whether each statement it true (**verdadero**) or false (**falso**). The speaker will confirm the correct answer.

2. Listen carefully to the dialogue. It will be read twice.

(*Diálogo 1*)

Now the speaker will make some statements about the dialogue you just heard. Tell whether each statement is true (**verdadero**) or false (**falso**). The speaker will confirm the correct answer.

3. Listen carefully to the dialogue. It will be read twice.

(*Diálogo 2*)

Now the speaker will ask some questions about the dialogue you just heard. Answer each question, omitting the subject. The speaker will confirm the correct answer. Repeat the correct answer.

Lección

10

1. The preterit of regular verbs
2. The preterit of *ser, ir,* **and** *dar*
3. Uses of *por* and *para*
4. **Weather expressions**

Vocabulario

COGNADOS

la **economía** economics	el **suéter** sweater
el **límite** limit	la **velocidad** velocity,
la **milla** mile	speed

NOMBRES
el **abrigo**   coat
la **aspiradora**   vacuum
   cleaner
el **avión**   plane
la **cocina**   kitchen
el (la) **cocinero(a)**   cook
la **escoba**   broom
el **impermeable**   raincoat
el (la) **ladrón(ona)**   thief,
   burglar, robber
la **lluvia**   rain
la **niebla**   fog
el **paraguas**   umbrella
el **queso**   cheese
la **suegra**   mother-in-law
el **suegro**   father-in-law
las **uvas**   grapes

VERBOS
   barrer   to sweep
   entrar   to enter,
      to come in

llevar   to carry, to take
llover (o:ue)   to rain
nevar (e:ie)   to snow
pasar (por)   to go by
planchar   to iron

ADJETIVO
   nublado(a)   cloudy

**OTRAS PALABRAS Y
EXPRESIONES**
   anoche   last night
   ayer   yesterday
   el límite de velocidad
      speed limit
   **¿Qué tiempo hace
   hoy?**   How's the weather
   today?

◀ 1. The preterit of regular verbs

Spanish has two simple past tenses: the preterit and the imperfect. (The imperfect will be studied in Lesson 11). The preterit of regular verbs is formed by dropping the infinitive ending and adding the appropriate preterit ending to the verb stem, as follows. Note that the endings for **-er** and **-ir** verbs are identical.

-ar *Verbs*	-er *Verbs*	-ir *Verbs*
entrar (*to enter*)	**comer** (*to eat*)	**escribir** (*to write*)
stem: **entr-**	**com-**	**escrib-**
entr**é**	com**í**	escrib**í**
entr**aste**	com**iste**	escrib**iste**
entr**ó**	com**ió**	escrib**ió**
entr**amos**	com**imos**	escrib**imos**
entr**aron**	com**ieron**	escrib**ieron**

yo **entré**   *I entered; I did enter*
Ud. **comió**   *you ate; you did eat*
ellos **escribieron**   *they wrote; they did write*

◆ The preterit tense is used to refer to actions or states that the speaker views as completed in the past. Note that Spanish has no equivalent for the English *did*, when used as an auxiliary verb in questions and negative sentences.

—¿Quién te **planchó** ese vestido? | *Who ironed this dress for you?*
—Lo **planché** yo. | *I ironed it.*

—¿Dónde **comió** Ud. anoche? | *Where did you eat last night?*
—**Comí** en la cafetería. | *I ate at the cafeteria.*

—¿**Abrió** Ud. las ventanas? | *Did you open the windows?*
—No, no las **abrí**. | *No, I didn't open them.*

—¿A qué hora te **acostaste** anoche? | *What time did you go to bed last night?*
—Me **acosté** a las once. | *I went to bed at eleven.*

ATENCIÓN: -ar and -er stem-changing verbs do not change stems in the preterit; they are regular: **Yo *volví* anoche y *cerré* la puerta.**

Práctica

A. Complete these sentences with the preterit of the verbs in parentheses:

1. ¿Dónde _____ (aprender) Ud. a hablar español?
2. ¿Qué _____ (decidir) Uds.? ¿Ir al hospital?
3. Yo no _____ (entender) su carta.
4. ¿Dónde _____ (comprar) tú esa maleta?

5. Lidia y Gerardo no _entraron_ (entrar) en la oficina.
6. ¿_ió_ (abrir) Ud. las puertas?
7. ¿Qué le _laron_ (preguntar) Uds. a la enfermera?
8. ¿A qué hora _aste_ (levantarse) tú ayer?
9. Carmen y yo _tomamos_ (tomar) café.
10. ¿Cuántas horas lo _espero_ (esperar) Ud.?

B. Tell what the following people did yesterday:

Modelo: Yo como sándwiches.
    Yo comí sándwiches ayer.

1. Oscar habla con sus padres. _habló_
2. Tú ves a Sandra. _viste_
3. Le escriben una carta a Rosa.
4. Me baño por la tarde. _bañe_ _en_
5. Cerramos las ventanas.
6. Gerardo se afeita por la mañana. _en_
7. Me quito los pantalones.
8. No te entiendo. _í_
9. María plancha el vestido de Ana. _ó_
10. Yo no me levanto temprano. _é_

to take notice

darse cuenta

2. The preterit of ser, ir, and dar

The preterit forms of **ser, ir,** and **dar** are irregular. Note that **ser** and **ir** have the same forms:

ser = ir

	ser (*to be*)	**ir** (*to go*)	**dar** (*to give*)
I was	fui	fui	*I:* di
you were	fuiste	fuiste	diste
he was *she, it*	fue	fue	*he she it gave* dio
We were	fuimos	fuimos	dimos
they were	fueron	fueron	dieron

—Ud. **fue** profesora en la Universidad de Arizona, ¿no?
 You were a professor at the University of Arizona, weren't you?

—Sí, yo **fui** profesora de economía.
 Yes, I was a professor of economics.

—¿Con quién **fue** Ud. al mercado ayer?
 With whom did you go to the market yesterday?

—**Fui** con mis amigos.
 I went with my friends.

—¿Quién le **dio** las uvas al niño?

—Se las **dio** la cocinera.

Who gave the grapes to the boy?

The cook gave them to him.

Práctica

A. Complete the following sentences with the preterit of the verbs **ir, ser,** or **dar,** as needed:

1. Yo _____ con mis padres al mercado.
2. Ella _____ mi profesora de economía el año pasado.
3. Nosotros no le _____ el dinero anoche.
4. ¿Le _____ Ud. las uvas al niño?
5. El doctor _____ al hospital.
6. Yo no te _____ el tenedor.
7. Nosotros no _____ sus estudiantes.
8. ¿Le _____ Ud. la maleta a la enfermera?
9. ¿Quién _____ el primer presidente de los Estados Unidos?
10. ¿A dónde _____ tú ayer? ¿Al parque?
11. Carlos y Roberto ¿ _____ al cine anoche?
12. ¿Le _____ tú el dinero a la cocinera?
13. María y yo _____ a Santiago el año pasado.
14. Yo les _____ esos pantalones a mis hermanos.

B. Write a short paragraph describing what you did yesterday.

3. Uses of por and para

◆ The preposition **por** is used to indicate:

1. Motion (*through, along, by*):

—¿**Por** dónde entró el ladrón?

—Entró **por** la ventana.

How (through where) did the burglar get in?

He got in through the window.

—¿A qué hora pasaste **por** mi casa ayer?

—Pasé **por** tu casa a las tres.

At what time did you go by my house yesterday?

I went by your house at three o'clock.

2. Cause or motive of an action (*because of, on account of, on behalf of*):

—¿Por qué no fueron
Uds. a clase ayer?
—No fuimos **por** la lluvia.

Why didn't you go to class yesterday?
We didn't go because of the rain.

3. Agency, means, manner, unit of measure (*by, for, per*):

—¿Vas a San Francisco
por avión?
—No, llevo el coche.
—¿Cuál es el límite de
velocidad en California?
—Cincuenta y cinco millas
por hora.

Are you going to San Francisco by plane?
No, I'm taking the car.
What's the speed limit in California?
Fifty-five miles per hour.

4. *In exchange for:*

—¿Cuánto pagaste **por** ese
abrigo?
—Pagué[1] cien dólares **por**
él.

How much did you pay for that coat?
I paid one hundred dollars for it.

◆ The preposition **para** is used to indicate:

1. Destination in space (*to*):

—¿A qué hora hay vuelos
para México?
—A las diez y a las doce
de la noche.

What time are there flights to Mexico?
At ten and twelve P.M.

2. Direction in time (*by, for*); a certain date in the future:

—¿Cuándo necesita Ud. la
aspiradora?
—La necesito **para** mañana.

When do you need the vacuum cleaner?
I need it by tomorrow.

3. Direction toward a recipient:

—¿**Para** quién es el queso?
—Es **para** mi suegra.

Who is the cheese for?
It's for my mother-in-law.

---

[1] Verbs ending in **-gar** change **g** to **gu** before **e** in the first person of the preterit in order to preserve the hard "g" sound. (See verb paradigms in Appendix B, p. 287.)

4. *In order to*; purpose:

—¿**Para** qué necesita Ud. la escoba?

—La necesito **para** barrer la cocina.

What do you need the broom for?

I need it (in order) to sweep the kitchen.

Práctica

Complete the following sentences using **para** or **por**, as needed:

1. Salimos _____ México mañana. Vamos _____ avión.
2. Necesito el coche __*para*__ mañana.
3. Anoche Juan pasó __*por*__ mi casa __*para*__ verme.
4. Hoy no hay vuelos __*para*__ Madrid.
5. El ladrón no entró __*por*__ la ventana.
6. ¿Cuánto pagaste __*por*__ esa escoba?
7. El queso no es __*para*__ mi suegro.
8. Conduzco mi coche a 55 millas __*por*__ hora. Ése es el límite de velocidad.
9. No puedo conducir a mucha velocidad __*por*__ la lluvia.
10. Pagué diez dólares __*por*__ estas sábanas.
11. Mi suegro me llamó __*por*__ teléfono.
12. El dinero es __*por*__ pagar las uvas.

4. Weather expressions

clima

In the following weather expressions, the verb **hacer** (*to make*) followed by a noun is used in Spanish, whereas the verb *to be* followed by an adjective is used in English:

Hace (mucho) frío.   *It is (very) cold.*
Hace (mucho) calor.   *It is (very) hot.*   *hace fresco (warm)*
Hace (mucho) viento.[1]   *It is (very) windy.*
Hace sol.[1]   *It is sunny.*

◆ **Hacer** is not used in weather expressions with **llover (o:ue)** *IRREGULAR* *llueve* (*to rain*) or **nevar (e:ie)** (*to snow*):

Llueve. Está lloviendo.   *It rains. It's raining.*
Nieva. Está nevando.   *It snows. It's snowing.*

◆ Other words and expressions related to the weather are

la **lluvia**   *rain*
la **niebla**   *fog*
Está nublado.   *It's cloudy.*

niebla - fog

[1] It is also correct to say: **hay viento, hay sol.**

♦ As in English, the Spanish impersonal verbs appear in the infinitive, present or past participle, and third person singular forms only.

—¿**Hace viento** hoy?   *Is it windy today?*
—Sí, y también **está**   *Yes, and it is raining a lot*
   lloviendo mucho.   *also.*

—¿Qué tiempo hace hoy,   *How's the weather today,*
   Marta? ¿**Hace** buen[1]   *Marta? Is it good*
   tiempo?   *(weather)?*
—No, **hace** mal[1] tiempo.   *No, we are having bad*
   Hace mucho **frío** y **está**   *weather. It is very cold*
   nevando.   *and it is snowing.*

Congelar —   *Me estoy congelando – I am freezing.*

Práctica " "   *muriéndo de frío – "*

A. Study these words, and then complete the following sentences:
de hambre
de calor

el **paraguas**   *umbrella*
el **impermeable**   *raincoat*
el **suéter**   *sweater*
el **abrigo**   *coat*

1. ¿Necesitas un paraguas? Sí, porque _____.
2. ¿No necesitas un abrigo? No, porque _____.
3. ¿Quieres un impermeable? No, no está _____.
4. ¿Necesitas un suéter? No, hoy _____.
5. Está nevando. Lleve el _abrigo_
6. Va a llover. Está _nublado._

B. How is the weather?

---

[1] **Bueno** and **malo** drop the **o** before a masculine singular noun.

buen día

esta lloviendo

3.

4.

Sudar - to sweat

5.

esta nevando

6.

hace sol.

neutral
tibio - warm -use w/food, peoples temps
but not climate.

agradable - warm - room, climate

no soy tibio - I don't want to get
involved

En el laboratorio

LECCIÓN 10

The following material is to be used with the tape in the language laboratory.

I. Vocabulario

Repeat each word after the speaker. When repeating words that are cognates, notice the difference in pronunciation between English and Spanish.

COGNADOS:	la economía el límite la milla el suéter la velocidad
NOMBRES:	el abrigo la aspiradora el avión la cocina el cocinero la escoba el impermeable el ladrón la lluvia la niebla el paraguas el queso la suegra el suegro las uvas
VERBOS:	barrer entrar llevar llover nevar pasar planchar
ADJETIVO:	nublado
OTRAS PALABRAS Y EXPRESIONES:	anoche ayer el límite de velocidad ¿Qué tiempo hace hoy?

II. Práctica

A. Answer the questions, using the cues provided. Repeat the correct answer after the speaker's confirmation. Listen to the model.

Modelo: —¿Con quién trabajaron Uds. ayer?   (con el director)
   —Trabajamos con el director.

1. (con el gerente)
2. (al cine)
3. (cien dólares)
4. (en la cafetería)
5. (cuatro horas)
6. (el doctor Lozano)
7. (a las doce)
8. (a Teresa)

B. Answer the questions, using the cues provided. Repeat the correct answer after the speaker's confirmation. Listen to the model.

Modelo: —¿Por dónde entraron Uds.?   (la ventana)
       —**Entramos por la ventana.**

1. (sí)	5. (cincuenta dólares)
2. (mañana)	6. (avión)
3. (Pepito)	7. (estudiar)
4. (la niebla)	8. (mañana)

C. Answer the questions, using the cue provided. Repeat the correct answer following the speaker's confirmation. Listen to the model.

Modelo: —¿Dónde hace mucho frío?   (Alaska)
       —**Hace mucho frío en Alaska.**

1. (Oregón)
2. (Arizona)
3. (otoño)
4. (Chicago)
5. (sí)

III. Para escuchar y entender

1. Listen carefully to the dialogue. It will be read twice.

(*Diálogo 1*)

Now the speaker will make statements about the dialogue you just heard. Tell whether each statement is true (**verdadero**) or false (**falso**). The speaker will confirm the correct answer.

2. Listen carefully to the dialogue. It will be read twice.

(*Diálogo 2*)

Now the speaker will ask some questions about the dialogue you just heard. Answer each question, omitting the subject. The speaker will confirm the correct answer. Repeat the correct answer.

¿Cuánto sabe usted ahora?

LECCIONES 6–10

Lección 6

A. Uses of the definite article

How would you say the following in Spanish?

1. Today is Wednesday.
2. Women want equality with men.
3. Education is important.
4. We're going to school next week.
5. I don't have classes on Fridays.

B. Stem-changing verbs (**o:ue**)

Answer the following questions:

1. ¿A qué hora vuelve Ud. a casa?
2. Cuando Uds. van a México, ¿vuelan o van en auto?
3. ¿Recuerdan Uds. los verbos irregulares?
4. ¿Cuántas horas duerme Ud.?
5. ¿Pueden Uds. ir a la iglesia hoy?

C. Affirmative and negative expressions

Change the following sentences to the affirmative:

1. Ellos no recuerdan nada.
2. No hay nadie en la escuela.
3. Yo no quiero volar tampoco.
4. No recibimos ningún regalo.
5. Nunca tiene éxito.

D. Uses of **tener que** and **hay que**

How would you say the following in Spanish?

1. To succeed, one must work.
2. You have to come back next week, Mr. Vega.
3. She has to work tomorrow.
4. One must start early.
5. Do we have to begin at eight? *Tenemos que empezar*

E. Pronouns as object of a preposition

How would you say the following in Spanish?

1. Can you come with me?
2. Are you going to work with them?
3. The money is for you, Anita.
4. The gift is not for me; it is for her. *Regalar - to gift*
5. No, Paco, I can't go with you.

F. Vocabulary

Complete the following sentences, using words learned in Lección 6.

1. ¿Cuándo vas a la _____ para comprar el billete? *boleto*
2. Todos los domingos voy a la _____.
3. Para mí, lo más importante es la _____.
4. Ella vuelve a trabajar el mes que _____ *viene (que entre)*
5. Quiero un pasaje de _____ y _____.
6. Su hermano nunca tiene _____.
7. Él _____ siete horas todas las noches.
8. Las clases comienzan la semana _____.

A. Stem-changing verbs (**e:i**)   **Lección 7**

Answer the following questions:

1. ¿Qué sirven Uds., sopa o ensalada?
2. ¿Qué pide Ud. para beber cuando va a un restaurante?
3. ¿Dice Ud. su edad?
4. ¿Sigue Ud. en la universidad?
5. ¿Uds. siempre piden postre?

B. Irregular first persons

Complete the sentences with the present indicative of the verbs in the following list. Use each verb once.

traer   conocer   traducir   hacer   saber
ver   salir   poner   conducir

1. Yo _____ mi coche.
2. Yo siempre _____ con ella.
3. Yo _____ la carne en la mesa.
4. Yo _____ del inglés al español.
5. Yo no _____ al maestro de mi hijo.
6. Yo _____ las cartas.
7. Yo _____ el postre.
8. Yo no _____ el regalo. ¿Dónde está?
9. Yo no _____ nadar.

C. Saber contrasted with **conocer**

How would you say the following in Spanish?

1. I know your son. *a su hijo*
2. He doesn't know French.
3. Do you know how to swim, Miss Vera?
4. Do you know the instructor? *al maestro*
5. Are the students familiar with Cervantes' novels?

D. The impersonal **se**

Answer the following questions:

1. ¿Qué idioma se habla en los Estados Unidos?
2. ¿Cómo se dice *often* en español?
3. ¿A qué hora se cierra la librería?
4. ¿Cómo se escribe su nombre? (S or Z)(B or V)
5. ¿A qué hora se abren las oficinas?

Deletrear—to spell

E. Direct object pronouns

Complete the following sentences with the Spanish equivalent of the direct object pronouns in parentheses. Follow the models.

Modelos: Yo veo *(him)*
Yo lo veo.

Yo quiero ver *(him)*
Yo quiero verlo.

1. Yo conozco *(them,* fem.*)*
2. Uds. van a comprar *(it,* masc.*)*
3. Nosotros no queremos ver *(you,* familiar*)*
4. Ella sirve *(it,* fem.*)*
5. ¿Ud. no conoce…? *(me)*
6. Él escribe *(them,* masc.*)*
7. Carlos va a visitar *(us)*
8. Nosotros no vemos *(you,* formal, sing., masc.*)*

F. Vocabulary

Complete the following sentences, using the words learned in Lección 7.

1. Un sinónimo de «carro» es _____.
2. Yo voy a _____ la ensalada ahora.
3. Mi hijo sabe de _____ todos los verbos.
4. Necesita las _____ para cambiar la cama.
5. Voy a la iglesia una _____ por semana.
6. Trabajo _____ los días.
7. "The Raven" es un _____ muy famoso de Poe.
8. Un sinónimo de «a menudo» es _____.

Lección 8   **A.** Demonstrative adjectives and pronouns

How would you say the following in Spanish?

1. I need these balls and those. *(over there)*
2. Do you want this notebook or that one?
3. I prefer these newspapers, not those *(over there)*.

4. Do you want to buy this racket or that one, Dad?
5. I don't want to eat at this restaurant. I prefer
   that one.   (*over there*)
6. I don't understand that.   (*neuter form*)

B. The present progressive

Complete the following sentences with the present progressive
of **leer, decir, estudiar, beber,** or **comer,** as needed:

1. Él _____ la lección.
2. Ella _____ en la cafetería.
3. Nosotros _____ el periódico.
4. Tú no _____ la verdad.
5. Yo _____ café.

C. Indirect object pronouns

Answer the following questions according to the model.

Modelo: —¿Qué me vas a traer de México?   (una frazada)
       —**Te voy a traer una frazada.**

1. ¿Qué te va a comprar Carlos?   (unos patines)
2. ¿Qué le das tú a Luis?   (el diario)
3. ¿En qué idioma les habla a Uds. el profesor?   (en español)
4. ¿Qué va a decirles Ud. a los niños?   (la verdad)
5. ¿Qué nos pregunta Ud.?   (la dirección de la oficina)
6. ¿A quién están escribiéndole Uds.?   (a nuestro padre)
7. ¿Cuándo le escribe Ud. a su abuelo?   (los lunes)
8. ¿A quién le da Ud. la información?   (al presidente)
9. ¿En qué idioma me hablas tú?   (en inglés)
10. ¿Qué te compran tus hijos?   (nada)

D. Direct and indirect object pronouns used together

How would you say the following in Spanish?

1. The money? I'm giving it to you tomorrow, Mr. Peña.
2. I know you need the dictionary, Anita, but I can't lend _____
   it to you.
3. I need my backpack. Can you bring it to me, Miss López?
4. The pens? She is bringing them to us.
5. When he needs skates, his mother buys them for him.

E. Pedir contrasted with **preguntar**

How would you say the following in Spanish?

1. I'm going to ask her where she lives.
2. I always ask my husband for money.
3. She always asks how you are, Mrs. Nieto.

4. They are going to ask me for the Spanish books.
5. I want to ask him how old he is.

F. Vocabulary

Complete the following sentences, using words learned in Lección 8.

1. Quiero leer la sección _____ del diario.
2. ¿Para _____ son esos patines? ¿Para tu hijo?
3. Para jugar al tenis, los niños necesitan una _____ y una de tenis.
4. Tenemos dos _____: un niño y una niña.
5. Un sinónimo de "diario" es _____.
6. El hermano de mi madre es mi _____.
7. Si prefieres comer _____ italiana, podemos ir al restaurante Roma.
8. Los niños están jugando en el _____.

Lección 9   **A.** Possessive pronouns

Answer the following questions in the negative, according to the model.

Modelo: —¿Estos pantalones son **de Juan?**
        —No, no son **de él.**

1. ¿Son **tuyas** estas maletas?
2. ¿Estos discos son de Julia?
3. ¿El vestido es **suyo,** señora?
4. ¿Es **de Uds.** esta cama?
5. ¿Esta tarjeta de crédito es **de tus padres?**
6. ¿Son **tuyos** estos documentos?
7. ¿Es **de Uds.** esta cinta?
8. ¿Es **nuestro** este dormitorio?

B. Reflexive constructions

How would you say the following in Spanish?

1. I get up at seven, I bathe, I get dressed, and I leave at seven-thirty.
2. What time do the children wake up?
3. She doesn't want to sit down.
4. He shaves every day.
5. Do you remember your teachers, Carlitos?
6. They are always complaining.
7. First she puts the children to bed, and then she goes to bed.
8. Do you want to try on these pants, Miss?

9. Where are you going to put the money, ladies?
10. The students always fall asleep in this class.

C. The command forms: **Ud.** and **Uds.**

Complete the sentences with the command forms of the verbs in the following list, as needed, and read each sentence aloud. Use each verb once:

escribir	venir	dar	hablar	doblar
servir	cerrar	volver	seguir	ser
estar	poner	ir	abrir	traer

1. _____ la puerta, señor Benítez.
2. _____ español, señores.
3. _____ sus documentos, señorita.
4. _____ mañana por la mañana, señoras.
5. No _____ la ventana, señorita. Hace calor.
6. _____ a la izquierda, señores.
7. _____ derecho, señorita.
8. _____ su nombre y dirección, señores.
9. _____ en la oficina mañana por la tarde, señores.
10. ¡No _____ tan impacientes, señoritas!
11. Señor Vega, _____ a la casa del director.
12. _____ el martes, señora. El doctor no está.
13. _____ el café en la terraza, señorita.
14. _____ las maletas aquí, señores.
15. _____ las cartas mañana, señoras.

D. Uses of object pronouns with command forms

How would you say the following in Spanish?

1. Tell them the truth, Mr. Mena.
2. The dessert? Don't bring it to me now, Miss Ruiz.
3. Don't tell (it to) my neighbor, please.
4. Bring the drinks, gentlemen. Bring them to the terrace.
5. Don't get up, Mrs. Miño.
6. The tea? Bring it to her at four o'clock in the afternoon, Mr. Vargas.

E. Vocabulary

Complete the following sentences, using words learned in Lección 9.

1. No tengo discos de Madonna, tengo _____.
2. Disneyland es un parque de _____.
3. Lleve los pantalones a la _____, señorita.
4. No tengo dinero; voy a pagar con la _____.

5. La librería no está a la derecha; está a la _____.
6. Pongan las _____ en la mesa, señores... La Coca-Cola, aquí...
7. Voy a _____ a los niños; ya son las nueve de la noche.
8. Para llegar a la universidad, siga Ud. _____.

Lección 10 **A.** Preterit of regular verbs / Preterit of **ser, ir,** and **dar**

Rewrite the following sentences according to the new beginnings. Follow the model.

Modelo: Voy al cine. (Ayer...)
        Ayer fui al cine.

1. Ella entra en la cafetería y come una ensalada. (Ayer...)
2. María le escribe a su suegra. (Ayer...)
3. Ella me presta su abrigo. (El viernes pasado...)
4. Ellos son los mejores estudiantes.
   (El año pasado...)
5. Ellos te esperan cerca del cine.
   (El sábado pasado...)
6. Mi hijo va a Buenos Aires. (El verano pasado...)
7. Le doy el impermeable. (Ayer por la mañana...)
8. Nosotros decidimos comprar la aspiradora.
   (El lunes pasado...)
9. Le pregunto la hora. (Anoche...)
10. Tú no pagas por el queso. (Anoche...)
11. Somos los primeros. (El jueves pasado...)
12. Me dan muchos problemas. (Ayer...)
13. Mi suegro no bebe café. (Anoche...)
14. Yo no voy a esquiar. (Ayer...)
15. Te damos el suéter. (La semana pasada...)

B. Uses of **por** and **para**

How would you say the following in Spanish?

1. The thief went in through the window.
2. She went by my house.
3. She didn't come because of the rain.
4. There are flights to Mexico on Saturdays.
5. We are going by plane.
6. The speed limit is fifty-five miles per hour.
7. I need the lesson on economics for tomorrow.
8. Who is the umbrella for?
9. I need the money to pay for the raincoat.
10. She paid two hundred dollars for that vacuum cleaner.

C. Weather expressions

How would you say the following in Spanish?

1. It is very windy today.
2. It is very cold, and it is also snowing.
3. It is very hot in Cuba.
4. How is the weather today?
5. Is it sunny or is it cloudy?
6. There are no flights because of the fog.

D. Vocabulary

Complete the following sentences, using words learned in Lección 10.

1. Necesito el _____ porque hace frío.
2. ¿Cuál es el _____ de velocidad?
3. Ella quiere ponerse el _____ porque va a llover.
4. ¿Dónde compraste las _____? ¿En el mercado?
5. Necesitamos la _____ para barrer.
6. Adela siempre _____ el vestido antes de ponérselo.
7. ¿Quién barrió la cocina? ¿La _____?
8. ¿Qué _____ hace hoy? ¿Hace frío?

Lección

11

1. **Time expressions with** *hacer*
2. **Irregular preterits**
3. **The imperfect tense**
4. **Command forms** (*tú*)

Vocabulario

COGNADOS

el **coctel** cocktail	**La Habana** Havana
el **favor** favor	la **limonada** lemonade

NOMBRES
el **arroz**   rice
los **guantes**   gloves
la **liquidación, venta**   sale _oferta_ _ontole en_
la **niña**   child, girl
el **niño**   child, boy
el **pollo**   chicken
los guantes de nieve —mittens.
la **zapatería**   shoe store

VERBOS
apagar   to turn off
caminar   to walk

ADJETIVOS
todo(a)   all
todos(as)   every

OTRAS PALABRAS Y EXPRESIONES
ahi, **allí**   there

arroz con pollo   chicken with rice
casi nunca   hardly ever
¿cuánto tiempo?   how long?
de vez en cuando   once in a while
en esa época   in those days
ir de compras   to go shopping
media hora   half an hour
otra vez   again
¡Rápido!   Quick!
Ten paciencia.   Be patient.
De nuevo—Again—(or) one more time.

◄ 1. Time expressions with hacer

Spanish uses the following formula to express how long something has been going on:

Hace + length of time + **que** + verb (in the present tense)
Hace   quince años   **que**   vivo en esta ciudad.
I have been living in this city for fifteen years.

—¿Cuánto tiempo **hace que** Ud. trabaja en la tienda?   *How long have you been working at the store?*
—**Hace** tres años **que** trabajo allí.   *I have been working there for three years.*

—¿Cuánto tiempo **hace que** Uds. están aquí?   *How long have you been here?*
—**Hace** media hora **que** estamos aquí.   *We have been here for half an hour.*

—¿Tienes hambre?   *Are you hungry?*
—Sí, **hace** ocho horas **que** no como.   *Yes, I haven't eaten for eight hours.*

Práctica

A. Answer the following questions according to the model:

Modelo: —¿Cuánto tiempo hace que Ud. trabaja allí?   (dos años)
          —**Hace dos años que trabajo allí.**

[handwritten: Hace cuanto que]

1. ¿Cuánto tiempo hace que Ud. estudia español?
   (tres meses)
2. ¿Cuánto tiempo hace que Ud. conoce a su novio(a)?
   (un año)
3. ¿Cuánto tiempo hace que Ud. no come?   (media hora)
4. ¿Cuánto tiempo hace que vive en esta ciudad?
   (seis semanas)
5. ¿Cuánto tiempo hace que no llueve aquí?   (cuatro meses)
6. ¿Cuánto tiempo hace que Ud. no ve a sus padres?
   (un mes)
7. ¿Cuánto tiempo hace que el presidente vive en
   Washington?   (dos años)
8. ¿Cuánto tiempo hace que Uds. no van a clase?
   (cinco días)

B. How would you say the following in Spanish?

1. It has been raining for three days. *[handwritten: Hace tres días que está lloviendo]*
2. My father-in-law has been sick for a week.
3. How long have you been living here? *[handwritten: ¿Cuánto tiempo hace que vives aquí?]*
4. He has been working at the store for fifteen years.
5. We haven't slept for twenty-four hours. *[handwritten: Hace veinte y cuatro horas que no dormimos]*

2. Irregular preterits

The following Spanish verbs are irregular in the preterit:

[handwritten: ejové amar - used for persons only.]

tener:	tuve, tuviste, tuvo, tuvimos, tuvieron
estar:	estuve, estuviste, estuvo, estuvimos, estuvieron
poder: *[to be able]*	pude, pudiste, pudo, pudimos, pudieron
poner: *[to place]*	puse, pusiste, puso, pusimos, pusieron
saber:	supe, supiste, supo, supimos, supieron
hacer:	hice, hiciste, hizo, hicimos, hicieron
venir:	vine, viniste, vino, vinimos, vinieron
querer:	quise, quisiste, quiso, quisimos, quisieron
decir:	dije, dijiste, dijo, dijimos, dijeron[1]
traer:	traje, trajiste, trajo, trajimos, trajeron[1]
conducir:	conduje, condujiste, condujo, condujimos, condujeron[1]
traducir:	traduje, tradujiste, tradujo, tradujimos, tradujeron[1]

[handwritten: use indirect object → means "to love" non ... means "to want"]

[handwritten: to handle a situation / to behave]

[1] Note that the **-i** is omitted in the third person plural ending of these verbs.

—¿Llamaste por teléfono a Juan?   *Did you phone Juan?*

—No, porque él **vino** a mi casa.   *No, because he came to my house.*

—¿Dónde **pusieron** Uds. el dinero?   *Where did you put the money?*

—Lo **pusimos** en el banco.   *We put it in the bank.*

—¿Qué **hizo** Ud. ayer?   *What did you do yesterday?*

—Fui de compras y caminé por la ciudad.   *I went shopping and I walked around the city.*

ATENCIÓN: Notice that the third person singular form of the verb **hacer** changes the **c** to **z** in order to maintain the soft sound of the **c** in the infinitive.

◆ The preterit of **hay** (from the verb **haber**) is **hubo**.

—Ayer **hubo** una fiesta en casa de Eva.   *Yesterday there was a party at Eva's house.*

—Sí. lo **supe** esta mañana.   *Yes, I found out (about it) this morning.*

◆ All verbs ending in **-ducir** follow the same pattern as the verb **conducir**, *e.g.*: **traducir**, *to translate*; **producir**, *to produce*.

—¿Qué lección **tradujeron** Uds.?   *What lesson did you translate?*

—**Tradujimos** la lección dos.   *We translated Lesson 2.*

Práctica

A. Complete the following paragraph with the preterit of the verbs in parentheses:

Isabel le escribe una carta a Teresa

Toledo, 15 de julio de 19..

Querida Teresa:

Ayer yo _estuve_ (estar) en Madrid, pero no _pude_ (poder) ir a verte. Salí de Toledo por la mañana y _conduje_ (conducir) por tres horas hasta llegar a Madrid. Allí _tuve_ (tener) que ir al hospital para ver a Gustavo. Caminé por la ciudad y _quise_ (querer) llamarte por teléfono, pero no _pude_ (poder) encontrar uno. Como siempre, ayer _hice_ (hacer) mucho calor. _Vine_ (Venir) de Madrid muy cansada. Esta mañana hablé por teléfono con Ramón. Él me _dije_ (decir) muchas cosas interesantes. ¡Ah...! Me _puso_ (poner) el vestido que compré en Madrid y salí con Jorge. El sábado vuelvo a Madrid para verte.

subrayar (underlined)

Tu amiga

Isabel

B. Change the boldface verbs to the preterit, to tell us what happened in the past:

1. Él **tiene** que ir al doctor porque está enfermo.
2. ¿Uds. no **pueden** venir, o no **quieren** venir?
3. Ella **viene** aquí y no **hace** nada.
4. Ellos **traen** los libros y los **ponen** en la mesa.
5. **Hay** una reunión en la universidad.
6. ¿Qué **dices** tú?
7. Yo **traduzco** las cartas.
8. Nosotros no lo **sabemos.**

C. Tell about yourself by answering these questions:

1. ¿A qué hora vino Ud. a la universidad hoy?
2. ¿Condujo su coche o caminó?
3. ¿Trajo sus libros de español?
4. ¿Pudo Ud. venir a clase la semana pasada?
5. ¿Tuvo que trabajar ayer?   *Tener que – to have to*
6. ¿Dónde estuvo Ud. anoche?
7. ¿Qué hizo anoche para la cena?
8. ¿En qué banco puso Ud. su dinero?

D. Using the **tú** form, ask a classmate all the questions in Práctica C.

3. The imperfect tense

There are two simple past tenses in Spanish: the preterit, which you studied in Lecciones 10 and 11, and the imperfect.

To form the imperfect tense, add the following endings to the stem of the verb:

The Imperfect Tense

-ar *Verbs*	-er *and* -ir *Verbs*	
hablar	comer	vivir
hablaba	comía	vivía
hablabas	comías	vivías
hablaba	comía	vivía
hablábamos	comíamos	vivíamos
hablaban	comían	vivían

◆ Notice that the endings of **-er** and **-ir** verbs are the same. Notice also that there is a written accent mark on the final **í** of **-er** and **-ir** verbs.

◆ The imperfect tense in Spanish is equivalent to three forms in English:

Yo **vivía** en Chicago. $\left\{\begin{array}{l} \textbf{\textit{I used to live}} \text{ in Chicago.} \\ \textbf{\textit{I was living}} \text{ in Chicago.} \\ \textbf{\textit{I lived}} \text{ in Chicago.} \end{array}\right.$

◆ The Spanish imperfect is used to refer to habitual or repeated actions in the past, with no reference to when they began or ended.

—¿**Comían** ellos arroz con pollo?
—Sí, lo **comían** de vez en cuando.

Did they used to eat chicken and rice?
Yes, they used to eat it once in a while.

—¿Dónde **vivía** Ud. en esa época?
—Yo **vivía** en La Habana.

Where did you live in those days?
I lived in Havana.

◆ The imperfect is also used to describe actions or events that the speaker views as in the process of happening in the past, again with no reference to when they began or ended.

Empezábamos a estudiar cuando él vino.

We were beginning to study when he came.

Práctica

Complete the following sentences with the imperfect tense of the verbs in this list. Use each verb once:

✓acostarse	✓preferir	✓servir	✓levantarse
✓poner	✓vivir	✓tener	✓hablar
✓poder	✓dar	✓dormir	✓comenzar

1. Ellos no _podían_ ir a la universidad porque las clases _comenzaban_ a las ocho de la mañana.
2. Mamá me _daba_ dinero para comprar café.
3. En esa época yo _vivía_ en Montevideo.
4. ¿Tú _ponías_ todo tu dinero en el banco?
5. ¿Qué _preferían_ Uds.? ¿Arroz con pollo o sopa?
6. Yo no _dormía_ muy bien por la noche.
7. Papá siempre _se levantaba_ a las cinco de la mañana.
8. Nosotros no _acostábamos_ muy temprano por la noche, porque _teníamos_ que ir a trabajar.

9. Yo siempre _servía_ la ensalada.
10. Nosotros _hablábamos_ inglés de vez en cuando.

Irregular imperfect forms

There are only three irregular verbs in the imperfect tense: **ser, ir,** and **ver.**

ser	ir	ver
era	iba	veía
eras	ibas	veías
era	iba	veía
éramos	íbamos	veíamos
eran	iban	veían

—¿Dónde vivías tú cuando **eras** niño?

Where did you live when you were a child?

—Yo vivía en Arizona cuando **era** niño.

I lived in Arizona when I was a child.

—Los vi esta mañana en la calle Quinta. ¿Adónde **iban** Uds.?

I saw you this morning on Fifth Street. Where were you going?

—**Íbamos** a la zapatería.

We were going to the shoe store.

—¿Cecilia **veía** a sus abuelos todos los sábados?

Did Cecilia used to see her grandparents every Saturday?

—**Veía** a su abuela a veces, pero casi nunca **veía** a su abuelo.

She used to see her grand-mother sometimes, but she hardly ever saw her grandfather.

Práctica

A. Change the verbs according to the new subjects. Make any additional changes needed:

1. Cuando yo **era** niña vivía con mis abuelos.   (nosotros / tú / Gustavo / ellos / Uds.)
2. Ellos casi nunca **iban** a la escuela.   (Yo / María / Nosotros / Tú / Uds.)
3. Nosotros los **veíamos** siempre.   (Ud. / Ellos / Yo / Tú / El Presidente)

B. Tell us what you used to do:

1. ¿Dónde vivía Ud. cuando era niño(a)?
2. ¿A qué escuela iba Ud.?
3. ¿Iban Uds. al cine a veces?
4. ¿Veía Ud. a sus abuelos todos los sábados?
5. ¿Hablaban Uds. español cuando eran niños?
6. Cuando Ud. era chico(a), ¿qué hacía los domingos?

◄ 4. Command forms (tú)

The affirmative command

The affirmative command for **tú** has exactly the same form as the third person singular of the present indicative.

Verb	Present Indicative Third Person Singular	Familiar Command (tú Form)
hablar	él habla	**habla**
comer	él come	**come**
abrir	él abre	**abre**
cerrar	él cierra	**cierra**
volver	él vuelve	**vuelve**
pedir	él pide	**pide**
traer	él trae	**trae**

—¿Qué pido? — *What shall I order?*
—**Pide** un coctel para mí y una limonada para ti. — *Order a cocktail for me and a lemonade for you.*

—**Cierra** las ventanas y **apaga** las luces antes de salir.[1] — *Close the windows and turn off the lights before going out.*
—Muy bien. **Espérame** en el coche. — *Very well. Wait for me in the car.*

—¿Necesitas los guantes? — *Do you need the gloves?*
—Sí, **tráe**melos, por favor. — *Yes, bring them to me, please.*

ATENCIÓN: Remember that direct, indirect, and reflexive pronouns are always attached to an affirmative command.

---

[1] The infinitive, not the *-ing* form, is used after a preposition in Spanish.

♦ Eight Spanish verbs have irregular affirmative familiar command forms:

decir:	**di** (*say, tell*)	salir:	**sal** (*go out, leave*)
hacer:	**haz** (*do, make*)	ser:	**sé** (*be*)
ir:	**ve** (*go*)	tener:	**ten** (*have*)
poner:	**pon** (*put*)	venir:	**ven** (*come*)

—Carlitos, **ven** aquí. **Haz**me   *Carlitos, come here. Do*
un favor. **Ve** y **di**le a   *me a favor. Go and tell*
tu mamá que quiero   *your mom that I want to*
hablar con ella. ¡Rápido!   *speak with her. Quick!*
—**Ten** paciencia. Ya voy.   *Be patient. I'm coming.*

The negative command

The negative command for **tú** is formed by adding -s to the command form for **Ud.**:

hable	no hables	*don't talk*
vuelva	no vuelvas	*don't return*
venga	no vengas	*don't come*
salga	no salgas	*don't leave*

—¿Voy con Roberto?   *Do I go with Roberto?*
—No, **no vayas** con él.   *No, don't go with him.*

—Hoy hay una liquidación   *Today there's a sale at La*
en La Francia.   *Francia.*
—¡**No** me **digas** que   *Don't tell me (that) you*
quieres ir de compras   *want to go shopping*
otra vez!   *again!*

ATENCIÓN: Remember that all object pronouns are placed *before* a negative command: No **me lo** traigas hoy.

Práctica

A. Confirm the following questions according to the model.

Modelo: —¿Traigo las raquetas?
        —Sí, **tráelas**, por favor.

1. ¿Pido el coctel?
2. ¿Hago la limonada?
3. ¿Apago la luz?
4. ¿Te espero en el coche?
5. ¿Me quito el abrigo?
6. ¿Vengo con Eva?

    7. ¿Lo pongo en la mesa?
    8. ¿Se lo digo?
    9. ¿Voy con Alberto? *Ve*
  10. ¿Salgo temprano? *Sal*
  11. ¿Me baño ahora?
  12. ¿Abro las ventanas?

B. Make the following commands negative.

    1. Vete. *no v*
    2. Dile que es verdad. *No di   , que es verdad*
    3. Sal con Roberto. *no se*
    4. Ven esta tarde. *no*
    5. Báñate ahora.
    6. Hazlo otra vez.
    7. Pon el dinero en el banco.
    8. Sé bueno.
    9. Ten una fiesta el sábado.
  10. Dale el dinero al gerente.

C. You are leaving a child home alone for a few hours. Using the *tú* form, tell the child what to do and what not to do. Give at least ten commands.

En el laboratorio

LECCIÓN 11

The following material is to be used with the tape in the language laboratory.

I. Vocabulario

Repeat each word after the speaker. When repeating words that are cognates, notice the difference in pronunciation between English and Spanish.

COGNADOS: el coctel   el favor   La Habana
     la limonada

NOMBRES: el arroz   los guantes   la liquidación
     la venta   la niña   el niño   el pollo
     la zapatería

VERBOS: apagar   caminar

ADJETIVOS: todo   todos

OTRAS PALABRAS Y EXPRESIONES: allí   arroz con pollo   casi nunca
     ¿cuánto tiempo?   de vez en cuando
     en esa época   ir de compras
     media hora   otra vez   ¡Rápido!
     Ten paciencia.

II. Práctica

A. Answer the following questions, using the cue provided. Repeat the correct answer after the speaker's confirmation. Listen to the model.

Modelo: —¿Cuánto tiempo hace que vives en La Habana?
          (tres años)
          —**Hace** tres años **que** vivo en La Habana.

B. Answer the following questions, using the cue provided. Repeat the correct answer after the speaker's confirmation. Listen to the model.

Modelo: —¿Qué tuviste que hacer ayer?   (estudiar español)
          —**Tuve que estudiar español.**

1. (vestidos)
2. (anoche)
3. (los estudiantes)
4. (a las siete)
5. (en la mesa)
6. (nada)

163

C. Explain what these people used to do by changing the following sentences to the imperfect:

Modelo: Mis abuelos **hablan** en español.
Mis abuelos **hablaban** en español.

1. Yo voy a la universidad todos los días.
2. Nosotros no vemos a nuestros amigos.
3. Yo tengo un buen coche.
4. Él es mi profesor.
5. Ellos comen arroz con pollo a veces.
6. Ud. me escribe de vez en cuando.

D. Change the following commands from the negative to the affirmative. Repeat the correct answer after the speaker's confirmation. Listen to the model.

Modelo: **No hables** inglés.
Habla inglés.

E. Change the following commands from the affirmative to the negative. Repeat the correct answer after the speaker's confirmation. Listen to the model.

Modelo: **Ponlo** en la mesa.
No lo pongas en la mesa.

III. Para escuchar y entender

1. Listen carefully to the dialogue. It will be read twice.

(*Diálogo 1*)

Now the speaker will make statements about the dialogue you just heard. Tell whether each statement is true (**verdadero**) or false (**falso**). The speaker will confirm the correct answer.

2. Listen carefully to the dialogue. It will be read twice.

(*Diálogo 2*)

Now the speaker will make statements concerning the conversation you just heard. Tell whether each statement is true (**verdadero**) or false (**falso**). The speaker will confirm the correct answer.

3. Listen carefully to the narration. It will be read twice.

(*Narración*)

Now the speaker will ask some questions about the narration you just heard. Answer each question, omitting the subject. The speaker will confirm the correct answer. Repeat the correct answer.

Lección

12

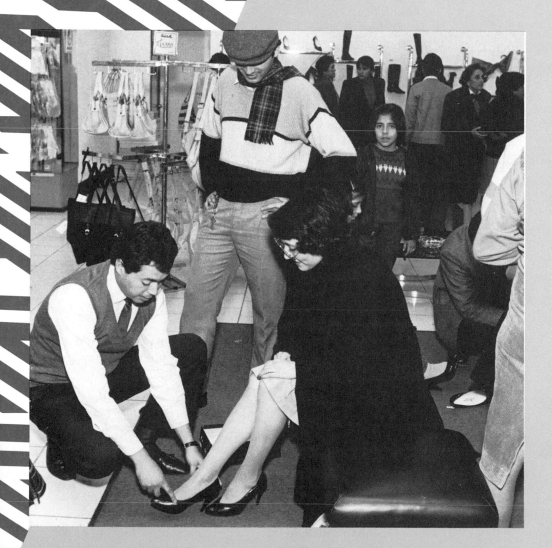

1. **The past progressive**
2. **The preterit contrasted with the imperfect**
3. **Changes in meaning with the imperfect and preterit of** *conocer, saber, querer,* **and** *poder*
4. *En* **and** *a* **as the equivalent of at**

Vocabulario

COGNADOS

el **aeropuerto** airport	la **farmacia** pharmacy
el **examen** exam	las **vacaciones**[1] vacation

NOMBRES
el **anillo** ring
los **aretes** earrings
la **cuñada** sister-in-law
el **cuñado** brother-in-law
la **joyería** jewelry store
la **máquina de escribir**
    typewriter
la **tarea** homework
el **traje de baño** bathing
    suit
la **vidriera, el escaparate**
    store window

VERBOS
    ayudar (a) to help
    encontrarse (con) (o:ue)
        to meet

mirar to look at
quedarse to stay, to
    remain
sentir(se) (e:ie) to feel

ADJETIVO
nuevo(a) new

**OTRAS PALABRAS Y
EXPRESIONES**
en casa at home
escribir a máquina to
    type
ir de vacaciones to go on
    vacation
juntos(as) together
sólo, solamente only
todo el día all day long

1. The past progressive

The past progressive indicates an action in progress in the past.
It is formed with the imperfect tense of the verb **estar** and the
Spanish equivalent of the *-ing* form of the main verb.

—¿Qué **estabas haciendo**
    cuando te llamé?
—**Estaba escribiendo** a
    máquina. Tengo una
    máquina de escribir
    nueva.

*What were you doing
when I called you?*
*I was typing. I have a new
typewriter.*

—¿Qué **estaban mirando**
    los chicos?
—**Estaban mirando** los
    anillos y los aretes que
    estaban en la vidriera.

*What were the boys look-
ing at?*
*They were looking at the
rings and the earrings
that were in the window.*

---

[1] *Vacaciones* is always used in the plural in Spanish.

—¿Qué te **estaba diciendo**
   Ana?

What was Ana saying to
*   you?*

—Me **estaba diciendo** que
   quería un traje de baño
   nuevo.

She was telling me that
*   she wanted a new bath-*
*   ing suit.*

Práctica

Tell what everybody was doing when a friend came to visit. Use
the cues provided.

Modelo: Elsa / hablar con Jorge.
           Elsa estaba hablando con Jorge.

1. yo / beber un refresco
2. Uds. / mirar televisión
3. tu mamá / leer un libro
4. Isabel / probarse el traje de baño nuevo
5. los niños / dormir
6. la cocinera / barrer la cocina
7. Carlos y papá / jugar a las cartas
8. tu hermana / escribir a máquina

2. The preterit contrasted with the imperfect

There are two simple past tenses in Spanish: the imperfect and the
preterit. The difference between the two can be visualized this way:

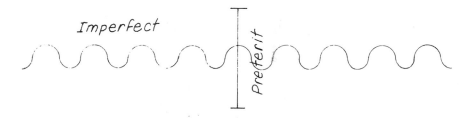

The continuous moving line of the imperfect represents an action or
state that was taking place in the past. We don't know when the
action started or ended. The vertical line of the preterit represents a
completed or finished event in the past.

The following table summarizes the uses of the preterit and the imperfect:

Preterit	Imperfect
1. Records, narrates, and reports an independent past act or event as a completed and undivided whole, regardless of its duration. 2. Sums up a past condition or state viewed as a whole.	1. Describes an action in progress in the past. 2. Indicates a continuous and habitual action: *used to . . .*[1] 3. Describes a physical, mental, or emotional state or condition in the past. 4. Expresses time in the past. 5. Is used in indirect speech.

The preterit:

—¿A qué hora **se acostó** Ud. anoche?
—Anoche **me acosté** a las once y media.

What time did you go to bed last night?
Last night I went to bed at eleven-thirty.

—Ayer **estuve** enferma todo el día.
—Yo también.

Yesterday I was sick all day long.
Me, too.

The imperfect:

—Cuando **íbamos** a la joyería, vimos a María Ortiz.
—¿Sí? Ella y yo siempre **íbamos** juntas de vacaciones.

As (when) we were going to the jewelry store, we saw María Ortiz.
Really? She and I always used to go on vacation together.

—¿Por qué te fuiste tan temprano? **Eran** sólo las ocho de la noche.
—Me fui porque no me **sentía** muy bien.

Why did you leave so early? It was only eight o'clock in the evening.
I left because I wasn't feeling very well.

—¿Qué dijo Eduardo?
—Dijo que Ana **estaba** en la farmacia.

What did Eduardo say?
He said Ana was at the pharmacy.

[1] Note that this use of the imperfect also corresponds to the English *would*, when used to describe a repeated action in the past: **Cuando yo era niña, comía pollo todos los domingos.** *When I was a child, I used to eat chicken every Sunday. (When I was a child, I would eat chicken every Sunday.)*

ATENCIÓN: In the first two exchanges, **íbamos** describes an action in progress, while in the fourth exchange, **sentía** describes a physical state. These verbs in the imperfect act as background for completed actions in the past, which are expressed by the preterit verbs **vimos, fui** and **dijo.** Notice an example of indirect speech in the last exchange.

Práctica

A. Complete the following sentences with the preterit or the imperfect of the verbs in parentheses, as needed:

1. Anoche él y yo _fueron_ (ir) a la joyería juntos.
2. Cuando nosotros _éramos_ (ser) chicos, _íbamos_ (ir) a casa de nuestros abuelos.
3. _Eran_ (Ser) las cuatro de la tarde cuando él _llegaba_ (llegar) ayer.
4. Ayer Roberto me _decía_ (decir) que _necesitaba_ (necesitar) el traje de baño.
5. La semana pasada yo _era_ (estar) muy enfermo también.
6. Yo _venía_ (venir) por la calle Octava cuando _vi_ (ver) a los niños que _eran_ (ir) a la farmacia.
7. Anoche ellos _se fueron_ (irse) porque no _se sen_ (sentirse) bien.
8. Yo siempre los _veía_ (ver) cuando ellos _iban_ (ir) al teatro.
9. Ellos no _estuvieron_ (estar) en casa anoche.
10. Ayer yo _compraba_ (comprar) una máquina de escribir.

B. Tell about yourself by answering the following questions:

1. ¿Dónde vivía Ud. cuando era niño(a)?
2. ¿Hablaba Ud. inglés o español con sus padres?
3. ¿A dónde iba de vacaciones todos los veranos?
4. ¿Veía Ud. a sus abuelos a menudo?
5. ¿A dónde fue Ud. anoche?
6. ¿A quién vio?
7. ¿Qué hora era cuando Ud. volvió a su casa ayer?
8. ¿Estuvo Ud. enfermo(a) ayer?
9. ¿Cómo se sentía Ud. hoy cuando salió de su casa?
10. ¿Le dijo su profesor(a) que Ud. hablaba bien el español?

C. How would you say the following in Spanish?

1. It was four o'clock when I got home yesterday.
2. Andrés was sick all day long yesterday.
3. When we were children, we lived in Chile. We always used to go to Argentina on vacation.

4. Raquel said that she wanted to go to the jewelry store.
5. We were going to the movies when we saw her.

D. Use your imagination to complete the following statements with either the preterit or the imperfect, as appropriate: *fuimos a la calle (out)*

1. Nosotros siempre comíamos en casa, pero ese día...
2. Ahora me levanto tarde, pero cuando era niño(a)...
3. Siempre iban de vacaciones a Madrid, pero el verano pasado...
4. Ahora estudio mucho, pero cuando era niño(a)... *estudiaba menos.*
5. Anoche, cuando mi amigo y yo íbamos a la biblioteca...
6. El profesor nos dijo que... *éramos*

3. Changes in meaning with the imperfect and preterit of conocer, saber, querer, **and** poder

In Spanish, a few verbs change their meaning when used in the preterit or the imperfect:

Preterit		*Imperfect*	
conocer		conocer	
conocí	*I met*	**conocía**	*I knew, I was acquainted with*
saber	*figured out*	saber	
supe	*I found out, I learned*	**sabía**	*I knew (a fact, how to)*
querer		querer	
no quise	*I refused*	**no quería**	*I didn't want to*
poder		poder	
pude	*I succeeded, I was able*	**podía**	*I could, I had the ability or chance*

*Lo vas a encontrar
Lo vas a saber –
You will figure
it out*

—Mario, ¿**conocías** a la cuñada de Luisa?
—No, la **conocí** ayer.

—Rita, ¿**sabías** que teníamos examen hoy?
—No, lo **supe** esta mañana.

Mario, did you know Louise's sister-in-law?
No, I met her yesterday.

Rita, did you know that we had an exam today?
No, I found out this morning.

—¿Por qué no **fuiste** el
  domingo a la fiesta?
—Porque Carlos no **quiso**
  llevarme. Tuve que
  quedarme en casa.

*Why didn't you go to the
  party on Sunday?*
*Because Carlos refused to
  take me. I had to stay
  home.*

—Ramón, ayer me dijiste
  que **podías** ayudarme
  con la tarea y no
  viniste.
—No **pude** salir porque
  mamá estaba enferma.

*Raymond, yesterday you
  told me you could help
  me with the homework,
  and you didn't come.*
*I wasn't able to go out be-
  cause mother was sick.*

Práctica

A. Complete the following dialogue, using the preterit or the imperfect of **saber, conocer, querer** or **poder**, as appropriate.

—¿Tú _conocías_ a Graciela?
—No, la _conocí_ anoche.
—¿Tú _sabías_ que ella era la esposa de Roberto?
—No, lo _supe_ anoche. Me lo dijo Raquel.
—¿Alberto fue a la fiesta anoche?
—Sí, fue. Él no _quiso_ ir, pero su hermano lo llevó.
—¿Y Rosa? ¿Por qué no fue? ¿No _pudo_ ir?
—No, Rosa no fue porque no _podía_

B. You are an interpreter. How would you say the following in
Spanish?

1. We met Julia's sister-in-law last night. _Conocimos la cuñada anoche_
2. She said she couldn't help you with the homework. _no podías_
3. My brother-in-law wasn't able to go with his wife to the _no pudo_
   party.
4. Yesterday they found out that they had an exam.
5. I didn't know your mother-in-law.
6. He refused to help me.
7. Did you know my address and my telephone number? _Sabías dirección_

4. En **and** a **as the equivalent of** *at*

_en - at
in
on_

◆ **En** is used in Spanish as the equivalent of *at* to indicate a certain
place or location:

—¿Dónde están los
  chicos? ¿No están **en**
  casa?

*Where are the boys?
  Aren't they (at) home?*

—No, están **en** el su-
  permercado.

*No, they're at the super-
  market.*

♦ **A** is used in Spanish as the equivalent of *at*

1. to refer to a specific moment in time:

—¿Cuándo se van a   *When are you going to*
    encontrar Uds.?   *meet?*
—Mañana **a** las once.   *Tomorrow at eleven.*

2. to indicate direction towards a point after the verb **llegar:**

—¿Cuándo llegaron **al**   *When did they arrive at*
    aeropuerto?   *the airport?*
—Llegaron **al** aeropuerto   *They arrived at the air-*
    ayer a las cinco.   *port yesterday at five.*

Práctica

¿**En** or **a**? Which one should you use?

1. Ellos están __en__ la universidad.
2. Hoy no voy a estar __en__ casa.
3. Mamá llegó __al__ aeropuerto __a__ las diez y media.
4. Llegó __a__ la tienda muy temprano.
5. Estoy __en__ la joyería en este momento.
6. La clase empezó __a__ las ocho.
7. ¿Están __en__ el aeropuerto?
8. Mañana llegan los chicos __a__ Bogotá.

En el laboratorio

LECCIÓN 12

The following material is to be used with the tape in the language laboratory.

I. Vocabulario

Repeat each word after the speaker. When repeating words that are cognates, notice the difference in pronunciation between English and Spanish.

COGNADOS:	el aeropuerto el examen la farmacia las vacaciones
NOMBRES:	el anillo los aretes la cuñada el cuñado la joyería la máquina de escribir la tarea el traje de baño la vidriera el escaparate
VERBOS:	ayudar encontrarse mirar quedarse sentir
ADJETIVO:	nuevo
OTRAS PALABRAS Y EXPRESIONES:	en casa escribir a máquina ir de vacaciones juntos sólo solamente todo el día

II. Práctica

A. Change the following from the imperfect to the past progressive. Repeat the correct answer after the speaker's confirmation. Listen to the model.

Modelo: Yo **comía** en la cafetería.
   Yo **estaba comiendo** en la cafetería.

B. Answer the questions, using the cues provided. Notice the use of the preterit or the imperfect. Repeat the correct answer after the speaker's confirmation. Listen to the model.

Modelo: —¿Qué hora era cuando él llegó?   (las nueve)
   —**Eran** las nueve cuando él **llegó.**

1. (en casa)
2. (en México)
3. (esta mañana)
4. (en una fiesta)
5. (sí)
6. (que no podían venir)
7. (sí)
8. (no, pero vine)
9. (No)
10. (a Luisa)

173

III. Para escuchar y entender

1. Listen carefully to the dialogue. It will be read twice.

   (*Diálogo 1*)

   Now the speaker will make statements about the dialogue you just heard. Tell whether each statement is true (**verdadero**) or false (**falso**). The speaker will confirm the correct answer.

2. Listen carefully to the dialogue. It will be read twice.

   (*Diálogo 2*)

   Now the speaker will ask some questions about the dialogue you just heard. Answer each question, omitting the subject. The speaker will confirm the correct answer. Repeat the correct answer.

Lección

13

ESTACIÓN DE SERVICIO

ES 3521

1. **The preterit of stem-changing verbs** (e:i **and** o:u)
2. **The expression** acabar de
3. **Special construction, with** gustar, doler, **and** hacer falta
4. **¿Qué? and** ¿cuál? **used with** ser

Vocabulario

COGNADOS

la **aspirina** aspirin	el **modelo** model
el (la) **dentista** dentist	la **temperatura** temperature
el **instrumento** instrument	el **termómetro** thermometer
el **mecánico** mechanic	

NOMBRES
el **aceite** oil
el **acumulador**, la **batería** battery
la **cabeza** head
el **dolor** pain
el **edificio** building
el (la) **empleado(a)** attendant, clerk
la **gasolinera, estación de servicio** gas station
el **limpiaparabrisas** windshield wiper
la **llanta**, la **goma**, el **neumático** tires
la **muela** tooth (molar)
el **traje** suit, outfit

VERBOS
despedirse (e:i) to say goodbye
divertirse (e:ie) to have a good time

doler (o:ue) to hurt, to ache
elegir (e:i) to choose, to select
encontrar (o:ue) to find
gustar to like, to be pleasing
medir (e:i) to measure
mentir (e:ie) to lie
morir (o:ue) to die
sacar to take out
usar to use
vender to sell

ADJETIVO
otro(a) other, another

OTRAS PALABRAS Y EXPRESIONES
acabar de to have just
hacer falta to need, to lack
sobre about

1. The preterit of stem-changing verbs (e:i and o:u)

e:i verbs

Stem-changing verbs of the **-ir** conjugation, whether they change **e** to **ie** or **e** to **i** in the present indicative, change **e** to **i** in the third person singular and plural of the preterit:

sentir		pedir	
sentí	sentimos	pedí	pedimos
sentiste		pediste	
sintió	sintieron	pidió	pidieron

♦ Some other verbs that follow the same **e** to **i** pattern are:

preferir	**repetir**
divertirse *(to have a good time)*	**elegir** *(to choose)*
	conseguir
mentir *(to lie)*	**despedirse** *(to say goodbye)*
servir	**seguir**

—Sra. López, ¿**sintió** Ud. dolor cuando el dentista le sacó la muela?
—No, no sentí nada.

Mrs. López, did you feel (any) pain when the dentist took out your tooth?
No, I didn't feel anything.

—¿A quién le **pidieron** Uds. el aceite?
—Se lo pedimos al empleado de la gasolinera.

Whom did you ask for the oil?
We asked the gas station attendant (for it).

—¿Llevó él el coche al mecánico?
—No, **prefirió** venderlo.

Did he take the car to the mechanic?
No, he preferred to sell it.

o:u verbs

Stem-changing verbs of the **-ir** conjugation that change **o** to **ue** in the present indicative change **o** to **u** in the third person singular and plural of the preterit:

dormir	
dormí	dormimos
dormiste	
durmió	durmieron

♦ Another verb that follows the same **o** to **u** pattern:

morir *(to die)*

—¿Cuántas horas **durmió** Ud. anoche?
—Yo dormí seis horas, pero Ana y Luis sólo **durmieron** tres.

How many hours did you sleep last night?
I slept six hours, but Ana and Luis slept only three.

Práctica

Complete the sentences with the preterit of the verb in parentheses:

1. Ellos _____ (despedirse) de Eva en el aeropuerto.
2. Ayer yo no _____ (sentir) dolor cuando me sacaron la muela.
3. Ella no me _____ (mentir). Me dijo la verdad.
4. ¿_____ (Servir) ellos los refrescos o los _____ (servir) tú?
5. El hijo de Carmen no _____ (conseguir) el aceite.
6. Pedro _____ (morir) anoche.
7. ¿Dónde _____ (dormir) Uds. anoche? Yo _____ (dormir) en el hotel.
8. ¿A quién le _____ (pedir) Ud. la maleta?
9. María _____ (elegir) el vestido verde.
10. Ellos _____ (divertirse) mucho en la fiesta ayer.

2. The expression acabar de

Acabar de means *to have just*. This formula is used in Spanish:

subject +	**acabar** (present tense) +		**de** +	*infinitive*
Pedro	**acaba**		**de**	**llegar.**

—¿Tiene Elena un acumulador nuevo?   *Does Elena have a new battery?*

—Sí, **acaba de** comprarlo.   *Yes, she (has) just bought it.*

—¿Tu coche necesita llantas nuevas?   *Does your car need new tires?*

—No, **acabo de** cambiarlas.   *No, I (have) just changed them.*

♦ Notice that the conjugation of **acabar** is regular.

Práctica

Tell us what everybody has just done by completing the following sentences with the correct form of **acabar de** + *infinitive*:

1. Juan _____ a esta ciudad.   (*has just arrived*)
2. Yo _____ esta casa.   (*have just bought*)
3. Ellas _____ el coche.   (*have just sold*)
4. Él _____ carne.   (*has just eaten*)
5. Elena _____.   (*has just gotten dressed*)
6. Uds. _____ a la gasolinera.   (*have just gone*)
7. Elena _____ la carta.   (*has just written*)

8. Tú _____ la revista.   *(have just read)*
9. Yo _____.   *(have just bathed)*
10. Ellos _____ la llanta.   *(have just changed)*

3. Special construction with gustar, doler, **and** hacer falta

The verb **gustar** means *to like (something or somebody)*. A special construction is required in Spanish to translate the English structure *to like (something or somebody)*. This is done by making the English direct object the subject of the Spanish sentence. The English subject then becomes the indirect object of the Spanish sentence.

English:	*I like your suit.*
	subj. d.o.
Spanish:	**Me gusta tu traje.**
	i.o. subj.
Literally:	*Your suit appeals to me.*

The two most commonly used forms of **gustar** are: (1) the third-person singular **gusta** if the subject is singular or if **gustar** is followed by one or more infinitives; and (2) the third-person plural **gustan** if the subject is plural.

Indirect Object Pronouns

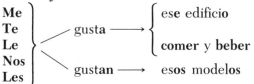

♦ Note that the verb **gustar** agrees with the subject of the sentence—that is, the person or thing *being liked*.

Me gusta **el café.**   Le gust**an las chicas altas.**

♦ Note that the person who does the liking is the *indirect object*.

Me gusta el café.   **Le** gustan las chicas altas.
I.O.   I.O.

—¿**Les gusta** el café?   *Do you (pl.) like coffee?*
—Sí, **nos gusta** mucho el   *Yes, we like coffee very*
café, pero **nos gusta**   *much, but we like tea*
más el té.   *better.*

ATENCIÓN: Note that the words **más** *(better)* and **mucho** immediately follow **gustar**.

◆ The verbs **doler** (*to hurt, to ache*) and **hacer falta** (*to need*) have the same construction as **gustar:**

—¿Qué **les hace falta,** señoras?	*What do you need, ladies?*
—**Nos hace falta** un limpiaparabrisas.	*We need a windshield wiper.*
—¿Por qué estás tomando aspirinas?	*Why are you taking aspirins?*
—Porque **me duele** la cabeza.	*Because my head hurts.*

ATENCIÓN: In Spanish, the definite article is generally used instead of the possessive adjective with parts of the body.

Práctica

A. Tell about yourself by answering the following questions:

1. ¿Cuándo toman Uds. aspirinas?
2. ¿Le duele a Ud. la cabeza a menudo?
3. ¿Qué le duele hoy?
4. ¿Qué le hace falta a Ud.?
5. ¿Les hacen falta a Uds. más toallas?
6. ¿Les gusta a Uds. el español?
7. ¿Le gusta caminar?
8. ¿Qué le gusta más, el café o el té?

B. What do you and these people like?

Modelo: (**José**) el café
 Le gusta el café.

1. (Elsa) ese modelo
2. (nosotros) el espanõl
3. (yo) ese traje
4. (ellos) comer y beber
5. (tú) las fiestas
6. (Uds.) los refrescos

C. You are an interpreter. How would you say the following in Spanish?

1. They like those buildings.
2. I need a suit.
3. I like this model.
4. We don't like to take aspirin.
5. Does your head hurt, madam?
6. Do you need a new battery?

◀4. ¿Qué? **and** ¿cuál? **used with** ser

◆ When asking for a definition, use ¿**qué**? to translate *what:*

—¿**Qué** es un   *What is a thermometer?*
    termómetro?
—Un termómetro es un   *A thermometer is an*
    instrumento que   *instrument we use to*
    usamos para medir la   *measure temperature.*
    temperatura.

◆ When asking for a choice, use ¿**cuál**? to translate *what (which).*
¿**Cuál**? carries the idea of selection from among many objects or
ideas:

—¿**Cuál** es su número de   *What is your social*
    seguro social?   *security number?*
—Mi número de seguro   *My social security number*
    social es 243-50-8139.   *is 243-50-8139.*

—¿**Cuáles** son sus ideas   *What are your ideas about*
    sobre la economía?   *the economy?*
—Yo no sé nada de la   *I don't know anything*
    economía.   *about the economy.*

Práctica

¿**Qué** or **Cuál**? Which one should you use?

1. ¿_____ es su número de seguro social?
2. ¿_____ es un termómetro? ¿Un instrumento para medir
    la temperatura?
3. ¿_____ son sus ideas sobre la educación?
4. ¿_____ es su estado civil?
5. ¿_____ es un impermeable? ¿Es algo para la lluvia?
6. ¿_____ es su número de teléfono?

En el laboratorio

LECCIÓN 13

The following material is to be used with the tape in the language laboratory.

I. Vocabulario

Repeat each word after the speaker. When repeating words that are cognates, notice the difference in pronunciation between English and Spanish.

COGNADOS:	la aspirina el dentista el instrumento el mecánico el modelo la temperatura el termómetro
NOMBRES:	el aceite el acumulador la batería la cabeza el dolor el edificio el empleado la gasolinera la estación de servicio el limpiaparabrisas la llanta la goma el neumático la muela el traje
VERBOS:	despedirse divertirse doler elegir encontrar gustar medir mentir morir sacar usar vender
ADJETIVO:	otro
OTRAS PALABRAS Y EXPRESIONES:	acabar de hacer falta sobre

II. Práctica

A. Change the verbs according to the new subjects. Repeat the correct answer after the speaker's confirmation. Listen to the model.

Modelo: Yo no lo conseguí.   (ella)
  Ella no lo consiguió.

1. (él)	6. (Ud.)
2. (ellos)	7. (Luis)
3. (Ana)	8. (ellos)
4. (Ud.)	9. (Carlos)
5. (Uds.)	10. (los niños)

B. Answer each question, using the expression **acabar de** + *infinitive*. Repeat the correct answer after the speaker's confirmation. Listen to the model.

Modelo: ¿Ya comiste?
Sí, **acabo de comer.**

C. Restate each statement or question, using **gusta más** to replace **preferir.** Repeat the correct answer.

Modelo: Yo **prefiero** este traje.
Me gusta más este traje.

1. Tú prefieres ir al cine.
2. Él prefiere ese modelo.
3. Ella prefiere esas habitaciones.
4. Nosotros preferimos tomar café.
5. Uds. prefieren ese hotel.
6. Yo prefiero viajar en avión.

D. Restate each statement or question, using the expression **hacer falta** to replace **necesitar.**

Modelo: Nosotros **necesitamos** dinero.
Nos hace falta dinero.

1. Yo necesito un acumulador.
2. Él necesita un limpiaparabrisas.
3. Ellos necesitan dos llantas nuevas.
4. ¿Tú necesitas ir a la gasolinera?
5. Nosotros necesitamos una casa más grande.

III. Para escuchar y entender

1. Listening carefully to the dialogue. It will be read twice.

(*Diálogo 1*)

Now the speaker will make statements about the dialogue you just heard. Tell whether each statement is true (**verdadero**) or false (**falso**). The speaker will confirm the correct answer.

2. Listen carefully to the dialogue. It will be read twice.

(*Diálogo 2*)

Now the speaker will ask some questions about the dialogue you just heard. Answer each question, omitting the subject. The speaker will confirm the correct answer. Repeat the correct answer.

Lección

14

1. *Hace* **meaning** *ago*
2. *The past participle*
3. *The present perfect tense*
4. *The past perfect (pluperfect) tense*

Vocabulario

COGNADOS

el **accidente** accident	las **matemáticas** mathematics
la **estación** station	el **tren** train

NOMBRES
el **boleto**   ticket
  (*e.g., for a bus, train*)
el **brazo**   arm
el **descuento**   discount
el **itinerario, horario**
  schedule
la **pierna**   leg
el **trabajo**   work, job
el **vuelto, cambio**   change

VERBOS
  casarse (con)   to get married
  cubrir   to cover
  perder   to miss
  (*e.g., a train*)

romper   to break
terminar, acabar   to finish

ADJETIVO
  contento(a)   happy, content

**OTRAS PALABRAS Y
EXPRESIONES**
  hacer cola   to stand in line
  llegar tarde   to be late
  por ciento   per cent
  por eso   that's why,
   therefore

◀ 1. Hace **meaning ago**

In sentences in the preterit and in some cases the imperfect, **hace** + *period of time* is equivalent to the English *ago*.[1]

Llegué **hace dos años.**   *I arrived two years ago.*

When **hace** is placed at the beginning of the sentence, the construction is as follows:

Hace + *period of time* +	**que** +	*verb* (*preterit*)	
Hace dos años	**que**	**llegué.**	

—¿Cuánto tiempo **hace
  que** llegó el tren?

—Llegó **hace dos horas.**

—¿Cuánto tiempo **hace
  que** Uds. se casaron?

—**Hace un año que** nos
  casamos.

*How long ago did the
  train arrive?*

It arrived two hours ago.

*How long ago did you get
  married?*

*We got married a year
  ago.*

---

[1] Sometimes the imperfect may be used with **hacer** to mean *ago:* **Hace dos años, yo vivía en Buenos Aires.** (*Two years ago, I lived in Buenos Aires.*)

Práctica

A. Tell us something about yourself.

1. ¿Cuánto tiempo hace que Uds. llegaron a la universidad?
2. ¿Cuánto tiempo hace que comenzó la clase?
3. ¿Cuánto tiempo hace que Ud. comió?
4. ¿Cuánto tiempo hace que Uds. empezaron a estudiar español?
5. ¿Cuánto tiempo hace que Ud. vino a esta ciudad?
6. ¿Cuánto tiempo hace que sus padres se conocieron?

B. You are an interpreter. How would you say the following in Spanish?

1. They bought the building five years ago.
2. I took two aspirins two hours ago.
3. How long ago did you arrive, Mr. Pérez?
4. We came to this city a month ago.
5. The train left an hour ago.

2. The past participle

> **Past participle**   a past form of a verb that may be used in conjunction with another (auxiliary) verb in certain past tenses. The past participle may also be used as an adjective: **gone, worked, written**

The past participle of regular verbs is formed by adding the following endings to the stem of the verb:

Past Participle Endings

-ar *Verbs*	-er *Verbs*	-ir *Verbs*
habl- **ado**	ten- **ido**	ven- **ido**

◆ The following verbs have irregular past participles in Spanish:

abrir	**abierto**	morir	**muerto**
cubrir	**cubierto**	poner	**puesto**
decir	**dicho**	ver	**visto**
escribir	**escrito**	volver	**vuelto**
hacer	**hecho**	romper	**roto**

◆ In Spanish, most past participles may be used as adjectives. As such, they agree in number and gender with the nouns they modify:

—¿Tuviste un accidente?   *Did you have an accident?*
—Sí, y tengo **la pierna**   *Yes, and I have a broken*
  rota.   *leg.*
—¿Y el brazo?   *And your arm?*
—No, **el brazo** no está   *No, my arm is not broken.*
  roto.

—¿**Las ventanas** están   *Are the windows open?*
  abiertas?
—No, están **cerradas.**   *No, they are closed.*

Práctica

A. What are the past participles of the following verbs?

1. dormir	6. cubrir	11. caminar	16. abrir
2. romper	7. recibir	12. pedir	17. ver
3. estar	8. hacer	13. decir	18. volver
4. comer	9. cerrar	14. comprar	19. aprender
5. poner	10. ser	15. morir	20. escribir

B. Using the elements from the two columns and the verb **estar,** create ten descriptive sentences. You may use a verb more than once:

Modelo: ventanas / cerrar
          Las ventanas **están cerradas.**

los hombres	servir
Pedro	romper
el libro	cerrar
la carta	morir
los instrumentos	dormir
las puertas	escribir (en español)
el café	hacer (de madera)
la mesa	abrir

◆ 3. The present perfect tense

The present perfect tense is formed by using the present tense of the auxiliary verb **haber** and the past participle of the verb to be conjugated.

This tense is equivalent to the use in English of the auxiliary verb *have* + past participle, as in *I have spoken.*

Present of **haber**[1] *(to have)*	
he	hemos
has	
ha	han

The Present Perfect Tense

	hablar	**tener**	**venir**
yo	**he** hablado	**he** tenido	**he** venido
tú	**has** hablado	**has** tenido	**has** venido
Ud. ⎫ él ⎬ ella ⎭	**ha** hablado	**ha** tenido	**ha** venido
nosotros	**hemos** hablado	**hemos** tenido	**hemos** venido
Uds. ⎫ ellos ⎬ ellas ⎭	**han** hablado	**han** tenido	**han** venido

—¿**Ha terminado** Ud. su
   lección de matemáticas?

*Have you finished your
   math lesson?*

—No, no la **he terminado**
   todavía.

*No, I haven't finished it
   yet.*

—¿Por qué **han llegado**
   tarde?

Why are[2] you late?

—**Hemos tenido** que
   hacer cola para
   comprar los boletos.

*We (have) had to stand in
   line to buy tickets.*

—¿Te **han dado** un
   descuento?

*Did they give[2] you a dis-
   count?*

—Sí, del diez por ciento.
   Estoy muy contento.

*Yes, ten per cent. I'm very
   happy.*

ATENCIÓN: Note that when the past participle is part of a perfect
tense, it is invariable and cannot be separated from the
auxiliary verb **haber:**

Siempre **ha escrito** las
   cartas a máquina.

*He has **always** typed the
   letters.*

---

[1] Note that the English verb *to have* has two equivalents in Spanish: **haber** (used only as
an auxiliary verb) and **tener.**

[2] Sometimes Spanish uses the present perfect where English would use the simple
present or the simple past tense.

Práctica

A. Tell what you and these people have or haven't done:

1. Ellos / terminar / lecciones
2. Ella / venir / a estudiar matemáticas
3. Yo / siempre / hacer bien / tarea
4. Nosotros / escribirlo / a máquina
5. Tú / nunca / tener que / hacer cola
6. Ud. / no decírselo

B. Tell about yourself by answering the following questions:

1. ¿Ha viajado Ud. por tren? ¿A dónde?
2. ¿Ha dicho Ud. siempre la verdad?
3. ¿Alguien ha abierto la ventana de su cuarto? ¿Quién?
4. ¿Ha visto Ud. a sus padres hoy?
5. ¿Han venido a clase todos los estudiantes hoy?
6. ¿Dónde han comprado Uds. el libro de español?
7. ¿Dónde han puesto Uds. los libros?
8. ¿Ha hecho Ud. toda la tarea?
9. ¿Han hablado Uds. con el profesor?
10. ¿Les ha dado muchos exámenes el profesor?

◀ 4. The past perfect (pluperfect) tense

The past perfect tense is formed by using the imperfect tense of the auxiliary verb **haber** and the past participle of the verb to be conjugated.

This tense is equivalent to the use, in English, of the auxiliary verb *had* + past participle, as in *I had spoken*. As in English, the past perfect tense in Spanish describes an action or event completed before some other past action or event.

Imperfect of **haber**	
había	habíamos
habías	
había	habían

The Past Perfect Tense

	estudiar	beber	ir
yo	**había** estudiado	**había** bebido	**había** ido
tú	**habías** estudiado	**habías** bebido	**habías** ido
Ud. él ella	**había** estudiado	**había** bebido	**había** ido
nosotros	**habíamos** estudiado	**habíamos** bebido	**habíamos** ido
Uds. ellos ellas	**habían** estudiado	**habían** bebido	**habían** ido

—¿Perdiste el tren?
—Sí, ya **había salido** cuando yo llegué a la estación. Por eso llegué tarde al trabajo.

Did you miss the train?
Yes, it had already left when I got to the station. That's why I was late to work.

—¿No trajiste el itinerario del tren?
—No, Juan ya lo **había traído**.

Didn't you bring the train schedule?
No, Juan had already brought it.

—¿Ya te **había dado** ella el vuelto?
—No, no me lo **había dado** todavía.

Had she already given you the change?
No, she hadn't given it to me yet.

Práctica

A. Using the verbs provided, complete these dialogues in the pluperfect tense.

1. —¿Cuándo tú llegaste los chicos ya _____ la cena? (hacer)
   —No, porque ellos no _____ de la universidad todavía. (volver)
2. —¡Yo no sabía que tú _____! (casarse)
   —¿No te lo dijo Ernesto? Yo se lo _____ a él. (decir)
3. —¿Uds. compraron los boletos para Eva y Luis?
   —No, ellos ya los _____. (comprar)
4. —¿A quién le _____ Uds. sobre ese problema? (escribir)
   —Le _____ al director. (escribir)

B. How would you say the following in Spanish?

1. When they arrived at the station, the train had already left. That's why they were late to work.
2. They had never given me a ten per cent discount before. I was very happy.
3. We had never missed the bus before, but that day we were late.
4. Had they given you the change?
5. I hadn't seen the schedule.

En el laboratorio

LECCIÓN 14

The following material is to be used with the tape in the language laboratory.

I. Vocabulario

Repeat each word after the speaker. When repeating words that are cognates, notice the difference in pronunciation between English and Spanish.

COGNADOS: el accidente   la estación   las matemáticas
el tren

NOMBRES: el boleto   el brazo   el descuento
el itinerario   el horario   la pierna
el trabajo   el vuelto   el cambio

VERBOS: casarse   cubrir   perder   romper
terminar   acabar

ADJETIVO: contento

**OTRAS PALABRAS Y
EXPRESIONES:** hacer cola   llegar tarde   por ciento
por eso

II. Práctica

A. Answer each question, using the cues provided below. Repeat the correct answer after the speaker's confirmation. Listen to the model.

1. tres meses
2. quince minutos
3. cinco años
4. dos semanas
5. cuatro horas

B. Answer each question using each past participle as an adjective. Repeat the correct answer after the speaker's confirmation. Listen to the model.

Modelo: —¿Terminaste la carta?
—Sí, ya **está terminada.**

C. Change each sentence to the present perfect tense. Repeat the correct answer following the speaker's confirmation. Listen to the model.

Modelo: Yo compro los regalos.
Yo **he comprado** los regalos.

193

D. Change the verbs according to the new subjects. Repeat the correct answer after the speaker's confirmation. Listen to the model.

Yo no lo había hecho todavía.
(Uds. / Nosotras / Tú / Eva / Ellos / Ud.)

III. *Para escuchar y entender*

1. Listen carefully to the narration. It will be read twice.

(*Narracion*)

Now the speaker will make statements concerning the narration you just heard. After each statement, say whether it is true (**verdadero**) or false (**falso**). The speaker will confirm the correct answer.

2. Listen carefully to the dialogue. It will be read twice.

(*Diálogo*)

Now the speaker will ask some questions about the dialogue you just heard. Answer each question, omitting the subject. The speaker will confirm the correct answer. Repeat the correct answer.

15

Anatomía Patológica

Urgencias

Entrada ala Norte P. **G**

Recepción de Enfermos

1. **Uses of** *hacía... que*
2. **The future tense**
3. **The conditional tense**
4. **Some uses of the prepositions** *a, de,* **and** *en*

Vocabulario

COGNADOS

la **ambulancia** ambulance
la **emergencia** emergency
el (la) **paciente** patient
el (la) **paramédico(a)**
 paramedic

el **plástico** plastic
el **resultado** result
el (la) **veterinario(a)**
 veterinarian

NOMBRES
el **análisis** test, analysis
la **herida** wound
la **inyección** shot, injection
el (la) **médico(a)** (medical)
 doctor
el **perro** dog
el **precio** price
los **puntos** stitches
la **radiografía** x-ray
la **sala de emergencia**
 emergency room

VERBOS
 arreglar to fix
 desinfectar to disinfect

enseñar to teach
mejorar to improve

OTRAS PALABRAS Y EXPRESIONES
 a tiempo on time
 después later, afterwards
 estar listo(a) to be ready
 poner una inyección to
 give a shot
 pronto soon
 sin falta without fail
 Yo creo que sí.
 I think so.

◀ 1. Uses of hacía... que

◆ To describe a situation that had been going on for a period of
 time and was still going on at a given moment in the past:

Hacía + *period of time* + **que** + *verb (imperfect)*
Hacía dos horas **que** **estudiábamos.**

—¿Cuánto tiempo **hacía**
 que Ud. vivía allí?
-—**Hacía diez años que**
 vivía allí.

*How long had you lived
 there?*
*I had lived there for ten
 years.*

◆ To describe a situation that had been going on in the past when
 something else happened:

—¿Cuánto tiempo **hacía**
 que esperabas cuando
 llegó la ambulancia?
—**Hacía media hora que**
 esperaba.

*How long had you been
 waiting when the ambu-
 lance arrived?*
*I had been waiting for a
 half hour.*

Práctica

> You are an interpreter. How would you say the following in Spanish?

1. She had been living there for two months when she met him.
2. How long had he been waiting for the ambulance?
3. They had been studying for four years.
4. I had been working for two weeks when she arrived.
5. How long had you known him?

2. The future tense

The English equivalent of the Spanish future is *will* or *shall* + a verb. As you have already learned, Spanish also uses the construction **ir a** + infinitive or the present tense with a time expression to express future actions or states, very much like the English present tense or the expression *going to*.

Vamos a ir al cine esta noche. ⎫
or: **Iremos** al cine esta noche. ⎭   *We're going (We'll go) to the movies tonight.*

Anita **toma** el examen mañana. ⎫
or: Anita **tomará** el examen mañana. ⎭   *Anita is taking (will take) the exam tomorrow.*

ATENCIÓN: The Spanish future is *not* used to make requests, as is the English future. In Spanish, requests are expressed with the verb **querer**.
¿Quieres llamar a Tomás? *Will you call Tomás?*

◆ Most Spanish verbs are regular in the future. The infinitive serves as the stem of almost all Spanish verbs. The endings are the same for all three conjugations.

The Future Tense

Infinitive		Stem	Endings
trabajar	yo	trabajar-	é
aprender	tú	aprender-	ás
escribir	Ud.	escribir-	á
hablar	él	hablar-	á
decidir	ella	decidir-	á
entender	nosotros	entender-	emos
caminar	Uds.	caminar-	án
perder	ellos	perder-	án
recibir	ellas	recibir-	án

ATENCIÓN: Notice that all the endings, except the one for the **nosotros** form, have written accent marks.

—¿**Llamarán** Uds. a los paramédicos?	*Will you call the paramedics?*
—No, nosotros lo **llevaremos** a la sala de emergencia.	*No, we will take him to the emergency room.*
—¿Cree Ud. que el paciente **mejorará** pronto?	*Do you think the patient will improve soon?*
—Yo creo que sí.	*I think so.*
—¿Cuándo **estarán** listos los análisis?	*When will the tests be ready?*
—**Estarán** listos mañana por la tarde.	*They will be ready tomorrow afternoon.*

Práctica

What *will happen* in the future?

1. Nosotros somos los primeros.
2. Los pacientes mejoran pronto.
3. Los estudiantes entienden la lección.
4. Los análisis están listos.
5. Él no entiende los problemas de la economía.
6. Tú aprendes español.
7. Yo compro las sábanas.
8. Uds. deciden a dónde ir.
9. Nosotros escribimos las cartas a máquina.
10. Ella va a clase todos los días.
11. Nosotros caminamos por la ciudad.
12. ¿Van Uds. a la sala de emergencia?

Irregular future forms

A few verbs are irregular in the future tense. These verbs use a modified form of the infinitive as a stem. The endings are the same as the ones for regular verbs:

Infinitive	*Stem*		*Future Tense*	
decir	dir-	yo	**dir-**	é
hacer	har-	tú	**har-**	ás
saber	sabr-	Ud.	**sabr-**	á
poder	podr-	ella	**podr-**	á
poner	pondr-	nosotros	**pondr-**	emos
venir	vendr-	Uds.	**vendr-**	án
tener	tendr-	ellos	**tendr-**	án
salir	saldr-	ellas	**saldr-**	án

—¿Le has dicho que le **pondrás** una inyección?

Have you told him that you will give him a shot?

—No, se lo **diré** después.

No, I'll tell him later.

—¿Cuándo **sabrán** Uds. el resultado de los análisis?

When will you know the result of the tests?

—Lo **sabremos** la semana próxima.

We will know next week.

—¿**Vendrá** hoy el médico a quitarle los puntos?

Will the doctor come today to remove the stitches?

—Sí, **vendrá** hoy, sin falta.

Yes, he'll come today, without fail.

◆ The future of **hay** (from the verb **haber**) is **habrá**.

Práctica

A. Using the verbs provided, complete these dialogues in the future tense:

1. —¿Qué le _____ Ud. al paciente?   (**decir**)
   —Le _____ que _____ que venir mañana.   (**decir / tener**)
   —¿Cuándo _____ el resultado de los análisis?   (**saber**)
   —Esta tarde.
2. —¿_____ el mecánico traer el coche?   (**Poder**)
   —Sí, él me ha dicho que _____ mañana.   (**venir**)
   —Muy bien, porque nosotros _____ para la capital por la noche.   (**salir**)
3. —¿Qué _____ Uds. el domingo?   (**hacer**)
   —Iremos a la fiesta que _____ en el Club.   (**haber**)
   —¿Qué te _____ para ir a la fiesta?   (**poner**)
   —El traje azul.

B. Tell about yourself by answering these questions:

1. ¿Podrá Ud. venir a clase mañana?
2. ¿Vendrán Uds. temprano?
3. ¿Habrá un examen mañana?
4. ¿Tendrán que estudiar mucho Uds.?
5. ¿A qué hora saldrán de la clase?
6. ¿A qué hora llegará Ud. a su casa hoy?
7. ¿A dónde irá Ud. el verano próximo?
8. ¿Qué hará Ud. el domingo?

3. The conditional tense

The conditional tense in Spanish is equivalent to the conditional in English, expressed by *would* plus *verb*.[1] Like the future tense, the conditional uses the infinitive as the stem and has only one set of endings for all three conjugations:

The Conditional Tense

Infinitive		Stem	Endings
trabajar	yo	trabajar-	ía
aprender	tú	aprender-	ías
escribir	Ud.	escribir-	ía
ir	él	ir-	ía
ser	ella	ser-	ía
dar	nosotros	dar-	íamos
servir	Uds.	servir-	ían
estar	ellos	estar-	ían
preferir	ellas	preferir-	ían

—¿**Vendería** Ud. su casa por cincuenta mil dólares? / *Would you sell your house for fifty thousand dollars?*

—No, yo no la **vendería** a ese precio. / *No, I wouldn't sell it at that price.*

—¿**Preferirían** Uds. ir conmigo al médico? / *Would you prefer to go with me to the doctor?*

—Sí, **preferiríamos** ir contigo. / *Yes, we would prefer to go with you.*

♦ The conditional is also used to express the future of a past action; that is, the conditional describes an event that in the past was perceived as occurring in the future.

—¿Qué te dijo el médico ayer? / *What did the doctor tell you yesterday?*

—Me dijo que me **desinfectaría** la herida. / *He told me that he would disinfect the wound (for me).*

---

[1] The imperfect, not the conditional, is used in Spanish as an equivalent of *used to:* **Cuando era pequeño siempre *iba* a la playa.** *When I was little I would always go to the beach.*

Práctica

These people don't agree with Ana's ideas. Using the cues in parentheses, explain what they wouldn't do:

Modelo: Ana va a vender su casa.   (yo)
    Yo **no** la **vendería.**

1. Ana va a comprar el coche a ese precio.   (Nosotros)
2. Ana va a escribirle.   (Yo)
3. Ana va a trabajar con los paramédicos.   (Uds.)
4. Ana va a ponerle una inyección.   (Ellos)
5. Ana va a arreglar el coche.   (Tú)
6. Ana va a ir en la ambulancia.   (Elsa)

Irregular conditional forms

The same verbs that are irregular in the future are also irregular in the conditional. The conditional endings are added to the modified form of the infinitive:

Infinitive	Stem	Conditional Tense		
decir	dir-	yo	**dir-**	ía
hacer	har-	tú	**har-**	ías
saber	sabr-	Ud.	**sabr-**	ía
poder	podr-	ella	**podr-**	ía
poner	pondr-	nosotros	**pondr-**	íamos
venir	vendr-	Uds.	**vendr-**	ían
tener	tendr-	ellos	**tendr-**	ían
salir	saldr-	ellas	**saldr-**	ían

ATENCIÓN: The conditional of **hay** is **habría.**

—¿Lo **harían** Uds.?	*Would you do it?*
—No, no lo **haríamos.**	*No, we wouldn't do it.*
—¿**Saldrías** conmigo?	*Would you go out with me?*
—No, no **saldría** contigo.	*No, I wouldn't go out with you.*
—¿**Podría** él llegar a tiempo?	*Would he be able to arrive on time?*
—No, no **podría** llegar a tiempo.	*No, he wouldn't be able to arrive on time.*

Práctica

A. What did these people say they would do?

Modelo: Dice que lo **hará.** (Dijo)
Dijo que lo haría.

1. Digo que vendré. (Dije)
2. Decimos que saldremos. (Dijimos)
3. Dices que lo pondrás en el banco. (Dijiste)
4. Ud. dice que lo sabrá mañana. (Ud. dijo)
5. Dicen que se lo dirán hoy. (Dijeron)
6. Dice que habrá una reunión. (Dijo)
7. Digo que no podré ir. (Dije)
8. Dices que lo tendrás listo hoy. (Dijiste)

B. You are an interpreter. How would you say the following in Spanish?

1. Would the men arrive on time?
2. My mother wouldn't do it.
3. They wouldn't know what to say.
4. Would you like to go with me?
5. How many stitches would he need?
6. We wouldn't tell (it to) him.
7. Didn't he say it would be better to disinfect the wound?
8. I said that she wouldn't be able to work.

◀ 4. Some uses of the prepositions a, de, **and** en

♦ The preposition **a** (*to, at, in*) is used:

1. To introduce the direct object when it is a person,[1] animal, or anything that is given personal characteristics:

Esperamos **a** los niños.
Llevé **a** mi perro al veterinario.

2. To indicate the time (hour) of day:

El análisis estará listo **a** las cinco.

3. To express destination or result after verbs of motion when they are followed by an infinitive, a noun, or a pronoun:

Siempre venimos **a** ver a mi sobrino.

---

[1] When the direct object is not a definite person, the personal **a** is not used: **Busco un buen maestro.**

4. After the verbs **enseñar, aprender, comenzar,** and **empezar** when they are followed by an infinitive:

Voy a **empezar** a arreglar el carro.
Él dijo que me **enseñaría** a conducir.

5. After the verb **llegar:**

Llegaremos a Lima mañana sin falta.

♦ The preposition **de** (*of, from, about*) is used:

1. To refer to a specific time of the day or night:

Dijeron que vendrían a las ocho **de** la noche.

2. To distinguish one from a group when using superlatives:

Mi sobrina es la más inteligente **de** la familia.

3. To indicate possession or relationship:

Carlos es el hijo **del** veterinario.
Esta es la radiografía **de** la señorita Varela.

4. To indicate the material something is made of:

La mesa es **de** plástico.

5. To indicate origin:

Ellos son **de** La Habana.

6. As a synonym of **sobre** or **acerca de** (*about*):

Hablaban **de** los precios de las casas.

♦ The preposition **en** (*at, in, on, inside, over*) is used:

1. to refer to a definite place:

Mi coche está **en** la gasolinera.

2. To indicate means of transportation:

Siempre viajábamos **en** autobús.

3. As a synonym of **sobre** (*on*):

Los libros están **en** la mesa.

ATENCIÓN: In México and in most Spanish-speaking countries of Latin America, **por** (*by*) is used with certain means of transportation, whereas **en** is used with other means:

Vamos por avión.
Vamos **por** tren.
but
Vamos **en** autobús.
Vamos **en** automóvil.

Práctica

Complete the following sentences using **a, de,** or **en,** as appropriate:

1. Llegaremos _____ Lima _____ las ocho _____ la mañana.
2. Esperaremos _____ la doctora para ver las radiografías.
3. Los niños están _____ casa.
4. Oscar siempre me está hablando _____ su perro.
5. ¿_____ qué hora van _____ empezar _____ estudiar?
6. Vienen _____ enseñarnos _____ conducir.
7. No me gusta viajar _____ autobús.
8. Llevé _____ mi perro al veterinario.
9. Esa niña es la más alta _____ la clase.
10. Los libros están _____ el escritorio.
11. La mesa _____ Juan es _____ plástico.
12. La sobrina _____ Luis es _____ Cuba.

En el laboratorio

LECCIÓN 15

The following material is to be used with the tape in the language laboratory.

I. Vocabulario

Repeat each word after the speaker. When repeating words that are cognates, notice the difference in pronunciation between English and Spanish.

COGNADOS:	la ambulancia la emergencia el paciente el paramédico el plástico el resultado el veterinario
NOMBRES:	el análisis la herida la inyección el médico el perro el precio los puntos la radiografía la sala de emergencia
VERBOS:	arreglar desinfectar enseñar mejorar
OTRAS PALABRAS Y EXPRESIONES:	a tiempo después estar listo poner una inyección pronto sin falta Yo creo que sí.

II. Práctica

A. Answer each question, using the cues provided. Repeat the correct answer after the speaker's confirmation.

1. tres horas
2. cinco años
3. dos meses
4. quince minutos
5. una semana

B. Change each sentence, using the future tense instead of the expression **ir a** + *infinitive*. Repeat the correct answer after the speaker's confirmation. Listen to the model.

Modelo: Vamos a salir muy tarde.
        Saldremos muy tarde.

C. Answer each question, always selecting the second alternative. Repeat the correct answer after the speaker's confirmation. Listen to the model.

Modelo: —¿Comprarías un coche o una casa?
    —**Compraría** una casa.

D. Answer the following questions in complete sentences, using the cue words provided. Repeat the correct answer after the speaker's confirmation.

1. María
2. las ocho
3. autobús
4. la mesa
5. Europa
6. hospital
7. Carlos
8. Sí

III. Para escuchar y entender

1. Listen carefully to the dialogue. It will be read twice.

(*Diálogo*)

Now the speaker will make statements about the dialogue you just heard. Tell whether each statement is true (**verdadero**) or false (**falso**). The speaker will confirm the correct answer.

2. Listen carefully to the narration. It will be read twice.

(*Narración*)

Now the speaker will ask some questions about the narration you just heard. Answer each question, omitting the subject. The speaker will confirm the correct answer. Repeat the correct answer.

¿Cuánto sabe usted ahora?

LECCIONES 11–15

A. Time expressions with **hacer**

Lección 11

Give the Spanish equivalent for each sentence. Follow the models.

Modelos: How long have you lived in California?
¿Cuánto tiempo hace que vive en California?

I have been living in California for two months.
Hace dos meses que vivo en California.

1. How long have you (*pl.*) been working in San Juan?
2. We have been working in San Juan for five years.
3. How long have they been waiting?
4. They have been waiting for three hours.
5. How long has she been studying Spanish?
6. She has been studying Spanish for two years.

B. Irregular preterits

Rewrite the sentences beginning with the expressions provided. Follow the model.

Modelo: Tenemos que salir.   (Ayer)
Ayer tuvimos que salir.

1. María está en la tienda.   (Ayer)
2. No pueden venir.   (Anoche)
3. Pongo el dinero en el banco.   (El mes pasado)
4. No haces nada.   (El domingo pasado)
5. Ella viene con Juan.   (Ayer)
6. No queremos venir a clase.   (El lunes pasado)
7. Yo no digo nada.   (Anoche)
8. Traemos la aspiradora.   (Ayer)
9. Yo conduzco mi coche.   (Anoche)
10. Ellos traducen las lecciones.   (Ayer)

C. The imperfect tense

Answer the following questions using the model as a guide:

Modelo: ¿Qué querían ellos?   (arroz con pollo)
Querían arroz con pollo.

1. ¿Dónde vivían Uds. cuando eran chicos?   (en Alaska)
2. ¿Qué idioma hablabas tú cuando eras chico(a)?   (inglés)
3. ¿A quién veías siempre cuando eras chico(a)?   (a mi abuela)

207

    4. ¿En qué banco depositaban Uds. el dinero? (en el Banco de América)

    5. ¿A qué hora se acostaban los niños? (a las nueve)

    6. ¿A dónde iba Rosa? (a la zapatería)

    7. ¿Qué compraba Ud.? (pollo)

    8. ¿En qué gastaban Uds. su dinero? (en libros)

D. The affirmative familiar command (**tú** form)

Change the commands from the **Ud.** (*formal*) form to the **tú** (*informal*) form. Follow the model.

Modelo: Salga con los niños.
         Sal con los niños.

    1. Venga acá, por favor.
    2. Hable con la maestra.
    3. Dígame su dirección.
    4. Lávese las manos.
    5. Póngase el abrigo.
    6. Tráiganos la limonada.
    7. Termine el trabajo.
    8. Hágame un favor.
    9. Apague la luz.
  10. Vaya de compras hoy.
  11. Salga temprano.
  12. Aféitese aquí.
  13. Tenga paciencia.
  14. Sea buena.
  15. Cene con nosotros.

E. The negative familiar command (**tú** form)

How would you say the following in Spanish?

    1. Don't tell (it to) him.
    2. Don't go out now.
    3. Don't get up.
    4. Don't bring the gloves now.
    5. Don't drink the lemonade.
    6. Don't break it (*masc.*).
    7. Don't talk to them.
    8. Don't go to the store.
    9. That dress? Don't put it on!
  10. Don't do that.

F. Complete the following sentences, using words learned in Lección 11:

    1. Ayer fui de _____ porque necesitaba un vestido.
    2. Ana, _____ la luz, por favor.

3. Los domingos nosotros siempre comíamos _____ con pollo.
4. No quiero un coctel; prefiero una _____.
5. Ayer hubo una gran _____ en Sears. Todo estaba muy barato.
6. En esa _____ nosotros vivíamos en La Habana.
7. Vamos a tomar un taxi porque ella no quiere _____.
8. Nosotros casi _____ comemos carne.
9. Yo uso guantes de vez en _____.
10. ¿Vas a salir otra _____?

A. The past progressive   **Lección 12**

Complete the sentences with the past progressive of the following verbs: **hacer, hablar, estudiar, comer, leer, trabajar, escribir, comprar.** Use each verb once.

1. Nosotros _____ arroz con pollo cuando llegó Elsa.
2. ¿Qué _____ tú cuando yo llamé?
3. Elena _____ a máquina cuando llegó el doctor Vargas.
4. Yo _____ por teléfono (*on the phone*) con mi cuñado.
5. ¿Uds. _____ los anillos en la joyería?
6. Ud. _____ el periódico cuando yo vine.
7. Los niños _____ la lección.
8. Roberto _____ en el garaje cuando yo lo vi.

B. The preterit contrasted with the imperfect.

How would you say the following in Spanish?

1. We went to bed at eleven last night.
2. She was typing when I saw her.
3. We used to go to Lima every summer.
4. It was ten-thirty when I called my sister-in-law.
5. She said she wanted to read.

C. Changes in meaning with imperfect and preterit of **conocer, saber, querer,** and **poder**

Complete the sentences with the preterit or the imperfect of the verbs **conocer, saber, querer,** and **poder** as appropriate:

1. Yo no _____ a los abuelos de María. Los _____ ayer.
2. Nosotros no _____ que ella era casada. Lo _____ anoche.
3. Pedro dijo que no _____ venir, pero vino a las dos.
4. Ellos no _____ llamarte por teléfono (*on the phone*) porque estaban trabajando. Por eso no te llamaron.
5. Mamá no vino a la fiesta porque no _____ venir.
6. Yo no _____ ir a la fiesta, pero cuando _____ que Carlos iba a ir, decidí ir también.

D. En and **a** for *at*

Write sentences using the words provided with **en** or **a**, as needed. Follow the model.

Modelo: Yo / estar / universidad.
        Yo estoy en la universidad.

1. Nosotros / llegar / aeropuerto / seis y media
2. Mi cuñada / estar / casa
3. Ellos / estar / joyería
4. La fiesta / ser / las doce
5. Yo / estar / la farmacia

E. Complete the following sentences, using the words learned in Lección 12:

1. Mi cuñada compró ayer un _____ de baño nuevo.
2. Ellos vieron el anillo en la _____ de la joyería.
3. No podemos irnos. Tenemos que _____ aquí _____ el día.
4. Necesito la _____ de escribir.
5. Compré las medicinas en la _____.
6. El mes pasado fuimos de _____ a México.
7. No quiero ir sola. ¿Por qué no vamos _____ tú y yo?
8. Tengo que estar en el _____ a las ocho porque el avión sale a las ocho y media.
9. El esposo de mi hermana es mi _____.
10. Ayer tuve un _____ en mi clase de español. Fue muy difícil.

Lección 13   A. Preterit of stem-changing verbs (**e:i** and **o:u**)

Rewrite the sentences beginning with the expressions provided. Follow the model.

Modelo: Él no pide dinero.   (Ayer)
        Ayer él no pidió dinero.

1. Él siente mucho dolor.   (Ayer)
2. Marta no duerme bien.   (Anoche)
3. No le pido nada.   (Ayer)
4. Ella te miente.   (La semana pasada)
5. Ellos sirven los refrescos.   (El sábado pasado)
6. No lo repito.   (Ayer)
7. Ella sigue estudiando.   (Anoche)
8. Tú no consigues nada.   (El lunes pasado)

B. The expression **acabar de**

Answer the following questions using the model as a guide:

Modelo: ¿Ya llegó Juan?
      Sí, acaba de llegar.

   1. ¿Ya encontraste el termómetro?
   2. ¿Ya le tomaste la temperatura?
   3. ¿Ya compraron ellos los instrumentos?
   4. ¿Ya midieron Uds. la ventana?
   5. ¿Ya te bañaste?
   6. ¿Ya llegaron los empleados?

C. Special construction with **gustar, doler,** and **hacer falta**

Complete the following sentences with the appropriate forms of **gustar, doler,** and **hacer falta:**

   1. No _____ esos edificios. Prefiero aquéllos.
   2. ¿Qué _____, señora? ¿Aceite?
   3. A Marta _____ la cabeza. ¿Tienes aspirinas?
   4. A nosotros no _____ dinero. No necesitamos comprar nada.
   5. ¿_____ a Ud. este modelo, o prefiere el otro?
   6. _____ un traje. ¿Puedes comprárselo?
   7. _____ una muela. Tengo que ir al dentista.
   8. No _____ caminar. ¿Podemos ir en coche?

D. **¿Qué?** and **¿cuál?** used with **ser**

How would you say the following in Spanish?

   1. What is a battery?
   2. What is your address?
   3. What is a thermometer?
   4. What is your telephone number?
   5. What are his ideas about this?

E. Complete the following sentences, using words learned in Lección 13:

   1. Voy a tomar una _____ porque me _____ la cabeza.
   2. El _____ es un instrumento que sirve para medir la temperatura.
   3. Nos hace _____ un limpiaparabrisas nuevo.
   4. El empleado _____ de llegar a la _____ de servicio.
   5. El dentista me sacó la _____
   6. Otro nombre para las llantas es _____.
   7. Nos _____ mucho en la fiesta.
   8. El _____ cambió el aceite de mi coche.

9. Otro nombre para batería es _____.
10. Nos _____ de los niños en el aeropuerto.

Lección 14   **A. Hace** meaning *ago*

Write 2 sentences for each set of items. Follow the model.

Modelo: Un año / yo / conocer / él
  Hace un año que yo lo conocí.
  Yo lo conocí hace un año.

1. tres meses / nosotros / llegar / a California
2. dos horas / el niño / tomar / un poco / café
3. dos días / ellos / terminar / el trabajo
4. veinte años / ella / ver / él
5. quince días / tú / venir / a esta ciudad

B. The past participle

Complete the following chart:

Infinitive	Past Participle
1. trabajar	1. trabajado
2. recibir	2. _____
3. _____	3. vuelto
4. usar	4. _____
5. escribir	5. _____
6. _____	6. ido
7. aprender	7. _____
8. _____	8. abierto
9. cubrir	9. _____
10. comer	10. _____
11. _____	11. visto
12. hacer	12. _____
13. ser	13. _____
14. _____	14. dicho
15. cerrar	15. _____
16. _____	16. muerto
17. _____	17. roto
18. dormir	18. _____
19. estar	19. _____
20. _____	20. puesto

C. Past participles used as adjectives:

How would you say the following in Spanish?

1. The book is written in English.
2. He has a broken leg.

3. The door is open.
4. Are the windows closed?
5. The work is finished.

D. The present perfect tense

Complete the sentences with the present perfect of the following verbs: **hablar, hacer, abrir, venir, decir, terminar, escribir, tener, poner, romperse, casarse.** Use each verb once.

1. Yo _____ muchas veces a este lugar.
2. ¿_____ Uds. la lección de matemáticas?
3. Nosotros todavía no _____ con el gerente del hotel.
4. Ellos me _____ que tengo que venir el sábado y el domingo.
5. ¿No _____ (tú) las cartas todavía?
6. Hoy nosotros no _____ nada, porque no _____ tiempo.
7. ¿Quién _____ las puertas?
8. ¿Dónde _____ Ud. las sillas?
9. Elena y Carlos no _____ todavía.
10. Yo _____ el brazo.

E. The past perfect (pluperfect) tense

How would you say the following in Spanish?

1. I had already brought the tickets.
2. They had given us a thirty per cent discount.
3. They had broken the pencils.
4. He had already seen the professor.
5. Had you covered the tables, Miss Peña?

F. Complete the following sentences, using words learned in Lección 14:

1. Él _____ el tren porque _____ tarde.
2. Tuvimos que hacer _____ para comprar los _____ para el tren.
3. Carlos quiere _____ con Rosa este mes.
4. Tuvo un accidente y tiene el brazo y la _____ rotos.
5. Me dieron un _____ del diez por _____ cuando compré el coche.
6. Necesitamos un _____ para saber a qué hora sale el tren.
7. La clase de _____ se acabó a las diez.
8. Pagué con veinte dólares y me dieron tres dólares de _____.

Lección 15   **A.** Uses of **hacía... que**

Answer the following questions using the model as a guide:

Modelo: ¿Cuánto tiempo hacía que Ud. vivía allí?   (tres años)
Hacía tres años que yo vivía allí.

1. ¿Cuánto tiempo hacía que Ud. no comía?   (diez horas)
2. ¿Cuánto tiempo hacía que Uds. lo esperaban cuando él llegó?   (media hora)
3. ¿Cuánto tiempo hacía que estudiabas español cuando fuiste a Madrid?
   (dos meses)
4. ¿Cuánto tiempo hacía que la paciente no bebía?   (dos horas)
5. ¿Cuánto tiempo hacía que Uds. trabajaban en la sala de emergencia?   (tres años)

B. The future tense
Answer the following questions using the model as a guide:

Modelo: ¿Cuándo comprarán Uds. un coche?   (el año próximo)
Compraremos un coche el año próximo.

1. ¿Cuándo será la fiesta del hospital?   (el sábado)
2. ¿Cuándo estarán listos los análisis?   (la semana que viene)
3. ¿Qué idioma enseñará Ud.?   (el español)
4. ¿Dónde estarán Uds. para esa fecha?   (en Florida)
5. ¿Qué le dirán Uds. al veterinario?   (que sí)
6. ¿Qué harás tú el domingo?   (nada)
7. ¿Cuándo sabremos el resultado de los análisis?   (hoy)
8. ¿Quién arreglará el coche?   (el mecánico)
9. ¿Quiénes podrán venir?   (los paramédicos)
10. ¿Quién le pondrá la inyección?   (la enfermera)
11. ¿Cuándo volverán los niños de México?   (el sábado)
12. ¿Cuándo vendrá la ambulancia?   (en una hora)
13. ¿Qué tendrán que hacer Uds.?   (estudiar para el examen)
14. ¿Cuándo me dará Ud. las radiografías?   (mañana sin falta)
15. ¿Con quiénes saldrán Uds. el sábado?   (con Raúl y con Mario)

C. The conditional tense

Complete the sentences with the conditional tense of the following verbs: **servir, poner, quejarse, haber, trabajar, seguir, vender, levantarse, preferir, ir.** Use each verb once.

1. Él dijo que nosotros _____ a Europa el verano próximo.
2. ¿Ellos _____ su casa a ese precio? Yo creo que sí.
3. ¿Dijo Ud. que _____ una clase esta tarde?
4. Yo no _____ el café en la terraza.

5. Tú no _____ en una gasolinera.
6. ¿_____ Ud. su dinero en ese banco?
7. ¿Qué _____ Uds.: ir a México o ir a Guatemala?
8. ¿_____ Uds. estudiando español?
9. ¿_____ tú a las tres de la mañana?
10. Nosotros no _____ del profesor.

D. Some uses of the prepositions **a, de,** and **en**

How would you say the following in Spanish?

1. We won't arrive at the university on time.
2. Did you take your dog to the vet, Mary?
3. Later we will travel by plane.
4. She's at the hospital. She's improving.
5. What are they talking about?

E. Complete the following sentences, using words learned in Lección 15:

1. Voy a llevar a mi perro al _____ porque está enfermo.
2. Mi hijo tuvo un accidente y ahora está en la sala de _____.
3. La enfermera le pondrá una _____ para el dolor.
4. Me dieron siete _____ en la herida.
5. Los análisis van a estar _____ mañana sin _____.
6. Trajeron al paciente al hospital en una _____.
7. Ellos te dirán el _____ de los análisis muy pronto.
8. Con estas medicinas la enferma va a _____ pronto.

Lección

16

1. **The present subjunctive**
2. **The subjunctive with verbs of volition**
3. **The absolute superlative**

Vocabulario

COGNADOS

la **familia** family	la **gasolina** gasoline

NOMBRES
la **cara**   face
el **correo**, la **oficina de**
   correos   post office
los **muebles**   furniture
el **paquete**   package
el **seguro**   insurance

VERBOS
  aconsejar   to advise
  alquilar   to rent
  asegurar   to insure
  gastar   to use, to spend
  mandar   to order
  mover (o:ue)   to move
  negar (e:ie)   to deny
  recomendar (e:ie)   to
  recommend

  rogar (o:ue)   to beg
  sugerir (e:ie)   to suggest

ADJETIVOS
  bello(a)   pretty
  bueno(a)   kind
  lento(a)   slow
  ocupado(a)   busy

**OTRAS PALABRAS Y
EXPRESIONES**
  de cambios mecánicos
    with standard shift
  sumamente   extremely,
  highly

◀1. The present subjunctive

Uses of the subjunctive

While the indicative mood is used to express events that are factual and definite, the subjunctive mood is used to refer to events or conditions that the speaker views as uncertain, unreal, or hypothetical. The subjunctive mood reflects feelings or attitudes towards events or conditions therefore, certain expressions of volition, doubt, surprise, fear, and so forth are followed by the subjunctive.

Except for its use in main clauses to express commands, the Spanish subjunctive is most often used in subordinate or dependent clauses.

The subjunctive is also used in English, although not as often as in Spanish. For example:

♦ *I suggest that he arrive tomorrow.*

The expression that requires the use of the subjunctive is in the main clause, *I suggest*. The subjunctive appears in the subordinate clause, *that he arrive tomorrow*. The subjunctive mood is used because the action of arriving is not yet realized; it is only what is *suggested* that he do.

♦ There are four main concepts that require the use of the subjunctive in Spanish:

1. *Volition:* demands, wishes, advice, persuasion, and other impositions of will

Ella **quiere** que yo **compre** muebles nuevos.	*She wants me to buy new furniture.*
Te **aconsejo** que **no vayas** a ese banco.	*I advise you not to go to that bank.*
Deseo que **vengas** con nosotros.	*I want you to come with us.*

2. *Emotion:* pity, joy, fear, surprise, hope, desire, etc.

Espero que Uds. **puedan** venir.	*I hope (that) you can come.*
Siento mucho que Luisa **esté** enferma.	*I'm very sorry that Luisa is sick.*

3. *Doubt, disbelief, and denial:* uncertainty, negated facts

Dudo que **paguen** un 10 por ciento de interés.	*I doubt (that) they pay 10 per cent interest.*
No es verdad que mi coche **gaste** mucha gasolina.	*It's not true that my car uses a lot of gas.*
Ella **niega** que Juan **sea** su esposo.	*She denies that Juan is her husband.*

4. *Unreality:* expectations, indefiniteness, nonexistence

¿Hay alguien que **hable** alemán?	*Is there anyone who speaks German?*
No hay nadie que lo **sepa**.	*There is nobody who knows (it).*

Formation of the present subjunctive

The present subjunctive is formed by dropping the **-o** from the stem of the first person singular of the present indicative and adding the following endings:

The Present Subjunctive of Regular Verbs		
-ar *Verbs*	**-er** *Verbs*	**-ir** *Verbs*
trabajar	**comer**	**vivir**
trabaj**e**	com**a**	viv**a**
trabaj**es**	com**as**	viv**as**
trabaj**e**	com**a**	viv**a**
trabaj**emos**	com**amos**	viv**amos**
trabaj**en**	com**an**	viv**an**

ATENCIÓN: Notice that the endings for **-er** and **-ir** verbs are the same.

The following table shows you how to form the first person singular of the present subjunctive from the infinitive of the verb.

Verb	First Person Singular (Indicative)	Stem	First Person Singular (Present Subjunctive)
hablar	hablo	**habl-**	hable
aprender	aprendo	**aprend-**	aprenda
escribir	escribo	**escrib-**	escriba
decir	digo	**dig-**	diga
hacer	hago	**hag-**	haga
traer	traigo	**traig-**	traiga
venir	vengo	**veng-**	venga
conocer	conozco	**conozc-**	conozca

Práctica

Give the present subjunctive of the following verbs:

1. **yo:** comer, venir, hablar, hacer, salir, ponerse
2. **tú:** decir, ver, traer, trabajar, escribir, conocer
3. **él:** vivir, aprender, salir, estudiar, levantarse, hacer
4. **nosotros:** escribir, caminar, poner, desear, tener, afeitarse
5. **ellos:** salir, hacer, llevar, conocer, ver, bañarse

Subjunctive forms of stem-changing verbs

Stem-changing **-ar** and **-er** verbs maintain the basic pattern of the present indicative. That is, their stems undergo the same changes in the present subjunctive:

recomendar (*to recommend*)		**recordar** (*to remember*)	
recomiende	recomendemos	recuerde	recordemos
recomiendes		recuerdes	
recomiende	recomienden	recuerde	recuerden

entender (*to understand*)		**mover** (*to move*)	
entienda	entendamos	mueva	movamos
entiendas		muevas	
entienda	entiendan	mueva	muevan

Stem-changing -ir verbs change the unstressed **e** to **i** and the unstressed **o** to **u** in the first person plural:

mentir *(to lie)*		dormir *(to sleep)*	
mienta	mintamos	duerma	durmamos
mientas		duermas	
mienta	mientan	duerma	duerman

Subjunctive forms of irregular verbs

dar	estar	saber	ser	ir
dé	esté	sepa	sea	vaya
des	estés	sepas	seas	vayas
dé	esté	sepa	sea	vaya
demos	estemos	sepamos	seamos	vayamos
den	estén	sepan	sean	vayan

◆ The subjunctive of **hay** (impersonal form of **haber**) is **haya**.

Práctica

Give the present subjunctive of the following verbs:

1. **yo:**   dormir, mover, cerrar, sentir, ser
2. **tú:**   mentir, volver, ir, dar, recordar
3. **ella:**   estar, saber, perder, dormir, ser
4. **nosotros:** pensar, recordar, dar, morir, cerrar
5. **ellos:**   ver, preferir, dar, ir, saber

2. The subjunctive with verbs of volition

All impositions of will, as well as indirect or implied commands, require the subjunctive in subordinate clauses. The subject in the main clause must be different from the subject in the subordinate clause.

◆ Some verbs of volition:

querer		rogar	*(to beg)*
mandar	*(to order)*	recomendar	*(to recommend)*
sugerir	*(to suggest)*	aconsejar	*(to advise)*
necesitar		pedir	

◆ Note the sentence structure for the use of the subjunctive in Spanish.

Yo quiero	que	**Ud. estudie.**
main clause		subordinate clause
I want		*you* to study.

—Quiero alquilar un coche.	*I want to rent a car.*
—Pues **te aconsejo** que **alquiles** uno de cambios mecánicos porque gasta menos gasolina.	*I advise you to rent a standard because it uses less gasoline.*
—Mi familia **quiere** que **asegure** el coche.	*My family wants me to insure the car.*
—Sí, es una buena idea tener seguro.	*Yes, it is a good idea to have insurance.*
—¿Qué quiere Ud. que yo **haga?**	*What do you want me to do?*
—Quiero que me **traiga** esos paquetes.	*I want you to bring me those packages.*

ATENCIÓN: If there is no change of subject, the infinitive is used:

—¿Qué quiere **hacer** Ud.?	*What do you want to do?*
—Yo quiero **traer** esos paquetes.	*I want to bring those packages.*

Práctica

A. What do you or other people want someone else to do? Use the present subjunctive of the verbs in parentheses:

1. Yo te sugiero que _____ (hacer) la tarea hoy.
2. Nosotros queremos que Ud. _____ (sentarse).
3. ¿Ud. me aconseja que yo _____ (asegurar) mi coche?
4. Ellos necesitan que él _____ (traer) los paquetes.
5. Él me pide que yo lo _____ (ayudar).
6. Necesito que tú me _____ (comprar) gasolina.
7. Ellos prefieren que nosotros no _____ (ir) hasta las nueve.
8. Él quiere que yo _____ (alquilar) un coche de cambios mecánicos.
9. Él nos recomienda que _____ (tener) seguro.
10. Yo no quiero que Uds. _____ (mover) esos muebles.

B. How would you say the following in Spanish?

1. My wife doesn't want me to rent that car.
2. I beg you to help me, Pedro.
3. They need me to take them to the gas station.
4. She always orders us to wash the car.
5. I want you to wash your hands, Paquito.
6. My father wants us to buy some furniture.

Omission of the main clause with verbs of volition

When the expression of the speaker's will is easily understood, the main clause that contains the verb of volition may be omitted:

¿Qué quiere Ud. que **haga** el niño?	*What do you want the boy to do?*
(Quiero) Que **se lave** la cara.	*I want him to wash his face.*
¿Va Ud. a hacer el trabajo?	*Are you going to do the work?*
No. Que lo **haga** Jorge.	*No. Let Jorge do it.*

Práctica

Respond, following the model.

Modelo: ¿Quién va a hacerlo? ¿Ud.?
   ¡Yo no! ¡Que lo haga ella!

1. ¿Quién va a salir? ¿Ud.?
2. ¿Quién va a alquilar el coche? ¿Ud.?
3. ¿Quién va a ir? ¿Ud.?
4. ¿Quién va a hablar? ¿Ud.?
5. ¿Quién va a traerlo? ¿Ud.?

Modelo: ¿No va a entrar Ud.?
   No, ¡que entren ellos!

1. ¿No va a dormir Ud.?
2. ¿No va a volver Ud.?
3. ¿No va a trabajar Ud.?
4. ¿No va a venir Ud.?
5. ¿No va a beber Ud.?

3. The absolute superlative

In Spanish, there are two ways of expressing a high degree of a given quality without comparing it to the same quality in another person or thing.

♦ By modifying the adjective with an adverb (**muy, sumamente**):

—¿Cómo es tu novia?	*What is your girlfriend like?*
—Es **muy** inteligente y **sumamente** buena.	*She is very intelligent and extremely kind.*

♦ By adding the suffix -**ísimo** (-**a, -os, -as**) to the adjective. This form is known as the absolute superlative. If the word ends in a vowel, the vowel is dropped before adding the suffix. Notice that the **í** of the suffix always has a written accent:

alto	alt-	**ísimo**	altísimo
ocupada	ocupad-	**ísima**	ocupadísima
lentos	lent-	**ísimos**	lentísimos
buenas	buen-	**ísimas**	buenísimas
difícil	dificil-	**ísimo**	dificilísimo

—¿Fuiste a Madrid el verano pasado?	*Did you go to Madrid last summer?*
—Sí, es una ciudad **bellísima**, pero es **dificilísimo** conducir allí.	*Yes, it is a very beautiful city, but it is extremely difficult to drive there.*
—¿Pueden ir al correo con nosotros?	*Can you go to the post office with us?*
—No, estamos **ocupadísimas**.	*No, we are extremely busy.*

Práctica

Change the underlined words in the following sentences to the absolute superlative:

1. Mi novia es <u>muy bella</u>.
2. Mi novio es <u>sumamente alto</u>.
3. Ellos están <u>muy ocupados</u>.
4. Es <u>muy fácil</u> llegar al correo.
5. Ellas son <u>muy buenas</u>.
6. La enfermera está <u>sumamente ocupada</u>.
7. Ellos son <u>muy lentos</u>.
8. Las clases son <u>sumamente difíciles</u> allí.

En el laboratorio

LECCIÓN 16

The following material is to be used with the tape in the language laboratory.

I. Vocabulario

Repeat each word after the speaker. When repeating words that are cognates, notice the difference in pronunciation between English and Spanish.

COGNADOS:	la familia la gasolina
NOMBRES:	la cara el correo la oficina de correos los muebles el paquete el seguro
VERBOS:	aconsejar alquilar asegurar gastar mandar mover negar recomendar rogar sugerir
ADJETIVOS:	bello bueno lento ocupado
OTRAS PALABRAS Y **EXPRESIONES:**	de cambios mecánicos sumamente

II. Práctica

A. What does Carmen want everybody to do? Use the present subjunctive with the cue words provided. Repeat the correct answer after the speaker's confirmation. Listen to the model.

Modelo: —¿Qué quiere Carmen que yo haga?   (escribir una carta)
　　　　　—**Carmen quiere que Ud. escriba una carta.**

1. ir al correo
2. traer el paquete
3. asegurar el auto
4. dar dinero
5. mover los muebles
6. lavarse la cara
7. alquilar un coche
8. comprar gasolina

B. Repeat each sentence, changing **muy** + *adjective* to the absolute superlative. Repeat the correct answer after the speaker's confirmation. Listen to the model.

Modelo: Mi novio es **muy alto.**
　　　　　Mi novio es **altísimo.**

III. Para escuchar y entender

1. Listen carefully to the narration. It will be read twice.

   (*Narración*)

   Now the speaker will make statements about the narration you just heard. Tell whether each statement is true (**verdadero**) or false (**falso**). The speaker will confirm the correct answer.

2. Listen carefully to the dialogue. It will be read twice.

   (*Diálogo 1*)

   Now the speaker will make statements about the dialogue you just heard. Tell whether each statement is true (**verdadero**) or false (**falso**). The speaker will confirm the correct answer.

3. Listen carefully to the dialogue. It will be read twice.

   (*Diálogo 2*)

   Now the speaker will ask some questions about the dialogue you just heard. Answer each question, omitting the subject. The speaker will confirm the correct answer. Repeat the correct answer.

Lección

17

1. **The subjunctive to express emotion**
2. **The subjunctive with some impersonal expressions**
3. **Formation of adverbs**

Vocabulario

COGNADOS

el **contrato** contract	**necesario(a)** necessary
especial special	**posible** possible
imposible impossible	**reciente** recent

NOMBRES
el (la) **abogado(a)**   lawyer
la **beca**   scholarship
la **conferencia**   lecture
el (la) **consejero(a)**   adviser
el **examen parcial**   midterm exam
la **física**   physics
la **matrícula**   tuition
la **nota**   grade
la **playa**   beach
la **química**   chemistry
el **requisito**   requirement

VERBOS
  alegrarse (de)   to be glad
  esperar   to hope
  firmar   to sign
  matricularse   to register

sentir (e:ie)   to regret, to be sorry
temer   to fear

ADJETIVOS
  cuidadoso(a)   careful
  rápido(a)   fast

OTRAS PALABRAS Y EXPRESIONES
  conviene   it is advisable
  en seguida   right away
  entonces   then, in that case
  es difícil   it's unlikely
  es lástima   it is a pity
  es seguro   it is certain
  esta noche   tonight
  ojalá   if only..., I hope

◀ 1. The subjunctive to express emotion

In Spanish, the subjunctive is always used in the subordinate clause when the verb in the main clause expresses any kind of emotion, such as fear, joy, pity, hope, pleasure, surprise, anger, regret and sorrow.

◆ Some verbs of emotion:

alegrarse (de)	*to be glad*	**sentir (e:ir)**	*to regret*
esperar	*to hope*	**temer**	*to fear*

—¿Vas a hablar con tu consejero hoy?

—Sí, y **espero** que me **diga** qué requisitos debo tomar.

Are you going to talk with your adviser today?

Yes, and I hope he'll tell me what requirements I have to take.

—Mañana tengo dos exámenes parciales, uno en química y otro en física. **Temo** que mis notas no **sean** muy buenas.	*Tomorrow I have two midterm exams, one in chemistry and the other in physics. I'm afraid that my grades aren't very good.*
—Entonces tienes que estudiar. **Siento** que no **puedas** ir con nosotros a la conferencia.	*Then you have to study. I'm sorry that you can't go with us to the lecture.*

ATENCIÓN: The subject of the subordinate clause must be different from that of the main clause. If there is no change of subject, the infinitive is used instead:

—¿Vas a terminar el trabajo para las cinco?	*Are you going to finish the work by five?*
—Temo no **poder** terminarlo tan pronto.	*I'm afraid I can't finish it so soon.*
—¿Cuándo se van Uds.?	*When are you leaving?*
—Esperamos **irnos** esta noche.	*We hope to leave tonight.*

Práctica

A. Complete the following sentences with the subjunctive or infinitive of the verbs in parentheses, as needed:

1. Espero que el consejero _____ (estar) en su oficina.
2. Me alegro de _____ (estar) aquí.
3. Temen no _____ (poder) terminar para la una.
4. Ella espera _____ (terminar) todos los requisitos este año.
5. Espero que el profesor me _____ (dar) una buena nota en química.
6. Siento mucho que ellos no _____ (volver) mañana.
7. Espero que no _____ (llover) hoy porque tengo que salir.
8. Espero que ellos me _____ (traer) el libro de física.
9. Siento no _____ (poder) ir a la conferencia.
10. Temo que él no _____ (tener) tiempo para vernos.
11. Temo no _____ (recordar) su dirección.
12. Me alegro de que nosotros no _____ (tener) el examen parcial hoy.

B. Use your imagination to finish the following with either the subjunctive or the infinitive, as appropriate:

1. Yo espero que mi profesor...
2. Nosotros nos alegramos de...

3. Yo temo...
4. Siento que Uds....
5. Ellos sienten no...
6. Yo me alegro de que mis padres...

2. The subjunctive with some impersonal expressions

In Spanish, some impersonal expressions that convey emotion, uncertainty, unreality, or an indirect or implied command are followed by a verb in the subjunctive. This occurs only when the verb of the subordinate clause has an expressed subject. The most common expressions are:

conviene	*it is advisable*
es difícil	*it is unlikely*
es importante	*it is important*
es (im)posible	*it is (im)possible*
es lástima	*it is a pity*
es mejor	*it is better*
es necesario	*it is necessary*
ojalá	*if only ...! or I hope ...*
puede ser	*it may be*

—¿Crees que va a llover mañana?

Do you think it's going to rain tomorrow?

—Ojalá que no **llueva** porque **es posible** que Enrique me **lleve** a la playa.

I hope it won't rain, because it's possible that Enrique will take me to the beach.

—¿Viene hoy el abogado?

Is the lawyer coming today?

—**Es difícil** que **venga** hoy.

It is unlikely that he'll come today.

—¿Cuándo quiere Ud. que yo escriba las cartas?

When do you want me to write the letters?

—**Es importante** que las **escriba** hoy.

It is important that you write them today.

—¿Cuándo quiere Ud. que los estudiantes tomen el examen?

When do you want the students to take the exam?

—**Es mejor** que lo **tomen** en seguida.

It is better that they take it right away.

—**Es lástima** que Ud. no
pueda conseguir una
beca.

*It is a pity that you can't
obtain a scholarship.*

—Sí, porque yo no tengo
dinero para pagar la
matrícula.

*Yes, because I don't have
money to pay the tuition.*

—¿Cuándo tengo que
matricularme?

*When do I have to
register?*

—**Es necesario** que **se
matricule** hoy.

*It is necessary that you
register today.*

ATENCIÓN: When the impersonal expression implies certainty,
the indicative is used:

¿Vienen ellos hoy?
Sí, **es seguro** que **vienen**
hoy.

Are they coming today?
*Yes, it is certain that
they'll come today.*

When a sentence is completely impersonal (that is, when no subject
is stated), the expressions on p. 230 are followed by the infinitive:

¿Cuándo vamos a firmar el
contrato?
Conviene firmarlo esta
semana.

*When are we going to sign
the contract?*
*It is advisable to sign it
this week.*

Práctica

A. Complete the following, using the infinitive, the indicative or
the subjunctive:

1. Conviene que Uds. _____ (tomar) los requisitos ahora.
2. Es imposible _____ (matricularse) a esta hora.
3. Es mejor que ellos no _____ (ir) a la conferencia.
4. Ojalá que el consejero _____ (venir) temprano.
5. Es seguro que el profesor nos _____ (dar) un examen
   hoy.
6. Es difícil que él _____ (conseguir) una beca.
7. Es seguro que el abogado _____ (tener) el contrato.
8. Es importante _____ (ir) a la conferencia de hoy.

B. You are an interpreter. How would you say the following in
Spanish?

1. It is unlikely that the lawyer will come today.
2. It is important that the students take the test right away.
3. It's a pity that your mother is sick.
4. It is necessary to finish the job today.
5. I hope he doesn't say anything.

6. It is certain that it is going to rain tonight.
7. Then it is better to pay the tuition tomorrow.
8. It is advisable to sign the contract this week.
9. It is certain that the adviser is in his office.
10. It is impossible to go to the beach now.

3. Formation of adverbs

> **Adverb** a word that modifies a verb, an adjective, or another adverb. It answers the questions "How?", "When?", "Where?": She walked **slowly**. She'll be here **tomorrow**. She is **here**.

Most Spanish adverbs are formed by adding **-mente** (the equivalent of *-ly* in English) to the adjective:

especial	*special*	especial**mente**	*specially, especially*
reciente	*recent*	reciente**mente**	*recently*
probable	*probable*	probable**mente**	*probably*

◆ If the adjective ends in **-o,** change the ending to **-a** before adding **-mente:**

lent**o**	*slow*	lent**amente**	*slowly*
rápid**o**	*rapid*	rápid**amente**	*rapidly*

◆ If two or more adverbs are used together, both change the **-o** to **-a,** but only the last adverb takes the **-mente** ending.

lent**a** y cuidados**amente**   *slowly and carefully*

◆ If the adjective has a written accent mark, the corresponding adverb retains it:

fácil   fácil**mente**

—Traigo estos libros **especialmente** para Ud.	*I'm bringing these books especially for you.*
—Gracias.	*Thanks.*
—El niño escribe la carta **lenta** y **cuidadosamente.**	*The child is writing the letter slowly and carefully.*
—¡Pero la escribe muy bien!	*But he is writing it very well!*

Práctica

You are an interpreter. How would you say the following in Spanish?

1. She reads slowly.
2. Do it carefully, Miss Peña.
3. The chair is especially for you, Sir.
4. She is going to do it rapidly but carefully.
5. When did you see her, Ma'am? Recently?
6. The lesson? We can translate it easily.

En el laboratorio

LECCIÓN 17

The following material is to be used with the tape in the language laboratory.

I. Vocabulario

Repeat each word after the speaker. When repeating words that are cognates, notice the difference in pronunciation between English and Spanish.

COGNADOS:	el contrato especial imposible necesario posible reciente
NOMBRES:	el abogado la beca la conferencia el consejero el examen parcial la física la matrícula la nota la playa la química el requisito
VERBOS:	alegrarse esperar firmar matricularse sentir temer
ADJETIVOS:	cuidadoso rápido
OTRAS PALABRAS Y ESPRESIONES:	conviene en seguida entonces es difícil es lástima es seguro esta noche ojalá

II. Práctica

A. Restate each of the following sentences, inserting the cue at the beginning and making any necessary changes. Repeat the correct answer after the speaker's confirmation. Listen to the model.

Modelo: El cliente firma el contrato.   (Espero)
   Espero que el cliente **firme** el contrato.

1. (Temo)	4. (Temo)
2. (Espero)	5. (Me alegro)
3. (Siento)	6. (Espero)

B. Restate each of the following sentences, inserting the cue at the beginning and making any necessary changes. Repeat the correct answer after the speaker's confirmation. Listen to the model.

Modelo: Él conduce muy rápido.   (Es difícil)
   Es difícil que él **conduzca** muy rápido.

1. (No conviene)
2. (Es necesario)
3. (Es imposible)
4. (Es mejor)

5. (Puede ser)
6. (Ojalá)
7. (Es lástima)
8. (Es importante)

C. Give the adverb that corresponds to each adjective. Repeat the correct answer after the speaker's confirmation. Listen to the model.

Modelo: especial
    especialmente

III. Para escuchar y entender

1. Listen carefully to the dialogue. It will be read twice.

   (*Diálogo 1*)

   Now the speaker will make statements about the dialogue you just heard. Tell whether each statement is true (**verdadero**) or false (**falso**). The speaker will confirm the correct answer.

2. Listen carefully to the dialogue. It will be read twice.

   (*Diálogo 2*)

   Now the speaker will make statements about the dialogue you just heard. Tell whether each statement is true (**verdadero**) or false (**falso**). The speaker will confirm the correct answer.

3. Listen carefully to the dialogue. It will be read twice.

   (*Diálogo 3*)

   Now the speaker will ask some questions about the dialogue you just heard. Answer each question, omitting the subject. The speaker will confirm the correct answer. Repeat the correct answer.

Lección

18

1. **The subjunctive to express doubt, disbelief, and denial**
2. **The subjunctive to express indefiniteness and non-existence**
3. **Diminutive suffixes**

Vocabulario

NOMBRES	**dudar** to doubt
el **almuerzo** lunch	**limpiar** to clean
el **árbol** tree	**quedar** to be located
el **centro** downtown (*area*)	
la **clase** kind, type	**ADJETIVOS**
el (la) **criado(a)** servant, maid	**frito(a)** fried
	libre free
el **fregadero** sink	**seguro(a)** sure
el **huevo** egg	
el (la) **jefe(a)** boss, chief	**OTRAS PALABRAS Y EXPRESIONES**
el (la) **viajero(a)** traveler	**adentro** inside
VERBOS	**afuera** outside
almorzar (o:ue) to have lunch	**poner la mesa** to set the table
buscar to look for	**todo el mundo** everybody
cenar to have supper	

◀1. The subjunctive to express doubt, disbelief, and denial

In Spanish, the subjunctive mood is always used in the subordinate clause when the main clause expresses doubt, uncertainty, or disbelief.

♦ Doubt or uncertainty

—¿Olga puede limpiar la casa esta tarde? *Can Olga clean the house this afternoon?*
—**Dudo que** ella **venga** hoy. *I doubt that she'll come today.*

—¿Está Ud. seguro de que él quiere huevos fritos para el almuerzo? *Are you sure that he wants fried eggs for lunch?*

—Sí, pero **no estoy seguro de que** él **quiera** almorzar ahora. *Yes, but I'm not sure that he wants to have lunch (right) now.*

ATENCIÓN: In the affirmative, the verb **dudar** (*to doubt*) takes the subjunctive in the subordinate clause even when there is no change of subject:

—¿Puedes ir conmigo al médico?	*Can you go to the doctor with me?*
—(**Yo**) **dudo** que (**yo**) **pueda** ir contigo hoy.	*I doubt that I can go with you today.*

When the speaker expresses no doubt and is certain of the reality, the indicative is used:

—¿Viene tu jefa hoy?	*Is your boss coming today?*
—**No dudo** que ella **viene.**	*I don't doubt (I'm sure) that she's coming.*
—¿Está Ud. seguro de que él sale mañana?	*Are you sure (that) he's leaving tomorrow?*
—Sí, **estoy seguro de que** él **sale** mañana.	*Yes, I'm sure (that) he's leaving tomorrow.*

◆   Disbelief

The verb **creer** (*to believe, to think*) is followed by the subjunctive when used in negative sentences in which it expresses disbelief.

—Carlos dice que él va a arreglar el fregadero antes de cenar.	*Carlos says he's going to fix the sink before having supper.*
—Yo **no creo que** él **pueda** arreglarlo.	*I don't think he can fix it.*

In the interrogative, if doubt is strongly implied, the subjunctive is also used:

—Carlitos tiene diez años. ¿Tú **crees** que él **quiera** ir a la conferencia?	*Carlos is ten years old. Do you think (that) he wants to go to the lecture?*
—**No, no creo** que **quiera** ir.	*No, I don't think he wants to go.*

ATENCIÓN: The verb **creer** is followed by the indicative in affirmative sentences in which it expresses belief.

—¿Los viajeros están afuera?	*Are the travelers outside?*
—No... **creo** que **están** adentro.	*No... I think they're inside.*

◆ Denial

When the main clause denies what is said in the subordinate clause, the subjunctive is used:

—¿Es verdad que tus padres tienen criada? — *Is it true that your parents have a maid?*

—No, **no es verdad que tengan** criada. — *No, it isn't true that they have a maid.*

ATENCIÓN: When the main clause confirms rather than denies what is said in the subordinate clause, the indicative is used: **Es verdad que** mis padres **tienen** criada.

Práctica

A. Complete the following sentences using the present indicative or the present subjunctive, whichever is appropriate:

1. Yo creo que la criada _____ (venir) hoy.
2. No es verdad que él _____ (estar) en la cárcel.
3. No creo que ellos _____ (poder) arreglar el fregadero ahora.
4. Estoy seguro de que nosotros _____ (tener) un examen hoy.
5. Dudan que yo _____ (limpiar) mi cuarto.
6. Es verdad que el postre _____ (ser) muy bueno.
7. No dudamos que ellos _____ (poder) conseguir una beca.
8. No estamos seguros de que ellos _____ (servir) el almuerzo antes de las doce.
9. No creo que ellos _____ (almorzar) con nosotros hoy.
10. Dudo que ellos _____ (querer) comer huevos fritos.

B. Finish the following, using your imagination:

1. Yo estoy seguro de que mis padres...
2. Dudo que la casa del profesor...
3. Es verdad que yo...
4. No estoy seguro de que mi amigo...
5. No es verdad que mi familia...
6. No creo que mi nota en esta clase...
7. No dudo que mis amigos...
8. Creo que el profesor...

2. The subjunctive to express indefiniteness and non-existence

The subjunctive is always used when the subordinate clause refers to someone or something that is indefinite, unspecified, or non-existent:

—¿Qué clase de casa necesitan ellos?

What kind of house do they need?

—Ellos buscan una casa **que sea** grande y **que quede** cerca del centro.

They're looking for a house that is big and (that is) located near the downtown area.

—¿**Hay alguien que no esté ocupado** y (**que**) **pueda** poner la mesa y servir la comida?

Is there anybody who is not busy and can set the table and serve the food?

—No, **no hay nadie que esté libre.** Todo el mundo está ocupado.

No, there is nobody who is free. Everybody is busy.

ATENCIÓN: If the subordinate clause refers to existent, definite, or specific persons or things, the indicative is used.

Ellos viven en una casa **que es grande** y **que queda** cerca del centro.

Aquí **hay alguien que no está ocupado y puede** poner la mesa y servir la comida.

Práctica

A. Complete the following sentences using the present subjunctive or the present indicative as appropriate:

1. No hay nadie que _____ (estar) libre esta tarde.
2. Yo quiero una casa que _____ (tener) cinco cuartos. Ahora vivo en una casa que _____ (tener) solamente tres.
3. ¿Hay algún restaurante que _____ (servir) comida mexicana?
4. Busco un empleado que _____ (querer) trabajar los domingos.
5. Hay una chica en mi clase que _____ (hablar) cinco idiomas.
6. No hay ninguna casa que _____ (quedar) cerca del centro y _____ (ser) barata.

7. Aquí hay alguien que _____ (poder) arreglar el fregadero.
8. Necesito una secretaria que _____ (saber) escribir muy bien a máquina.

B. Finish the following, using your imagination:

1. Yo quiero una casa que...
2. No hay ningún restaurante que...
3. En mi familia no hay nadie que...
4. Yo vivo en una casa que...
5. Conozco a una chica / un chico que...
6. En mi clase de español hay muchos estudiantes que...
7. En la ciudad donde yo vivo hay muchos restaurantes que...
8. Yo no conozco a nadie que...

◆3. Diminutive suffixes

To express the idea of small size, and also to denote affection, special suffixes are used in Spanish. The most common suffixes are **-ito(a)** and **-cito(a)**. There are no set rules for forming the diminutive, but usually if the word ends in **-a** or **-o,** the vowel is dropped and **- ito(a)** is added:

niño	niñ + **ito** =	**niñito**	*(little boy)*
niña	niñ + **ita** =	**niñita**	*(little girl)*
abuelo	abuel + **ito** =	**abuelito**	*(grandpa)*
Ana	An + **ita** =	**Anita**	*(Annie)*

◆ If the word ends in a consonant other than **-n** or **-r,** the suffix **ito(a)** is added:

árbol + **ito** =	**arbolito**	*(little tree)*
Luis + **ito** =	**Luisito**	*(Louie)*

◆ If the word ends in **-e, -n** or **-r,** the suffix **-cito(a)** is added:

coche + **cito** =	**cochecito**	*(little car)*
mujer + **cita** =	**mujercita**	*(little woman)*
Carmen + **cita** =	**Carmencita**	*(Carmen)*

—Hola, **abuelito.** ¿Me trajiste el **arbolito** de Navidad?
—Sí, **Tomasito.**

Hello, grandpa. Did you bring me the little Christmas tree?
Yes, Tommy.

—Me gusta tu **cochecito.**
—Gracias, **Carmencita.**

I like your little car.
Thanks, Carmen.

Práctica

Give the diminutive corresponding to each of the following:

1. primo
2. escuela
3. árbol
4. Raúl
5. coche

6. hermana
7. favor
8. Juan
9. Adela
10. mamá

En el laboratorio

LECCIÓN 18

The following material is to be used with the tape in the language laboratory.

I. Vocabulario

Repeat each word after the speaker. When repeating words that are cognates, notice the difference in pronunciation between English and Spanish.

NOMBRES:	el almuerzo el árbol el centro la clase el criado el fregadero el huevo el jefe el viajero
VERBOS:	almorzar buscar cenar dudar limpiar quedar
ADJETIVOS:	frito libre seguro
OTRAS PALABRAS Y EXPRESIONES:	adentro afuera poner la mesa todo el mundo

II. Práctica

A. Restate each of the following sentences, inserting the cue at the beginning and making any necessary changes. Repeat the correct answer after the speaker's confirmation. Listen to the model.

Modelo: No dudo que ella viene hoy.   (Dudo)
   Dudo que ella **venga** hoy.

1. (No estoy seguro)
2. (No creo)
3. (No es verdad)
4. (Buscamos)
5. (Necesito una secretaria)
6. (No hay nadie)

III. Para escuchar y entender

1. Listen carefully to the narration. It will be read twice.

(*Narración*)

Now the speaker will make statements about the narration you just heard. Tell whether each statement is true (**verdadero**) or false (**falso**). The speaker will confirm the correct answer.

2. Listen carefully to the dialogue. It will be read twice.

   (*Diálogo 1*)

   Now the speaker will make statements concerning the conversation you just heard. After each statement, say whether it is true (**verdadero**) or false (**falso**). The speaker will confirm the correct answer.

3. Listen carefully to the dialogue. It will be read twice.

   (*Diálogo 2*)

   Now the speaker will ask some questions about the dialogue you just heard. Answer each question, omitting the subject. The speaker will confirm the correct answer. Repeat the correct answer.

Lección

19

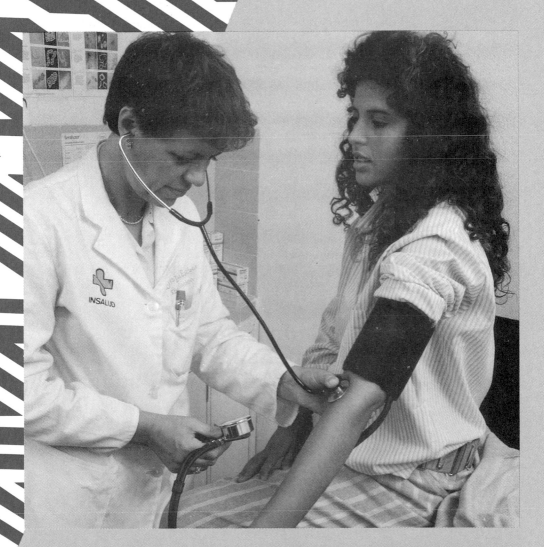

1. The subjunctive after conjunctions implying uncertainty or unfulfillment
2. The present perfect subjunctive
3. Uses of the present perfect subjunctive

Vocabulario

COGNADOS

horrible horrible	el **testamento** testament,
el (la) **pasajero(a)** passenger	will

NOMBRES
la **autopista** freeway
el (la) **ayudante** assistant
el (la) **cirujano(a)** surgeon
la **cuenta** bill, account
la **fiebre** fever,
   temperature
el **informe** report
el (la) **oculista** eye doctor
la **operación, cirugía**
   surgery
la **pastilla** pill
el **peso** weight

VERBOS
bajar to go down
chocar to collide
revisar, chequear to
   check
sobrevivir to survive

**OTRAS PALABRAS Y
EXPRESIONES**
a menos que unless
antes de que before
echar al correo to mail
en caso de que in case
**en cuanto, tan pronto
   como** as soon as
hacer ejercicio to
   exercise
hasta que until
para que in order that
ponerse a dieta to go on
   a diet
por lo menos at least
sacar copia (de) to
   photocopy
sin que without

◆1. The subjunctive after conjunctions implying uncertainty or unfulfillment

The subjunctive is used after conjunctions of time when the main clause refers to the future or is a command.

◆ Some conjunctions of time:

tan pronto como	*as soon as*
en cuanto	*as soon as*
hasta que	*until*
cuando	*when*

—Eva, ¿cuándo va a
  llamarte el doctor?
—Me llamará **tan pronto
  como sepa** el resultado
  de los análisis.

*Eva, when is the doctor
  going to call you?*
*He is going to call me as
  soon as he finds out the
  results of the tests.*

—Carlos, ¿a qué hora van
a empezar la operación?

*Carlos, at what time are
they going to begin the
surgery?*

—La van a empezar **en
cuanto lleguen** los
cirujanos.

*They are going to begin
(it) as soon as the sur-
geons arrive.*

—Tomás, ¿cuándo vamos
a salir para el
aeropuerto?

*Thomas, when are we
going to leave for the
airport?*

—No podemos salir **hasta
que** el carro **esté**
arreglado.

*We can't leave until the
car is fixed.*

—**Cuando llegue** David,
dígale que saque copia
de estas cartas y las
eche al correo.

*When David arrives, tell
him to photocopy these
letters and mail them.*

—Muy bien, se lo diré
cuando venga.

*OK, I'll tell him when he
arrives.*

ATENCIÓN: If the action already happened or if there is no
indication of a future action, the indicative is used after the
conjunction of time.

—Eva, ¿cuándo te llamó
el doctor?

*Eva, when did the doctor
call you?*

—Me llamó **tan pronto
como supo** el resultado
de los análisis.

*He called me as soon as he
found out the result of
the tests.*

—Carlos, ¿a qué hora van
a empezar la
operación.

*Carlos, at what time are
they going to begin the
surgery?*

—Siempre empiezan **en
cuanto llegan** los
cirujanos.

*They always begin as soon
as the surgeons arrive.*

—Tomás, ¿cuándo salieron
Uds. para el
aeropuerto?

*Thomas, when did you
leave for the airport?*

—No pudimos salir **hasta
que** el coche **estuvo**
arreglado.

*We were not able to leave
until the car was fixed.*

There are some conjunctions that by their very meaning imply
uncertainty or conditional fulfillment and are therefore *always* followed by the subjunctive.

◆ Some conjunctions that always take the subjunctive:

a menos que	*unless*	**en caso de que**	*in case*
antes de que	*before*	**para que**	*in order to*
con tal que	*provided that*	**sin que**	*without*

—¿Va Ud. a firmar el
   testamento hoy?

*Are you going to sign the
   will today?*

—No puedo firmarlo **sin
   que** mi abogado lo **lea.**

*I can't sign it without my
   lawyer reading it.*

—¿Vas a tomar las pastillas
   esta noche?

*Are you going to take the
   pills tonight?*

—Sí, voy a tomarlas **a
   menos que** me **baje** la
   fiebre.

*Yes, I'm going to take
   them unless the fever
   goes down.*

Práctica

A. Complete the sentences with the subjunctive or the indicative of
the verbs in the following list, as needed. Use each verb only
once.

arreglar	salir	dar
llegar	pedir	comenzar
firmar	llover	estar
preguntar	ver	terminar

1. Vamos a echar las cartas al correo tan pronto como el
   jefe las _____.
2. Siempre cierro las ventanas cuando _____.
3. Me llamó tan pronto como _____ al hospital.
4. No puede salir sin que ellos lo _____.
5. No me lo dirán a menos que se lo _____.
6. No podré comprar las pastillas hasta que Uds. me _____
   el dinero.
7. Le dimos el carro tan pronto como nos lo _____.
8. Dígale al empleado que saque copia del testamento en
   cuanto _____ terminado.
9. Siempre espero hasta que él _____ del trabajo.
10. Te llamaré por teléfono cuando _____ de escribir las
    cartas.
11. Voy a llamar al cirujano antes de que _____ la
    operación.
12. Trae el coche mañana para que lo _____ el mecánico.

B. Use your imagination to complete the following with the indicative or the subjunctive, as necessary:

1. No te bajará la fiebre a menos que...
2. El cirujano va a comenzar la operación en cuanto...
3. Siempre me llama tan pronto como...
4. Anoche lo esperé hasta que...
5. Voy a limpiar la casa en caso de que...
6. Él siempre llama a su abogado cuando...
7. No puedo echar las cartas al correo antes de que...
8. No puedo comprarte el anillo sin que mis padres...

2. The present perfect subjunctive

The present perfect subjunctive is formed with the present subjunctive of the auxiliary verb **haber** and the past participle of the main verb.

The Present Perfect Subjunctive

Present Subjunctive of haber + *Past Participle of the Main Verb*		
yo	haya	hablado
tú	hayas	comido
Ud. él ella	haya	vivido
nosotros	hayamos	hecho
Uds. ellos ellas	hayan	puesto

Práctica

Conjugate the following verbs in the present perfect subjunctive for each subject given.

1. **yo:** hacer, venir, comer, levantarse
2. **tú:** trabajar, poner, decir, acostarse
3. **ella:** escribir, cerrar, abrir, sentarse
4. **nosotros:** morir, hablar, llegar, vestirse
5. **ellos:** romper, vender, alquilar, bañarse

3. Uses of the present perfect subjunctive

The present perfect subjunctive is used to describe events that have ended in the present or that will end prior to a given time or event in the future. It is equivalent to the English *have* or *has* + past participle, when the main clause calls for the use of the subjunctive.

—¿Ya han pagado Uds. la cuenta del oculista?	*Have you already paid the eye doctor's bill?*
—No recuerdo... no, **no creo** que la **hayamos pagado** todavía.	*I don't remember . . . No, I don't think **we've paid** it yet.*
—Hubo un accidente en la autopista. Chocaron dos autobuses, y **temo** que **hayan muerto** todos los pasajeros.	*There was an accident on the freeway. Two buses collided and I fear that all the passengers (**have**) died.*
—¡Qué horrible![1] **Ojalá** que algunos **hayan sobrevivido.**	*How horrible! I hope that some (of them) (**have**) survived.*
—Inés se ha puesto a dieta.	*Ines has gone on a diet.*
—Sí, pero **no creo** que **haya perdido** mucho peso porque nunca hace ejercicio.	*Yes, but I don't think **she has lost** a lot of weight because she never exercises.*

Práctica

A. Complete the sentences below with the present perfect subjunctive of the verbs in the following list. Use each verb only once:

estar	sobrevivir	pagar	poder	morir
ir	conseguir	chocar	revisar	llegar

1. No creo que ellos _____ la cuenta del oculista.
2. Siento que tú _____ tan ocupado.
3. Espero que Uds. _____ los informes.
4. Ojalá que mi ayudante _____ a la oficina.
5. No es verdad que _____ dos autobuses.
6. Temo que ninguno de los pasajeros del avión _____.
7. Dudo que él _____ vender la casa a ese precio.

[1]The Spanish equivalent of *how* + adjective is **qué** + adjective.

8. Ojalá que no _____ todos los pasajeros en el accidente.
9. No creo que todos los cirujanos _____ a la reunión.
10. Siento que tú no _____ el puesto.

B. You are an interpreter. How would you say the following in Spanish?

1. I don't think my husband has exercised.
2. I hope he has gone on a diet because he needs it.
3. It's not true that she has lost weight.
4. I doubt that they have photocopied the report.
5. He is not going to call you unless he has seen his lawyer.

En el laboratorio

LECCIÓN 19

The following material is to be used with the tape in the language laboratory.

I. Vocabulario

Repeat each word after the speaker. When repeating words that are cognates, notice the difference in pronunciation between English and Spanish.

COGNADOS:	horrible el pasajero el testamento
NOMBRES:	la autopista el ayudante el cirujano la cuenta la fiebre el informe el oculista la operación la cirugía la pastilla el peso
VERBOS:	bajar chocar revisar chequear sobrevivir
OTRAS PALABRAS Y EXPRESIONES:	a menos que antes de que echar al correo en caso de que en cuanto tan pronto como hacer ejercicio hasta que para que ponerse a dieta por lo menos sacar copia sin que

II. Práctica

A. Restate each of the following sentences, inserting the cue at the beginning and making any necessary changes. Repeat the correct answer after the speaker's confirmation. Listen to the model.

Modelo: Siempre me llama tan pronto como llega.   (Me va a llamar)
Me va a llamar tan pronto como llegue.

1. (Le voy a hablar)
2. (Se lo va a dar)
3. (Van a trabajar)
4. (Lo echaré)
5. (Sacaré)
6. (Se lo diré)

B. Restate each of the following sentences, inserting the cue at the beginning and making any necessary changes. Use the present perfect subjunctive. Listen to the model.

Modelo: El abogado ha llegado.   (Espero)
Espero que el abogado haya llegado.

1. Ojalá	6. Es imposible
2. Dudo	7. Temo
3. No creo	8. Es una lástima
4. No es verdad	9. No es posible
5. Dudan	10. Puede ser

III. Para escuchar y entender

1. Listen carefully to the dialogue. It will be read twice.

   (*Diálogo 1*)

   Now the speaker will make statements about the dialogue you just heard. Tell whether each statement is true (**verdadero**) or false (**falso**). The speaker will confirm the correct answer.

2. Listen carefully to the dialogue. It will be read twice.

   (*Diálogo 2*)

   Now the speaker will make statements about the dialogue you just heard. Tell whether each statement is true (**verdadero**) or false (**falso**). The speaker will confirm the correct answer.

3. Listen carefully to the dialogue. It will be read twice.

   (*Diálogo 3*)

   Now the speaker will ask some questions about the dialogue you just heard. Answer each question, omitting the subject. The speaker will confirm the correct answer. Repeat the correct answer.

Lección

20

1. **The imperfect subjunctive**
2. **Uses of the imperfect subjunctive**
3. **If clauses**

Vocabulario

COGNADOS

el **aniversario** anniversary	el **consulado** consulate
el **banquete** banquet	la **ostra** oyster

NOMBRES
el **cordero** lamb
la **matrícula** registration
el **mozo** waiter
la **propina** tip

VERBOS
  asistir to attend
  celebrar to celebrate
  dejar to leave (behind)
  devolver (o:ue) to return
  (something), to
  give back
  recoger to pick up

ADJETIVOS
  asado(a) roasted
  raro(a) strange

**OTRAS PALABRAS Y
EXPRESIONES**
el **aniversario de bodas**
  wedding anniversary
el **puré de papas** mashed
  potatoes

1. The imperfect subjunctive

The imperfect subjunctive is the simplest past tense of the subjunctive. It is formed in the same way for all verbs, regular and irregular. The **-ron** ending of the third person plural of the preterit is dropped and the following endings are added to the stem: **-ra, -ras, -ra, -ramos, -ran.**[1]

The Imperfect Subjunctive

Verb	Preterit, Third Person Plural	Stem	Imperfect Subjunctive	
hablar	hablaron	**habla-**	que yo habla-	ra
comer	comieron	**comie-**	que tú comie-	ras
vivir	vivieron	**vivie-**	que Ud. vivie-	ra
traer	trajeron	**traje-**	que él traje-	ra
ir	fueron	**fue-**	que ella fue-	ra
saber	supieron	**supie-**	que nosotros supié-	ramos
decir	dijeron	**dije-**	que Uds. dije-	ran
poner	pusieron	**pusie-**	que ellos pusie-	ran
estar	estuvieron	**estuvie-**	que ellas estuvie-	ran

[1] See Appendix B: Verbs, for the other set of endings of the imperfect subjunctive, the **-se** endings.

♦ Notice the written accent mark in the first person plural form.

Práctica

Give the imperfect subjunctive of the following verbs:

1. **yo:** bajar, aprender, abrir, cerrar, estar, acostarse
2. **tú:** salir, sentir, temer, recordar, venir, ponerse
3. **Ud.:** llevar, romper, morir, revisar, volar, alegrarse
4. **nosotros:** esperar, traer, pedir, volver, servir, vestirse
5. **ellos:** tener, ser, dar, estar, poder, irse

◆2. Uses of the imperfect subjunctive

♦ The imperfect subjunctive is always used in the subordinate clause when the verb of the main clause is in the past and requires the subjunctive mood:

—¿Qué te sugirió él?

What did he suggest (to you)?

—Me **sugirió** que **pidiera** cordero asado y puré de papás.

He suggested that I order roast lamb and mashed potatoes.

—Ella pidió ostras.

She ordered oysters.

—¡Qué raro! Yo **no creía** que le **gustaran** las ostras.

How strange! I didn't think she liked oysters.

—Carlitos, te **dije** que le **dejaras** una buena propina al mozo.

Carlitos, I told you to leave the waiter a good tip.

—Y yo te **dije** que me **dieras** más dinero.

And I told you to give me more money.

♦ The imperfect subjunctive is also used when the verb of the main clause is in the present, but the subordinate clause refers to the past:

—**Es** una lástima que no **asistieras** ayer al banquete.

It's a pity that you didn't attend the banquet yesterday.

—No pude, porque tuve que ir al consulado a recoger mi pasaporte.

I wasn't able to (make it) because I had to go to the consulate to pick up my passport.

◆ The imperfect subjunctive form of **querer** (**quisiera**) is used as a polite form of request:

Quisiera pedirle un favor.   *I would like to ask you a favor.*

Práctica

A. Complete the sentences with the imperfect subjunctive of the following verbs. Use each verb once:

escribir	sacar	lavarse	recoger
asistir	pedir	venir	firmar

1. El mozo me sugirió que _____ cordero asado.
2. Sentí mucho que Ud. no _____ al banquete.
3. Le pedí a papá que _____ mi pasaporte en el consulado.
4. Ella no les dijo que _____ las cartas en inglés.
5. Es una lástima que el abogado no _____ ayer a la oficina.
6. El director me pidió que _____ copias de los informes.
7. El profesor quería que nosotros _____ las cartas.
8. Tú no me dijiste que _____ la cara y las manos antes de hacer la tarea.

B. You are an interpreter. How would you say the following in Spanish?

1. They wanted me to leave a good tip.
2. I told you not to order oysters, Roberto.
3. I'm sorry you were sick yesterday, Mr. Vera.
4. They asked them to attend the banquet? How strange!
5. He told us to make mashed potatoes.
6. I'm glad you were able to come last Friday.

◣ 3. *If* clauses

In Spanish, the imperfect subjunctive is used in a clause introduced by **si** (*if*) when it refers to statements considered contrary to fact, hypothetical, or unlikely to happen. The resultant clause usually has a verb in the conditional:

Si yo fuera Ud....   *If I were you . . .*

—**Si** yo **tuviera** dinero, iría de vacaciones con Uds.   *If I had money, I would go on vacation with you.*

—¿No te lo puede prestar tu padre?   *Can't your father lend it to you?*

—No, porque si mi padre
me lo **prestara,** tendría
que devolvérselo antes
de septiembre, y yo
necesito el dinero para
pagar la matrícula.

*No, because if my father
were to lend it to me,[1] I
would have to give it
back to him before Sep-
tember, and I need the
money to pay for regis-
tration.*

—Si ellos **vinieran** hoy,
podríamos ir a la playa
o al parque.

*If they came today, we
could go to the beach or
to the park.*

—Ellos no van a venir
porque hoy celebran su
aniversario de bodas.

*They're not going to come
because they're cele-
brating their wedding
anniversary today.*

◆ When an if-clause is *not* contrary to fact or hypothetical, or
when there is a possibility that it will happen, the indicative is
used:

Si los muchachos vienen
hoy, **podemos** ir a la
playa.

*If the boys come today,
we can go to the
beach.*

◆ The present subjunctive is *never* used with an if-clause.

Práctica

A. Complete the following sentences with the present indicative or
the imperfect subjunctive of the verbs in parentheses, as
needed:

1. Si yo _____ (tener) tiempo, te llevaré al banquete.
2. Si tú _____ (poder), ¿lo harías?
3. Si Federico me _____ (devolver) el dinero, podré
   pagar la matrícula.
4. Si ella _____ (venir), iríamos a la playa.
5. Si la jefa me _____ (dar) una semana de vacaciones,
   iría a París.
6. Nosotros visitaríamos a nuestros abuelos si (nosotros) no
   _____ (estar) enfermos.
7. Compraré la casa si _____ (conseguir) el dinero.
8. Si yo _____ (ser) tú, no dejaría esa propina.
9. Mamá dice que me va a comprar el vestido si (ella) _____
   (salir) temprano de la oficina.
10. Si ellos lo _____ (saber), te lo dirían.

---

[1] Many colloquial English speakers use the simple past tense to express a contrary-to-fact
or hypothetical situation, *e.g.,* ". . . *if my father* **lent** *it to me.*"

B. You are an interpreter. How would you say the following in Spanish?

1. I would help you if I could, Charlie.
2. If she has time, she'll take you to the consulate.
3. If you celebrate your wedding anniversary, I will come to the party.
4. We would go on vacation if we had the money.
5. I would attend the banquet if I weren't sleepy.
6. We are going to go to the park if he comes back early.

En el laboratorio

LECCIÓN 20

The following material is to be used with the tape in the language laboratory.

I. Vocabulario

Repeat each word after the speaker. When repeating words that are cognates, notice the difference in pronunciation between English and Spanish.

COGNADOS: el aniversario   el banquete
el consulado   la ostra

NOMBRES: el cordero   la matrícula   el mozo
la propina

VERBOS: asistir   celebrar   dejar   devolver
recoger

ADJETIVOS: asado   raro

**OTRAS PALABRAS Y
EXPRESIONES:** el aniversario de bodas
el puré de papas

II. Práctica

A. Restate each of the following sentences, inserting the cue at the beginning and making any necessary changes. Repeat the correct answer after the speaker's confirmation. Listen to the model.

Modelo: Ella quiere que yo vaya con él.   (Ella quería)
Ella quería que yo **fuera** con él.

1. Fue una lástima
2. No creí
3. Esperaba
4. Dudábamos
5. No había nadie
6. Necesitaba
7. No quería
8. No creían

B. Restate each of the following sentences, inserting the cue at the beginning and making any necessary changes. Repeat the correct answer after the speaker's confirmation. Listen to the model.

Modelo: Iré si tengo tiempo.   (Iría)
Iría si **tuviera** tiempo.

1. Le hablaría
2. Lo compraríamos
3. Lo harían
4. Se lo diría

263

5. Vendríamos	7. Lo compraría
6. Me alegraría	8. Lo haríamos

III. Para escuchar y entender

1. Listen carefully to the narration. It will be read twice.

   (*Narración*)

   Now the speaker will make statements about the narration you just heard. After each statement, say whether it is true (**verdadero**) or false (**falso**). The speaker will confirm the correct answer.

2. Listen carefully to the dialogue. It will be read twice.

   (*Diálogo 1*)

   Now the speaker will make statements about the dialogue you just heard. After each statement, say whether it is true (**verdadero**) or false (**falso**). The speaker will confirm the correct answer.

3. Listen carefully to the dialogue. It will be read twice.

   (*Diálogo 2*)

   Now the speaker will ask some questions about the dialogue you just heard. Answer each question, omitting the subject. The speaker will confirm the correct answer. Repeat the correct answer.

¿Cuánto sabe usted ahora?

LECCIONES 16–20

A. The subjunctive

Lección 16

Complete the sentences with the Spanish equivalent of the verbs in parentheses. Use the present subjunctive. Follow the model.

Modelo: ...que yo _____ (*speak*)
     ...que yo hable

1. ...que nosotros _____ (*advise*)
2. ...que yo _____ (*rent*)
3. ...que Uds. _____ (*write*)
4. ...que tú _____ (*live*)
5. ...que él _____ (*say*)
6. ...que Ud. _____ (*close*)
7. ...que ellos _____ (*come*)
8. ...que ella _____ (*get up*)
9. ...que yo _____ (*ask for, request*)
10. ...que Uds. _____ (*do*)
11. ...que Ana _____ (*bring*)
12. ...que Ud. _____ (*recommend*)
13. ...que nosotros _____ (*spend*)
14. ...que yo _____ (*go*)
15. ...que Luis _____ (*shave*)
16. ...que nosotros _____ (*sleep*)
17. ...que ella _____ (*give*)
18. ...que ellos _____ (*know*)
19. ...que yo _____ (*go out*)
20. ...que tú _____ (*have*)

B. The subjunctive with verbs of volition

How would you say the following in Spanish?

1. She wants me to bring the packages.
2. I prefer that we go to the post office.
3. At what time do you want me to be there tomorrow, Mr. Acevedo?
4. Ask him to rent the car, Mrs. Portillo.
5. Tell them to wash their faces now.
6. (Let) your boyfriend do it.
7. (Let) them come in.
8. He wants me to be his girlfriend.
9. Do you need them to bring you the furniture, sir?
10. I don't want you to do anything, Johnny.

C. The absolute superlative

Answer the following questions according to the model.

Modelo: ¿Es inteligente el hijo de Yolanda?
¡Ah, sí! Es inteligentísimo.

1. ¿Es alto Roberto?
2. ¿Es cara la gasolina?
3. ¿Son lentos los trenes?
4. ¿Es buena la profesora?
5. ¿Es difícil esta lección?
6. ¿Es bella la ciudad donde viven Uds.?
7. ¿Es fácil el español?
8. ¿Estás ocupado este fin de semana?

D. Complete the following sentences, using words learned in Lección 16:

1. Voy a _____ un coche de cambios _____ porque _____ menos gasolina.
2. Debes lavarte la _____ ahora, Pepito.
3. Voy a comprar algunos _____ para mi dormitorio.
4. Fueron a la oficina de _____ a llevar unas cartas.
5. No pudo hacerlo hoy porque estaba muy _____.
6. Ellos me recomiendan que _____ el coche con esa compañía.
7. Ella es muy bonita. Es sumamente _____.

Lección 17 **A.** The subjunctive to express emotion

How would you say the following in Spanish?

1. I hope you can talk with your adviser today, Ana.
2. I'm glad your mother is feeling better, Mr. Gómez.
3. I'm afraid we can't sign the contract tomorrow, Mrs. Herrero.
4. We're glad to be here today.
5. She hopes to leave tomorrow morning.
6. I hope you can come to the lecture, Mr. Peña.
7. We're afraid we can't finish the job tonight.
8. I'm sorry you are so sick, Mrs. Treviño.

B. The subjunctive with impersonal expressions

Complete the following sentences with the subjunctive, the indicative, or the infinitive of the verb in parentheses, as appropriate:

1. Es difícil que ellos _____ (matricularse) hoy.
2. Es necesario _____ (estudiar) mucho.
3. Es mejor _____ (escribir) ahora mismo.

4. Es verdad que nosotros _____ (terminar) mañana.
5. Es lástima que el consejero no _____ (estar) aquí hoy.
6. Es importante _____ (sacar) buenas notas.
7. Es seguro que ellos _____ (llegar) el lunes.
8. Es posible _____ (firmar) los contratos hoy.

C. Formation of adverbs

Write the adverbs corresponding to the following adjectives:

1. feliz
2. especial
3. rápido

4. fácil
5. lento y cuidadoso

D. Complete the following sentences, using words learned in Lección 17:

1. Necesito dinero para pagar la _____ de la universidad.
2. Quiero hablar con mi _____ antes de firmar el contrato.
3. ¿Qué _____ espera en este examen? ¿Una «A»?
4. La Dra. Salcedo da una _____ hoy, pero no puedo ir porque tengo un examen _____ en mi clase de química.
5. No tiene que pagar la matrícula porque tiene una _____.
6. Voy a hablar con mi _____ porque tengo muchos problemas con mis clases.
7. La física y la _____ son muy difíciles para mí.
8. Esta _____ no puedo ir. Iré mañana por la mañana.
9. Es _____ que él esté enfermo.
10. Él escribe lenta y _____.

A. The subjunctive to express doubt, disbelief and denial   **Lección 18**

Change the following sentences according to the model:

Modelo: Estoy seguro de que el jefe **viene** hoy.   (Dudo)
    Dudo que el jefe venga hoy.

1. Dudo que el café ya **esté** frío.   (Estoy seguro de que)
2. Creo que Pedro **va** con nosotros.   (No creo que)
3. Es verdad que María **está** muy enferma.   (No es verdad que)
4. No dudo que la criada **está** aquí.   (Dudo que)
5. No es verdad que ella **quiera** huevos fritos.   (Es cierto que)
6. Es cierto que ella **almuerza** aquí.   (No es cierto que)

B. The subjunctive to express indefiniteness and nonexistence

Change the following sentences according to the new beginning:

1. Tengo una casa que queda cerca del centro.   (Busco una casa que)

2. ¿Hay alguien aquí que sepa escribir a máquina?   (Aquí hay una chica que)
3. ¿Hay alguien que puede arreglar el fregadero?   (No hay nadie que)
4. Necesito una empleada que pueda trabajar los domingos.   (Tengo una empleada que)
5. Aquí no hay nadie que pueda poner la mesa ahora.   (Hay dos personas que)
6. Conozco un restaurante que sirve comida mexicana. (Busco un restaurante que)

C. Diminutive suffixes

Complete the following sentences with the Spanish equivalent of the words in parentheses:

1. Yo ya compré el _____ de Navidad.   (*little tree*)
2. Mi _____ se llama _____.   (*little sister / little Theresa*)
3. ¿Puedes hacerme un _____ para mi _____?   (*little dress / little daughter*)
4. Fuimos a Disneylandia con _____.   (*Johnny*)
5. Tenemos un _____ muy bueno.   (*little car*)

D. Complete the following sentences, using words learned in Lección 18:

1. La _____ no vino hoy, así que yo tengo que _____ la casa.
2. Hoy no estoy ocupado. Estoy _____ y puedo ir con Uds.
3. Necesito el mantel para _____ la mesa.
4. Todo el _____ vino a la fiesta.
5. Ayer compré un _____ de Navidad para mis hijos.
6. La casa _____ cerca del centro.
7. Nosotros siempre _____ a las doce y media del día.
8. No quiero arroz con pollo. Quiero pollo _____.

Lección 19   **A.** The subjunctive after conjunctions implying uncertainty or unfulfillment

How would you say the following in Spanish?

1. I'll speak to him as soon as I see the surgeon.
2. Stay here in case he has a fever, Mrs. Ortega.
3. He wrote to me as soon as he arrived.
4. We are going to wait until he comes.
5. I can't go without my parents knowing (it).
6. We'll go to the eye doctor when we have (the) money.

B. The present perfect subjunctive

Complete the following sentences with the Spanish equivalent of the verbs in parentheses. Use the present perfect subjunctive. Follow the model.

Modelo: ...que él _____ (*speak*)
  ...que él haya hablado

1. ...que yo _____ (*see*)
2. ...que Uds. _____ (*do*)
3. ...que tú _____ (*learn*)
4. ...que ellos _____ (*sign*)
5. ...que Ud. _____ (*fix*)
6. ...que nosotros _____ (*bajar*)
7. ...que Ana _____ (*return*)
8. ...que Luis _____ (*go to bed*)

C. Uses of the present perfect subjunctive

Write sentences using the following items. Follow the model.

Modelo: Yo / alegrarse / tú / venir
  Yo me alegro de que tú hayas venido.

1. Ellos / sentir / Uds. / estar enfermos
2. Rosa / no creer / yo / hacerlo
3. Nosotros / temer / él / morir
4. No es verdad / nosotros / ponernos a dieta
5. Ojalá / papá / hacer / ejercicio / hoy

D. Complete the following sentences, using words learned in Lección 19:

1. Tengo que ir al _____ mañana porque no veo muy bien.
2. El _____ le hizo la operación ayer.
3. Voy a darle dos aspirinas para bajarle la _____.
4. Mi hermano tiene que perder _____. Necesita ponerse a _____ y hacer más _____.
5. Voy a echar estas cartas al _____, pero antes voy a sacarle _____.
6. Chocaron dos autobuses en la _____ y murieron muchos pasajeros. ¡Qué _____!
7. Necesito ver a mi abogado para hacer mi _____.
8. Mi _____ va a revisar todos los informes porque yo no puedo hacerlo.
9. No murieron todos. Por lo menos ocho personas _____.
10. Voy a tomar las _____ para el dolor tan _____ como tú me las traigas.

Lección 20   **A.** The imperfect subjunctive

Complete the sentences with the Spanish equivalent of the verbs in parentheses. Use the imperfect subjunctive. Follow the model:

Modelo: ...que yo _____ (*live*)
     ...que yo viviera

1. ...que nosotros _____ (*attend*)
2. ...que tú _____ (*leave behind*)
3. ...que ellos _____ (*wash themselves*)
4. ...que yo _____ (*pick up*)
5. ...que Ud. _____ (*can*)
6. ...que Carlos _____ (*bring*)
7. ...que Uds. _____ (*give back*)
8. ...que ella _____ (*have*)

B. Uses of the imperfect subjunctive

Change the following sentences according to the models:

Modelo 1: Me dice que hable con él.   (Me dijo)
     Me dijo que hablara con él.

Modelo 2: Siento que tú estés enferma.   (ayer)
     Siento que tú estuvieras enferma ayer.

1. Le pido que venga en seguida.   (Le pedí)
2. Me alegro de que puedas terminarlo.   (anoche)
3. No creo que ella lo haga.   (No creí)
4. No es verdad que ellos celebren su aniversario de bodas.   (ayer)
5. Temen que ella no deje propina.   (anoche)
6. Dudo que el banquete sea hoy.   (el sábado pasado)

C. *If* clauses

Complete the following sentences:

1. Yo compraría una casa si...
2. Iremos a verte si...
3. Yo iría al médico si...
4. Mañana saldremos si...
5. Ellos nos ayudarían si...
6. Nosotros se lo diremos si...
7. Yo dormiría si...
8. Vamos a comer algo si...

D. Complete the following sentences, using words learned in Lección 20:

1. Mis padres van a _____ su aniversario de _____ con un banquete.
2. No quiero pollo _____; prefiero pollo frito.
3. Voy a ir al _____ de México para pedir una visa.
4. Ellos van a comer _____ asado y sopa de _____.
5. No quiero pedir _____ de papas; prefiero papas fritas.
6. Voy a dejarle una buena _____ al mozo porque el servicio fue excelente.
7. No puedo _____ a clase hoy porque no me siento bien.
8. Este vestido no me gusta. Lo voy a _____.
9. Voy a la oficina de correos para _____ un paquete.
10. Ana siempre está en casa a esta hora, pero hoy no está. ¡Qué _____!

Appendix A

Spanish Pronunciation

Vowels

There are five distinct vowels in Spanish: **a, e, i, o,** and **u.** Each vowel has only one basic, constant sound. The pronunciation of each vowel is constant, clear, and brief. The length of the sound is practically the same whether it is produced in a stressed or unstressed syllable.[1]

While producing the sounds of the English stressed vowels that most closely resemble the Spanish ones, the speaker changes the position of the tongue, lips, and lower jaw, so that the vowel actually starts as one sound and then *glides* into another. In Spanish, however, the tongue, lips, and jaw keep a constant position during the production of the sound.

> **English:** banana   **Spanish:** banana

The stress falls on the same vowel and syllable in both Spanish and English, but the English stressed *a* is longer than the Spanish stressed **a.**

> **English:** banana   **Spanish:** banana

Note also that the English stressed *a* has a sound different from the other *a*'s in the word, while the Spanish **a** sound remains constant.

a in Spanish sounds similar to the English *a* in the word *father*.

alta	casa	palma	Ana
cama	Panamá	alma	apagar

e is pronounced like the English *e* in the word *eight*.

mes	entre	este	deje
ese	encender	teme	prender

i has a sound similar to the English *ee* in the word *see*.

fin	ir	sí	sin	dividir	Trini	difícil

o is similar to the English *o* in the word *no*, but without the glide.

toco	como	poco	roto
corto	corro	solo	loco

---

[1] In a stressed syllable, the prominence of the vowel is indicated by its loudness.

u is pronounced like the English *oo* sound in the word *shoot*, or the *ue* sound in the word *Sue*.

su	Lulú	Úrsula	cultura
un	luna	sucursal	Uruguay

Diphthongs and Triphthongs

When unstressed **i** or **u** falls next to another vowel in a syllable, it unites with that vowel to form what is called a *diphthong*. Both vowels are pronounced as one syllable. Their sounds do not change; they are only pronounced more rapidly and with a glide. For example:

traiga	Lidia	treinta	siete	oigo	adiós
Aurora	agua	bueno	antiguo	ciudad	Luis

A *triphthong* is the union of three vowels: a stressed vowel between two unstressed ones (**i** or **u**) in the same syllable. For example: Paraguay, estudiéis.

NOTE: Stressed **i** and **u** do not form diphthongs with other vowels, except in the combinations **iu** and **ui**. For example, rí-o, sa-**bí**-ais.

In syllabication, diphthongs and triphthongs are considered a single vowel; their components cannot be separated.

Consonants

p   Spanish **p** is pronounced in a manner similar to the English *p* sound, but without the puff of air that follows after the English sound is produced.

pesca	pude	puedo	parte	papá
postre	piña	puente	Paco	

k   The Spanish **k** sound, represented by the letters **k, c** before **a, o, u,** or a consonant, and **qu**, is similar to the English *k* sound, but without the puff of air.

casa	comer	cuna	clima	acción	que
quinto	queso	aunque	kiosko	kilómetro	

t   Spanish **t** is produced by touching the back of the upper front teeth with the tip of the tongue. It has no puff of air as in the English *t*.

todo	antes	corto	Guatemala	diente
resto	tonto	roto	tanque	

d   The Spanish consonant **d** has two different sounds depending on its position. At the beginning of an utterance and after **n** or **l**, the tip of the tongue presses the back of the upper front teeth.

día	doma	dice	dolor	dar
anda	Aldo	caldo	el deseo	un domicilio

In all other positions the sound of **d** is similar to the *th* sound in the English word *they*, but softer.

medida	todo	nada	nadie	medio
puedo	moda	queda	nudo	

g   The Spanish consonant **g** is similar to the English *g* sound in the word *guy* except before **e** or **i**.

goma	glotón	gallo	gloria	lago	alga
gorrión	garra	guerra	angustia	algo	Dagoberto

j   The Spanish sound **j** (or **g** before **e** and **i**) is similar to a strongly exaggerated English *h* sound.

gemir	juez	jarro	gitano	agente
juego	giro	bajo	gente	

b, v   There is no difference in sound between Spanish **b** and **v**. Both letters are pronounced alike. At the beginning of an utterance or after **m** or **n**, **b** and **v** have a sound identical to the English *b* sound in the word *boy*.

vivir	beber	vamos	barco	enviar
hambre	batea	bueno	vestido	

When pronounced between vowels, the Spanish **b** and **v** sound is produced by bringing the lips together but not closing them, so that some air may pass through.

sábado	autobús	yo voy	su barco

y, ll   In most countries, Spanish **ll** and **y** have a sound similar to the English sound in the word *yes*.

el llavero	trayecto	su yunta	milla
oye	el yeso	mayo	yema
un yelmo	trayectoria	llama	bella

NOTE: When it stands alone or is at the end of a word, Spanish **y** is pronounced like the vowel **i**.

rey	hoy	y	doy	buey
muy	voy	estoy	soy	

r   The sound of Spanish **r** is similar to the English *dd* sound in the word *ladder*.

crema	aroma	cara	arena	aro
harina	toro	oro	eres	portero

rr   Spanish **rr** and also **r** in an initial position and after **n, l,** or **s** are pronounced with a very strong trill. This trill is produced by bringing the tip of the tongue near the alveolar ridge and letting it vibrate freely while the air passes through the mouth.

rama	carro	Israel	cierra	roto
perro	alrededor	rizo	corre	Enrique

s   Spanish **s** is represented in most of the Spanish world by the letters **s**, **z**, and **c** before **e** or **i**. The sound is very similar to the English sibilant *s* in the word *sink*.

sale	sitio	presidente	signo
salsa	seda	suma	vaso
sobrino	ciudad	cima	canción
zapato	zarza	cerveza	centro

h   The letter **h** is silent in Spanish.

hoy	hora	hilo	ahora
humor	huevo	horror	almohada

ch   Spanish **ch** is pronounced like the English *ch* in the word *chief*.

hecho	chico	coche	Chile
mucho	muchacho	salchicha	

f   Spanish **f** is identical in sound to the English *f*.

difícil	feo	fuego	forma
fácil	fecha	foto	fueron

l   Spanish **l** is similar to the English *l* in the word *let*.

dolor	lata	ángel	lago	sueldo
los	pelo	lana	general	fácil

m   Spanish **m** is pronounced like the English *m* in the word *mother*.

mano	moda	mucho	muy
mismo	tampoco	multa	cómoda

n   In most cases, Spanish **n** has a sound similar to the English *n*.

nada	nunca	ninguno	norte
entra	tiene	sienta	

The sound of Spanish **n** is often affected by the sounds that occur around it. When it appears before **b**, **v**, or **p**, it is pronounced like an **m**.

tan bueno	toman vino	sin poder
un pobre	comen peras	siguen bebiendo

ñ   Spanish **ñ** is similar to the English *ny* sound in the word *canyon*.

señor	otoño	ñoño	uña
leña	dueño	niños	años

x   Spanish **x** has two pronunciations depending on its position. Between vowels the sound is similar to English *ks*.

examen   exacto   boxeo   éxito
oxidar   oxígeno   existencia

When it occurs before a consonant, Spanish **x** sounds like *s*.

expresión   explicar   extraer   excusa
expreso   exquisito   extremo

NOTE: When **x** appears in **México** or in other words of Mexican origin, it is pronounced like the Spanish letter **j**.

Rhythm

Rhythm is the variation of sound intensity that we usually associate with music. Spanish and English each regulate these variations in speech differently, because they have different patterns of syllable length. In Spanish the length of the stressed and unstressed syllables remains almost the same, while in English stressed syllables are considerably longer than unstressed ones. Pronounce the following Spanish words, enunciating each syllable clearly.

es-tu-dian-te   bue-no   Úr-su-la
com-po-si-ción   di-fí-cil   ki-ló-me-tro
po-li-cí-a   Pa-ra-guay

Because the length of the Spanish syllables remains constant, the greater the number of syllables in a given word or phrase, the longer the phrase will be.

Linking

In spoken Spanish, the different words in a phrase or a sentence are not pronounced as isolated elements but are combined together. This is called *linking*.

Pepe come pan.   Pe-pe-co-me-pan
Tomás toma leche.   To-más-to-ma-le-che
Luis tiene la llave.   Luis-tie-ne-la-lla-ve
La mano de Roberto.   La-ma-no-de-Ro-ber-to

1. The final consonant of a word is pronounced together with the initial vowel of the following word.

Carlos anda   Car-lo-san-da
un ángel   u-nán-gel
el otoño   e-lo-to-ño
unos estudios interesantes   u-no-ses-tu-dio-sin-te-re-san-tes

2. A diphthong is formed between the final vowel of a word and the initial vowel of the following word. A triphthong is formed when there is a combination of three vowels (see rules for the formation of diphthongs and triphthongs on page 274).

su hermana	suher-ma-na
tu escopeta	tues-co-pe-ta
Roberto y Luis	Ro-ber-toy-Luis
negocio importante	ne-go-cioim-por-tan-te
lluvia y nieve	llu-viay-nie-ve
ardua empresa	ar-duaem-pre-sa

3. When the final vowel of a word and the initial vowel of the following word are identical, they are pronounced slightly longer than one vowel.

A-nal-can-za Ana alcanza		tie-ne-so	tiene eso
lol-vi-do	lo olvido	Ada-tien-de Ada atiende	

The same rule applies when two identical vowels appear within a word.

cres	crees
Te-rán	Teherán
cor-di-na-ción	coordinación

4. When the final consonant of a word and the initial consonant of the following word are the same, they are pronounced as one consonant with slightly longer than normal duration.

e-la-do	el lado	tie-ne-sed tienes sed
Car-lo-sal-ta	Carlos salta	

Intonation

Intonation is the rise and fall of pitch in the delivery of a phrase or a sentence. In general, Spanish pitch tends to change less than English, giving the impression that the language is less emphatic.

As a rule, the intonation for normal statements in Spanish starts in a low tone, raises to a higher one on the first stressed syllable, maintains that tone until the last stressed syllable, and then goes back to the initial low tone, with still another drop at the very end.

Tu amigo viene mañana.	José come pan.
Ada está en casa.	Carlos toma café.

Syllable Formation in Spanish

General rules for dividing words into syllables:

Vowels

1. A vowel or a vowel combination can constitute a syllable.

    a-lum-no   a-bue-la   Eu-ro-pa

2. Diphthongs and triphthongs are considered single vowels and cannot be divided.

    bai-le   puen-te   Dia-na   es-tu-diáis   an-ti-guo

3. Two strong vowels (**a, e, o**) do not form a diphthong and are separated into two syllables.

    em-ple-ar   vol-te-ar   lo-a

4. A written accent on a weak vowel (**i** or **u**) breaks the diphthong, thus the vowels are separated into two syllables.

    trí-o   dú-o   Ma-rí-a

Consonants

1. A single consonant forms a syllable with the vowel that follows it.

    po-der   ma-no   mi-nu-to

    NOTE: **ch, ll,** and **rr** are considered single consonants: **a-ma-ri-llo, co-che, pe-rro.**

2. When two consonants appear between two vowels, they are separated into two syllables.

    al-fa-be-to   cam-pe-ón   me-ter-se   mo-les-tia

    EXCEPTION: When a consonant cluster composed of **b, c, d, f, g, p,** or **t** with **l** or **r** appears between two vowels, the cluster joins the following vowel: **so-bre, o-tros, ca-ble, te-lé-gra-fo.**

3. When three consonants appear between two vowels, only the last one goes with the following vowel.

    ins-pec-tor   trans-por-te   trans-for-mar

    EXCEPTION: When there is a cluster of three consonants in the combinations described in rule 2, the first consonant joins the preceding vowel and the cluster joins the following vowel: **es-cri-bir, ex-tran-je-ro, im-plo-rar, es-tre-cho.**

Accentuation

In Spanish, all words are stressed according to specific rules. Words that do not follow the rules must have a written accent to indicate the change of stress. The basic rules for accentuation are as follows.

1. Words ending in a vowel, **n**, or **s** are stressed on the next-to-the-last syllable.

hi-jo	**ca**-lle	**me**-sa	fa-**mo**-sos
flo-**re**-cen	**pla**-ya	**ve**-ces	

2. Words ending in a consonant, except **n** or **s**, are stressed on the last syllable.

ma-**yor**	a-**mor**	tro-pi-**cal**
na-**riz**	re-**loj**	co-rre-**dor**

3. All words that do not follow these rules must have the written accent.

ca-**fé**	**lá**-piz	**mú**-si-ca	sa-**lón**
án-gel	**lí**-qui-do	fran-**cés**	**Víc**-tor
sim-**pá**-ti-co	rin-**cón**	a-**zú**-car	**dár**-se-lo
sa-**lió**	**dé**-bil	e-**xá**-me-nes	**dí**-me-lo

4. Pronouns and adverbs of interrogation and exclamation have a written accent to distinguish them from relative pronouns.

¿Qué comes?	*What are you eating?*
La pera que él no comió.	*The pear that he did not eat.*
¿Quién está ahí?	*Who is there?*
El hombre a quien tú llamaste.	*The man whom you called.*
¿Dónde está?	*Where is he?*
En el lugar donde trabaja.	*At the place where he works.*

5. Words that have the same spelling but different meanings take a written accent to differentiate one from the other.

el	*the*	él	*he, him*	te	*you*	té	*tea*
mi	*my*	mí	*me*	si	*if*	sí	*yes*
tu	*your*	tú	*you*	mas	*but*	más	*more*

Verbs

Regular Verbs

Model -ar, -er, -ir *verbs*

INFINITIVE		
amar (*to love*)	**comer** (*to eat*)	**vivir** (*to live*)

GERUND		
amando (*loving*)	**comiendo** (*eating*)	**viviendo** (*living*)

PAST PARTICIPLE		
amado (*loved*)	**comido** (*eaten*)	**vivido** (*lived*)

Simple Tenses

Indicative Mood

PRESENT		
(*I love*)	(*I eat*)	(*I live*)
amo	como	vivo
amas	comes	vives
ama	come	vive
amamos	comemos	vivimos
amáis[1]	coméis	vivís
aman	comen	viven

IMPERFECT		
(*I used to love*)	(*I used to eat*)	(*I used to live*)
amaba	comía	vivía
amabas	comías	vivías
amaba	comía	vivía
amábamos	comíamos	vivíamos
amabais	comíais	vivíais
amaban	comían	vivían

[1]**Vosotros amáis**: The vosotros form of the verb is used primarily in Spain. This form has not been used in this text.

PRETERIT

(*I loved*)	(*I ate*)	(*I lived*)
amé	comí	viví
amaste	comiste	viviste
amó	comió	vivió
amamos	comimos	vivimos
amasteis	comisteis	vivisteis
amaron	comieron	vivieron

FUTURE

(*I will love*)	(*I will eat*)	(*I will live*)
amaré	comeré	viviré
amarás	comerás	vivirás
amará	comerá	vivirá
amaremos	comeremos	viviremos
amaréis	comeréis	viviréis
amarán	comerán	vivirán

CONDITIONAL

(*I would love*)	(*I would eat*)	(*I would live*)
amaría	comería	viviría
amarías	comerías	vivirías
amaría	comería	viviría
amaríamos	comeríamos	viviríamos
amaríais	comeríais	viviríais
amarían	comerían	vivirían

Subjunctive Mood

PRESENT

([*that*] I [*may*] love)	([*that*] I [*may*] eat)	([*that*] I [*may*] live)
ame	coma	viva
ames	comas	vivas
ame	coma	viva
amemos	comamos	vivamos
améis	comáis	viváis
amen	coman	vivan

IMPERFECT

(two forms: **ara, ase**)

([*that*] I [*might*] love)	([*that*] I [*might*] eat)	([*that*] I [*might*] live)
amara(-ase)	comiera(-iese)	viviera(-iese)
amaras(-ases)	comieras(-ieses)	vivieras(-ieses)
amara(-ase)	comiera(-iese)	viviera(-iese)
amáramos(-ásemos)	comiéramos(-iésemos)	viviéramos(-iésemos)
amarais(-aseis)	comierais(-ieseis)	vivierais(-ieseis)
amaran(-asen)	comieran(-iesen)	vivieran(-iesen)

Imperative Mood (Command Forms)

(*love*)	(*eat*)	(*live*)
ama (tú)	come (tú)	vive (tú)
ame (Ud.)	coma (Ud.)	viva (Ud.)
amemos (nosotros)	comamos (nosotros)	vivamos (nosotros)
amad (vosotros)	comed (vosotros)	vivid (vosotros)
amen (Uds.)	coman (Uds.)	vivan (Uds.)

Compound Tenses

PERFECT INFINITIVE

haber amado	haber comido	haber vivido

PERFECT PARTICIPLE

habiendo amado	habiendo comido	habiendo vivido

Indicative Mood

PRESENT PERFECT

(*I have loved*)	(*I have eaten*)	(*I have lived*)
he amado	he comido	he vivido
has amado	has comido	has vivido
ha amado	ha comido	ha vivido
hemos amado	hemos comido	hemos vivido
habéis amado	habéis comido	habéis vivido
han amado	han comido	han vivido

PLUPERFECT

(*I had loved*)	(*I had eaten*)	(*I had lived*)
había amado	había comido	había vivido
habías amado	habías comido	habías vivido
había amado	había comido	había vivido
habíamos amado	habíamos comido	habíamos vivido
habíais amado	habíais comido	habíais vivido
habían amado	habían comido	habían vivido

FUTURE PERFECT

(*I will have loved*)	(*I will have eaten*)	(*I will have lived*)
habré amado	habré comido	habré vivido
habrás amado	habrás comido	habrás vivido
habrá amado	habrá comido	habrá vivido
habremos amado	habremos comido	habremos vivido
habréis amado	habréis comido	habréis vivido
habrán amado	habrán comido	habrán vivido

CONDITIONAL PERFECT

(*I would have loved*)	(*I would have eaten*)	(*I would have lived*)
habría amado	habría comido	habría vivido
habrías amado	habrías comido	habrías vivido
habría amado	habría comido	habría vivido
habríamos amado	habríamos comido	habríamos vivido
habríais amado	habríais comido	habríais vivido
habrían amado	habrían comido	habrían vivido

Subjunctive Mood

PRESENT PERFECT

([*that*] *I* [*may*] *have loved*)	([*that*] *I* [*may*] *have eaten*)	([*that*] *I* [*may*] *have lived*)
haya amado	haya comido	haya vivido
hayas amado	hayas comido	hayas vivido
haya amado	haya comido	haya vivido
hayamos amado	hayamos comido	hayamos vivido
hayáis amado	hayáis comido	hayáis vivido
hayan amado	hayan comido	hayan vivido

PLUPERFECT

(two forms: **-ra, -se**)

([*that*] *I* [*might*] *have loved*)	([*that*] *I* [*might*] *have eaten*)	([*that*] *I* [*might*] *have lived*)
hubiera(-iese) amado	hubiera(-iese) comido	hubiera(-iese) vivido
hubieras(-ieses) amado	hubieras(-ieses) comido	hubieras(-ieses) vivido
hubiera(-iese) amado	hubiera(-iese) comido	hubiera(-iese) vivido
hubiéramos(-iésemos) amado	hubiéramos(-iésemos) comido	hubiéramos(-iésemos) vivido
hubierais(-ieseis) amado	hubierais(-ieseis) comido	hubierais(-ieseis) vivido
hubieran(-iesen) amado	hubieran(-iesen) comido	hubieran(-iesen) vivido

Stem-Changing Verbs

The -ar *and* -er *stem-changing verbs*

Stem-changing verbs are those that have a change in the root of the verb. Verbs that end in **-ar** and **-er** change the stressed vowel **e** to **ie**, and the stressed **o** to **ue**. These changes occur in all persons, except the first- and second-persons plural of the present indicative, present subjunctive, and command.

INFINITIVE	PRESENT INDICATIVE	IMPERATIVE	PRESENT SUBJUNCTIVE
cerrar	cierro	—	cierre
(*to close*)	cierras	cierra	cierres
	cierra	cierre	cierre
	cerramos	cerremos	cerremos
	cerráis	cerrad	cerréis
	cierran	cierren	cierren
perder	pierdo	—	pierda
(*to lose*)	pierdes	pierde	pierdas
	pierde	pierda	pierda
	perdemos	perdamos	perdamos
	perdéis	perded	perdáis
	pierden	pierdan	pierdan
contar	cuento	—	cuente
(*to count,*	cuentas	cuenta	cuentes
to tell)	cuenta	cuente	cuente
	contamos	contemos	contemos
	contáis	contad	contéis
	cuentan	cuenten	cuenten
volver	vuelvo	—	vuelva
(*to return*)	vuelves	vuelve	vuelvas
	vuelve	vuelva	vuelva
	volvemos	volvamos	volvamos
	volvéis	volved	volváis
	vuelven	vuelvan	vuelvan

Verbs that follow the same pattern are:

acertar   to guess right
acordarse   to remember
acostar(se)   to go to bed
almorzar   to have lunch
atravesar   to go through
cegar   to blind
cocer   to cook
colgar   to hang
comenzar   to begin
confesar   to confess
costar   to cost
demostrar   to demonstrate, to show
despertar(se)   to wake up
empezar   to begin
encender   to light, to turn on
encontrar   to find

entender   to understand
llover   to rain
mover   to move
mostrar   to show
negar   to deny
nevar   to snow
pensar   to think, to plan
probar   to prove, to taste
recordar   to remember
resolver   to decide on
rogar   to beg
sentar(se)   to sit down
soler   to be in the habit of
soñar   to dream
tender   to stretch, to unfold
torcer   to twist

The -ir stem-changing verbs

There are two types of stem-changing verbs that end in -ir: one type
changes stressed **e** to **ie** in some tenses and to **i** in others, and stressed
o to **ue** or **u**; the second type always changes stressed **e** to **i** in the
irregular forms of the verb.

Type I **ir:** **e:ie** or **i**
o:ue or **u**

These changes occur as follows:

Present Indicative: all persons except the first and second plural change
e to **ie** and **o** to **ue**. *Preterit:* third person, singular and plural, changes
e to **i** and **o** to **u**. *Present Subjunctive:* all persons change **e** to **ie** and **o**
to **ue**, except the first- and second-persons plural, which change **e** to **i**
and **o** to **u**. *Imperfect Subjunctive:* all persons change **e** to **i** and **o** to **u**.
Imperative: all persons except the second-person plural change **e** to **ie**
and **o** to **ue**; first-person plural changes **e** to **i** and **o** to **u**. *Present
Participle:* changes **e** to **i** and **o** to **u**.

	Indicative		*Imperative*	*Subjunctive*	
INFINITIVE	PRESENT	PRETERIT		PRESENT	IMPERFECT
sentir	siento	sentí	—	sienta	sintiera(-iese)
(to feel)	sientes	sentiste	siente	sientas	sintieras
	siente	sintió	sienta	sienta	sintiera
PRESENT	sentimos	sentimos	sintamos	sintamos	sintiéramos
PARTICIPLE	sentís	sentisteis	sentid	sintáis	sintierais
sintiendo	sienten	sintieron	sientan	sientan	sintieran
dormir	duermo	dormí	—	duerma	durmiera(-iese)
(to sleep)	duermes	dormiste	duerme	duermas	durmieras
	duerme	durmió	duerma	duerma	durmiera
PRESENT	dormimos	dormimos	durmamos	durmamos	durmiéramos
PARTICIPLE	dormís	dormisteis	dormid	durmáis	durmierais
durmiendo	duermen	durmieron	duerman	duerman	durmieran

Other verbs that follow the same pattern are:

advertir   to warn
arrepentir(se)   to repent
consentir   to consent, to
pamper
convertir(se)   to turn into
discernir   to discern
divertir(se)   to amuse
(oneself)

herir   to wound, to hurt
mentir   to lie
morir   to die
preferir   to prefer
referir   to refer
sugerir   to suggest

Type II -ir: e:i

The verbs in this second category are irregular in the same tenses as those of the first type. The only difference is that they only have one change: e:i in all irregular persons.

	Indicative		Imperative	Subjunctive	
INFINITIVE	PRESENT	PRETERIT		PRESENT	IMPERFECT
pedir	pido	pedí	—	pida	pidiera(-iese)
(to ask for,	pides	pediste	pide	pidas	pidieras
request)	pide	pidió	pida	pida	pidiera
PRESENT	pedimos	pedimos	pidamos	pidamos	pidiéramos
PARTICIPLE	pedís	pedisteis	pedid	pidáis	pidierais
pidiendo	piden	pidieron	pidan	pidan	pidieran

Verbs that follow this pattern are:

concebir	to conceive	**reir(se)**	to laugh
competir	to compete	**repetir**	to repeat
despedir(se)	to say goodbye	**reñir**	to fight
elegir	to choose	**seguir**	to follow
impedir	to prevent	**servir**	to serve
perseguir	to pursue	**vestir(se)**	to dress

Orthographic-Changing Verbs

Some verbs undergo a change in the spelling of the stem in certain tenses, in order to maintain the original sound of the final consonant. The most common verbs of this type are those with the consonants **g** and **c**. Remember that **g** and **c** have a soft sound in front of **e** or **i**, and have a hard sound in front of **a**, **o**, or **u**. In order to maintain the soft sound in front of **a**, **o**, and **u**, **g** and **c** change to **j** and **z**, respectively. And in order to maintain the hard sound of **g** and **c** in front of **e** and **i**, **u** is added to the **g** (**gu**) and **c** changes to **qu**.

The following important verbs undergo spelling changes in the tenses listed below:

1. Verbs ending in **-gar** change **g** to **gu** before **e** in the first person of the preterit and in all persons of the present subjunctive.

    pagar *(to pay)*
    Preterit: pagué, pagaste, pagó, etc.
    Pres. Subj.: pague, pagues, pague, paguemos, paguéis, paguen

    Verbs that follow the same pattern: **colgar, llegar, navegar, negar, regar, rogar, jugar.**

2. Verbs ending in **-ger** and **-gir** change **g** to **j** before **o** and **a** in the first person of the present indicative and in all the persons of the present subjunctive.

proteger (*to protect*)
Pres. Ind.:   protejo, proteges, protege, etc.
Pres. Subj.: proteja, protejas, proteja, protejamos, protejáis, protejan

Verbs that follow the same pattern: **coger, dirigir, elegir, escoger, exigir, recoger, corregir.**

3. Verbs ending in **-guar** change **gu** to **gü** before **e** in the first person of the preterit and in all persons of the present subjunctive.

averiguar (*to find out*)
Preterit: averigüé, averiguaste, averiguó, etc.
Pres. Subj.: averigüe, averigües, averigüe, averigüemos, averigüéis, averigüen

The verb **apaciguar** follows the same pattern.

4. Verbs ending in **-guir** change **gu** to **g** before **o** and **a** in the first person of the present indicative and in all persons of the present subjunctive.

conseguir (*to get*)
Pres. Ind.:   consigo, consigues, consigue, etc.
Pres. Subj.: consiga, consigas, consiga, consigamos, consigáis, consigan

Verbs that follow the same pattern: **distinguir, perseguir, proseguir, seguir.**

5. Verbs ending in **-car** change **c** to **qu** before **e** in the first person of the preterit and in all persons of the present subjunctive.

tocar (*to touch, to play* [*a musical instrument*])
Preterit: toqué, tocaste, tocó, etc.
Pres. Subj.: toque, toques, toque, toquemos, toquéis, toquen

Verbs that follow the same pattern: **atacar, buscar, comunicar, explicar, indicar, sacar, pescar.**

6. Verbs ending in **-cer** and **-cir** preceded by a consonant change **c** to **z** before **o** and **a** in the first person of the present indicative and in all persons of the present subjunctive.

torcer (*to twist*)
Pres. Ind.:   tuerzo, tuerces, tuerce, etc.
Pres. Subj.: tuerza, tuerzas, tuerza, torzamos, torzáis, tuerzan

Verbs that follow the same pattern: **convencer, esparcir, vencer.**

7. Verbs ending in -**cer** and -**cir** preceded by a vowel change **c** to **zc** before **o** and **a** in the first person of the present indicative and in all persons of the present subjunctive.

conocer (*to know, to be acquainted with*)
Pres. Ind.:   conozco, conoces, conoce, etc.
Pres. Subj.: conozca, conozcas, conozca, conozcamos, conozcáis,
         conozcan.

Verbs that follow the same pattern: **agradecer, aparecer, carecer, establecer, entristecer, lucir, nacer, obedecer, ofrecer, padecer, parecer, pertenecer, relucir, reconocer.**

8. Verbs ending in -**zar** change **z** to **c** before **e** in the first person of the preterit and in all persons of the present subjunctive.

rezar (*to pray*)
Preterit: recé, rezaste, rezó, etc.
Pres. Subj.: rece, reces, rece, recemos, recéis, recen

Verbs that follow the same pattern: **alcanzar, almorzar, comenzar, cruzar, empezar, forzar, gozar, abrazar.**

9. Verbs ending in -**eer** change the unstressed **i** to **y** between vowels in the third-person singular and plural of the preterit, in all persons of the imperfect subjunctive, and in the present participle.

creer (*to believe*)
Preterit: creí, creíste, creyó, creímos, creísteis, creyeron
Imp. Subj.: creyera, creyeras, creyera, creyéramos, creyerais,
         creyeran
Pres. Part.: creyendo

Leer and **poseer** follow the same pattern.

10. Verbs ending in -**uir** change the unstressed **i** to **y** between vowels (except -**quir**, which has the silent **u**) in the following tenses and persons:

huir (*to escape, to flee*)
Pres. Part.: huyendo
Pres. Ind.: huyo, huyes, huye, huimos, huís, huyen
Preterit: huí, huiste, huyó, huimos, huisteis, huyeron
Imperative: huye, huya, huyamos, huid, huyan
Pres. Subj.: huya, huyas, huya, huyamos, huyáis, huyan
Imp. Subj.: huyera(ese), huyeras, huyera, huyéramos, huyerais,
         huyeran

Verbs that follow the same pattern: **atribuir, concluir, constituir, construir, contribuir, destituir, destruir, disminuir, distribuir, excluir, incluir, influir, instruir, restituir, sustituir.**

11. Verbs ending in **-eír** lose one **e** in the third-person singular and plural of the preterit, in all persons of the imperfect subjunctive, and in the present participle.

reír(se) (*to laugh*)
Preterit: reí, reíste, rió, reímos, reísteis, rieron
Imp. Subj.: riera(ese), rieras, riera, rieramos, rierais, rieran
Pres. Part.: riendo

Sonreír and **freír** follow the same pattern.

12. Verbs ending in **-iar** add a written accent to the **i**, except in the first- and second-persons plural of the present indicative and subjunctive.

fiar(se) (*to trust*)
Pres. Ind.: fío, fías, fía, fiamos, fiais, fían
Pres. Subj.: fíe, fíes, fíe, fiemos, fiéis, fíen

Verbs that follow the same pattern: **ampliar, criar, desviar, enfriar, enviar, guiar, telegrafiar, vaciar, variar.**

13. Verbs ending in **-uar** (except **-guar**) add a written accent to the **u**, except in the first- and second-persons plural of the present indicative and subjunctive.

actuar (*to act*)
Pres. Ind.: actúo, actúas, actúa, actuamos, actuáis, actúan
Pres. Subj.: actúe, actúes, actúe, actuemos, actuéis, actúen

Verbs that follow the same pattern: **continuar, acentuar, efectuar, exceptuar, graduar, habituar, insinuar, situar.**

14. Verbs ending in **-ñir** remove the **i** of the diphthongs **ie** and **ió** in the third-person singular and plural of the preterit and in all persons of the imperfect subjunctive. They also change the **e** of the stem to **i** in the same persons.

teñir (*to dye*)
Preterit: teñí, teñiste, **tiñó,** teñimos, teñisteis, **tiñeron**
Imp. Subj.: tiñera(ese), tiñeras, tiñera, tiñéramos, tiñerais, tiñeran

Verbs that follow the same pattern: **ceñir, constreñir, desteñir, estreñir, reñir.**

Some Common Irregular Verbs

Only those tenses with irregular forms are given below.

adquirir (*to acquire*)
Pres. Ind.: adquiero, adquieres, adquiere, adquirimos, adquirís, adquieren
Pres. Subj.: adquiera, adquieras, adquiera, adquiramos, adquiráis, adquieran
Imperative: adquiere, adquiera, adquiramos, adquirid, adquieran

andar (*to walk*)
Preterit: anduve, anduviste, anduvo, anduvimos, anduvisteis,
                anduvieron
Imp. Subj.:   anduviera (anduviese), anduvieras, anduviera,
                anduviéramos, anduvierais, anduvieran

avergonzarse (*to be ashamed, to be embarrassed*)
Pres. Ind.:   me avergüenzo, te avergüenzas, se avergüenza, nos
                avergonzamos, os avergonzáis, se avergüenzan
Pres. Subj.: me avergüence, te avergüences, se avergüence, nos
                avergoncemos, os avergoncéis, se avergüencen
Imperative: avergüénzate, avergüéncese, avergoncémonos,
                avergonzaos, avergüénzense

caber (*to fit, to have enough room*)
Pres. Ind.:   quepo, cabes, cabe, cabemos, cabéis, caben
Preterit: cupe, cupiste, cupo, cupimos, cupisteis, cupieron
Future: cabré, cabrás, cabrá, cabremos, cabréis, cabrán
Conditional: cabría, cabrías, cabría, cabríamos, cabríais, cabrían
Imperative: cabe, quepa, quepamos, cabed, quepan
Pres. Subj.:   quepa, quepas, quepa, quepamos, quepáis, quepan
Imp. Subj.:   cupiera (cupiese), cupieras, cupiera, cupiéramos, cupierais,
                cupieran

caer (*to fall*)
Pres. Ind.:   caigo, caes, cae, caemos, caéis, caen
Preterit: caí, caíste, cayó, caímos, caísteis, cayeron
Imperative: cae, caiga, caigamos, caed, caigan
Pres. Subj.:   caiga, caigas, caiga, caigamos, caigáis, caigan
Imp. Subj.:   cayera (cayese), cayeras, cayera, cayéramos, cayerais,
                cayeran
Past Part.:   caído

conducir (*to guide, to drive*)
Pres. Ind.:   conduzco, conduces, conduce, conducimos, conducis,
                conducen
Preterit: conduje, condujiste, condujo, condujimos, condujisteis,
                condujeron
Imperative: conduce, conduzca, conduzcamos, conducid, conduzcan
Pres. Subj.: conduzca, conduzcas, conduzca, conduzcamos, conduzcáis,
                conduzcan
Imp. Subj.:   condujera (condujese), condujeras, condujera,
                condujéramos, condujerais, condujeran

                (All verbs ending in **-ducir** follow this pattern.)

convenir (*to agree*) See **venir**.

dar (*to give*)
Pres. Ind.:   doy, das, da, damos, dais, dan
Preterit: di, diste, dio, dimos, disteis, dieron

Imperative: da, dé, demos, dad, den
Pres. Subj.: dé, des, dé, demos, deis, den
Imp. Subj.: diera (diese), dieras, diera, diéramos, dierais, dieran

decir (*to say, to tell*)
Pres. Ind.: digo, dices, dice, decimos, decís, dicen
Preterit: dije, dijiste, dijo, dijimos, dijisteis, dijeron
Future: diré, dirás, dirá, diremos, diréis, dirán
Conditional: diría, dirías, diría, diríamos, diríais, dirían
Imperative: di, diga, digamos, decid, digan
Pres. Subj.: diga, digas, diga, digamos, digáis, digan
Imp. Subj.: dijera (dijese), dijeras, dijera, dijéramos, dijerais, dijeran
Pres. Part.: diciendo
Past. Part.: dicho

detener (*to stop, to hold, to arrest*) See **tener.**

entretener (*to entertain, to amuse*) See **tener.**

errar (*to err, to miss*)
Pres. Ind.: yerro, yerras, yerra, erramos, erráis, yerran
Imperative: yerra, yerre, erremos, errad, yerren
Pres. Subj.: yerre, yerres, yerre, erremos, erréis, yerren

estar (*to be*)
Pres. Ind.: estoy, estás, está, estamos, estáis, están
Preterit: estuve, estuviste, estuvo, estuvimos, estuvisteis,
estuvieron
Imperative: está, esté, estemos, estad, estén
Pres. Subj.: esté, estés, esté, estemos, estéis, estén
Imp. Subj.: estuviera (estuviese), estuvieras, estuviera, estuviéramos,
estuvierais, estuvieran

haber (*to have*)
Pres. Ind.: he, has, ha, hemos, habéis, han
Preterit: hube, hubiste, hubo, hubimos, hubisteis, hubieron
Future: habré, habrás, habrá, habremos, habréis, habrán
Conditional: habría, habrías, habría, habríamos, habríais, habrían
Imperative: he, haya, hayamos, habed, hayan
Pres. Subj.: haya, hayas, haya, hayamos, hayáis, hayan
Imp. Subj.: hubiera (hubiese), hubieras, hubiera, hubiéramos,
hubierais, hubieran

hacer (*to do, to make*)
Pres. Ind.: hago, haces, hace, hacemos, hacéis, hacen
Preterit: hice, hiciste, hizo, hicimos, hicisteis, hicieron
Future: haré, harás, hará, haremos, haréis, harán
Conditional: haría, harías, haría, haríamos, haríais, harían
Imperative: haz, haga, hagamos, haced, hagan
Pres. Subj.: haga, hagas, haga, hagamos, hagáis, hagan

Imp. Subj.: hiciera (hiciese), hicieras, hiciera, hiciéramos, hicierais, hicieran
Past Part.: hecho

imponer *(to impose, to deposit)* See **poner.**

introducir *(to introduce, to insert, to gain access)* See **conducir.**

ir *(to go)*
Pres. Ind.:   voy, vas, va, vamos, vais, van
Imp. Ind.:   iba, ibas, iba, íbamos, ibais, iban
Preterit: fui, fuiste, fue, fuimos, fuisteis, fueron
Imperative: ve, vaya, vayamos, id, vayan
Pres. Subj.: vaya, vayas, vaya, vayamos, vayáis, vayan
Imp. Subj.:   fuera (fuese), fueras, fuera, fuéramos, fuerais, fueran

jugar *(to play)*
Pres. Ind.:   juego, juegas, juega, jugamos, jugáis, juegan
Imperative: juega, juegue, juguemos, jugad, jueguen
Pres. Subj.: juegue, juegues, juegue, juguemos, juguéis, jueguen

obtener *(to obtain)* See **tener.**

oír *(to hear)*
Pres. Ind.:   oigo, oyes, oye, oímos, oís, oyen
Preterit: oí, oíste, oyó, oímos, oísteis, oyeron
Imperative: oye, oiga, oigamos, oid, oigan
Pres. Subj.: oiga, oigas, oiga, oigamos, oigáis, oigan
Imp. Subj.:   oyera (oyese), oyeras, oyera, oyéramos, oyerais, oyeran
Pres. Part.: oyendo
Past Part.:   oído

oler *(to smell)*
Pres. Ind.:   huelo, hueles, huele, olemos, oléis, huelen
Imperative: huele, huela, olamos, oled, huelan
Pres. Subj.: huela, huelas, huela, olamos, oláis, huelan

poder *(to be able)*
Pres. Ind.:   puedo, puedes, puede, podemos, podéis, pueden
Preterit: pude, pudiste, pudo, pudimos, pudisteis, pudieron
Future: podré, podrás, podrá, podremos, podréis, podrán
Conditional: podría, podrías, podría, podríamos, podríais, podrían
Imperative: puede, pueda, podamos, poded, puedan
Pres. Subj.: pueda, puedas, pueda, podamos, podáis, puedan
Imp. Subj.:   pudiera (pudiese), pudieras, pudiera, pudiéramos, pudierais, pudieran
Pres. Part.: pudiendo

poner *(to place, to put)*
Pres. Ind.:   pongo, pones, pone, ponemos, ponéis, ponen

Preterit: puse, pusiste, puso, pusimos, pusisteis, pusieron
Future: pondré, pondrás, pondrá, pondremos, pondréis, pondrán
Conditional: pondría, pondrías, pondría, pondríamos, pondríais,
                 pondrían
Imperative: pon, ponga, pongamos, poned, pongan
Pres. Subj.: ponga, pongas, ponga, pongamos, pongáis, pongan
Imp. Subj.:   pusiera (pusiese), pusieras, pusiera, pusiéramos, pusierais,
                 pusieran
Past. Part.: puesto

querer (*to want, to wish, to like*)
Pres. Ind.:   quiero, quieres, quiere, queremos, queréis, quieren
Preterit: quise, quisiste, quiso, quisimos, quisisteis, quisieron
Future: querré, querrás, querrá, querremos, querréis, querrán
Conditional: querría, querrías, querría, querríamos, querríais, querrían
Imperative: quiere, quiera, queramos, quered, quieran
Pres. Subj.: quiera, quieras, quiera, queramos, queráis, quieran
Imp. Subj.:   quisiera (quisiese), quisieras, quisiera, quisiéramos,
                 quisierais, quisieran

resolver (*to decide on*)
Past Part.:   resuelto

saber (*to know*)
Pres. Ind.:   sé, sabes, sabe, sabemos, sabéis, saben
Preterit: supe, supiste, supo, supimos, supisteis, supieron
Future: sabré, sabrás, sabrá, sabremos, sabréis, sabrán
Conditional: sabría, sabrías, sabría, sabríamos, sabríais, sabrían
Imperative: sabe, sepa, sepamos, sabed, sepan
Pres. Subj.: sepa, sepas, sepa, sepamos, sepáis, sepan
Imp. Subj.:   supiera (supiese), supieras, supiera, supiéramos, supierais,
                 supieran

salir (*to leave, to go out*)
Pres. Ind.:   salgo, sales, sale, salimos, salís, salen
Future: saldré, saldrás, saldrá, saldremos, saldréis, saldrán
Conditional: saldría, saldrías, saldría, saldríamos, saldríais, saldrían
Imperative: sal, salga, salgamos, salid, salgan
Pres. Subj.: salga, salgas, salga, salgamos, salgáis, salgan

ser (*to be*)
Pres. Ind.:   soy, eres, es, somos, sois, son
Imp. Ind.:   era, eras, era, éramos, erais, eran
Preterit: fui, fuiste, fue, fuimos, fuisteis, fueron
Imperative: sé, sea, seamos, sed, sean
Pres. Subj.: sea, seas, sea, seamos, seáis, sean
Imp. Subj.:   fuera (fuese), fueras, fuera, fuéramos, fuerais, fueran

suponer (*to assume*) See **poner.**

tener (*to have*)
Pres. Ind.:   tengo, tienes, tiene, tenemos, tenéis, tienen
Preterit: tuve, tuviste, tuvo, tuvimos, tuvisteis, tuvieron
Future: tendré, tendrás, tendrá, tendremos, tendréis, tendrán
Conditional: tendría, tendrías, tendría, tendríamos, tendríais, tendrían
Imperative: ten, tenga, tengamos, tened, tengan
Pres. Subj.:   tenga, tengas, tenga, tengamos, tengáis, tengan
Imp. Subj.:   tuviera (tuviese), tuvieras, tuviera, tuviéramos, tuvierais,
                tuvieran

traducir (*to translate*)
Pres. Ind.:   traduzco, traduces, traduce, traducimos, traducís, traducen
Preterit: traduje, tradujiste, tradujo, tradujimos, tradujisteis,
                tradujeron
Imperative: traduce, traduzca, tradúzcamos, traducid, traduzcan
Pres. Subj.:   traduzca, traduzcas, traduzca, traduzcamos, traduzcáis,
                traduzcan
Imp. Subj.:   tradujera (tradujese), tradujeras, tradujera, tradujeramos,
                tradujerais, tradujeran

traer (*to bring*)
Pres. Ind.:   traigo, traes, trae, traemos, traéis, traen
Preterit: traje, trajiste, trajo, trajimos, trajisteis, trajeron
Imperative: trae, traiga, traigamos, traed, traigan
Pres. Subj.:   traiga, traigas, traiga, traigamos, traigáis, traigan
Imp. Subj.:   trajera (trajese), trajeras, trajera, trajéramos, trajerais,
                trajeran
Pres. Part.:   trayendo
Past Part.:   traído

valer (*to be worth*)
Pres. Ind.:   valgo, vales, vale, valemos, valéis, valen
Future: valdré, valdrás, valdrá, valdremos, valdréis, valdrán
Conditional: valdría, valdrías, valdría, valdríamos, valdríais, valdrían
Imperative: vale, valga, valgamos, valed, valgan
Pres. Subj.:   valga, valgas, valga, valgamos, valgáis, valgan

venir (*to come*)
Pres. Ind.:   vengo, vienes, viene, venimos, venís, vienen
Preterit: vine, viniste, vino, vinimos, vinisteis, vinieron
Future: vendré, vendrás, vendrá, vendremos, vendréis, vendrán
Conditional: vendría, vendrías, vendría, vendríamos, vendríais,
                vendrían
Imperative: ven, venga, vengamos, venid, vengan
Pres. Subj.:   venga, vengas, venga, vengamos, vengáis, vengan
Imp. Subj.:   viniera (viniese), vinieras, viniera, viniéramos, vinierais,
                vinieran
Pres. Part.:   viniendo

ver (*to see*)
Pres. Ind.:   veo, ves, ve, vemos, veis, ven
Imp. Ind.:   veía, veías, veía, veíamos, veíais, veían
Preterit: vi, viste, vio, vimos, visteis, vieron
Imperative: ve, vea, veamos, ved, vean
Pres. Subj.:   vea, veas, vea, veamos, veáis, vean
Imp. Subj.:   viera (viese), vieras, viera, viéramos, vierais, vieran
Past. Part.:   visto

volver (*to return*)
Past Part.:   vuelto

Appendix C

Careers and Occupations

accountant **contador**
actor **actor**
actress **actriz**
administrator **administrador**
agent **agente**
architect **arquitecto**
artist **artista**
baker **panadero**
bank officer **empleado bancario**
bank teller **cajero**
banker **banquero**
barber **barbero**
bartender **barman, cantinero**
bill collector **cobrador**
bookkeeper **tenedor de libros**
brickmason (bricklayer) **albañil**
buyer **comprador**
cameraman **camarógrafo**
carpenter **carpintero**
cashier **cajero**
chiropractor **quiropráctico**
clerk **dependiente** (*store*), **oficinista** (*office*)
computer operator **computista**
contractor **contratista**
construction worker **obrero de la construcción**
constructor **constructor**
cook **cocinero**
copilot **copiloto**
counselor **consejero**
craftsman **artesano**
dancer **bailarín**
decorator **decorador**

dental hygienist **higienista dental**
dentist **dentista**
designer **diseñador**
detective **detective**
dietician **especialista en dietética**
diplomat **diplomático**
director **director**
dockworker **obrero portuario**
doctor **doctor, médico**
draftsman **dibujante**
dressmaker **modista**
driver **conductor**
economist **economista**
editor **editor**
electrician **electricista**
engineer **ingeniero**
engineering technician **ingeniero técnico**
eye doctor **oculista**
farmer **agricultor**
fashion designer **diseñador de alta costura, modisto**
fireman **bombero**
fisherman **pescador**
flight attendant **auxiliar de vuelo, azafata**
foreman **capataz, encargado**
funeral director **empresario de pompas fúnebres**
garbage collector **basurero**
gardener **jardinero**
guard **guardia**
guide **guía**
hairdresser **peluquero**
home economist **economista doméstico**

housekeeper **ama de llaves**
inspector **inspector**
instructor **instructor**
insurance agent **agente de seguros**
interior designer **diseñador de interiores**
interpreter **intérprete**
investigator **investigador**
janitor **conserje**
jeweler **joyero**
journalist **periodista**
judge **juez**
lawyer **abogado**
librarian **bibliotecario**
machinist **maquinista**
maid **criada**
mail carrier **cartero**
manager **gerente**
meat cutter **carnicero**
mechanic **mecánico**
midwife **comadrona, partera**
military **militar**
miner **minero**
model **modelo**
musician **músico**
night watchman **sereno, guardián**
nurse **enfermero**
optician **óptico**
optometrist **optometrista**
painter **pintor**
paramedic **paramédico**
pharmacist **farmacéutico**
photographer **fotógrafo**
physical therapist **terapista físico**
physician **médico**
pilot **piloto, aviador**
plumber **plomero**
policeman **policia**
printer **impresor**
psychologist **psicólogo**
public relations agent **agente de relaciones públicas**
real estate agent **agente de bienes raíces**
receptionist **recepcionista**
reporter **reportero, periodista**
sailor **marinero**
salesman **vendedor**
scientist **científico**
seamstress **costurera, modista**
secretary **secretario**
social worker **trabajador social**
sociologist **sociólogo**
stenographer **estenógrafo**
stewardess **azafata, auxiliar de vuelo**
stockbroker **bolsista**
student **estudiante**
supervisor **supervisor**
surgeon **cirujano**
systems analyst **analista de sistemas**
tailor **sastre**
taxi driver **chofer de taxi, conductor**
teacher **maestro** (*elem. school*), **profesor** (*high school and college*)
technician **técnico**
telephone operator **telefonista**
therapist **terapista**
television and radio technician **técnico de radio y televisión**
television and radio announcer **locutor**
teller **cajero**
travel agent **agente de viajes**
traveling salesman **viajante de comercio**

truck driver   **camionero**
typist   **mecanógrafa,
dactilógrafa**
undertaker   **director de
pompas fúnebres**
veterinarian   **veterinario**

waiter   **mozo, camarero**
waitress   **camarera**
watchmaker   **relojero**
watchman   **sereno, guardián**
worker   **obrero**
writer   **escritor**

Appendix D

Lección 1

A. 1. nosotros / nosotras   2. ellos   3. ellas   4. ustedes
5. ellos   6. nosotros / nosotras

B. 1. desean   2. necesitamos   3. estudias   4. tomo
5. trabaja

C. 1. ¿(Ella) necesita las cucharas? / No, (ella) no necesita las cucharas; necesita los tenedores.   2. ¿Hablan (Uds.) italiano? / No, (nosotros) no hablamos italiano; hablamos español.   3. ¿El señor Vega trabaja en Lima? / No, (él) no trabaja en Lima; trabaja en Santiago.

D. 1. trescientos cuarenta y uno   2. setecientos ochenta y tres   3. mil   4. quinientos setenta y cinco   5. cuatrocientos sesenta y siete   6. ochocientos noventa y seis

E. 1. servilletas   2. inglés; italiano; francés   3. tenedor
4. restaurante   5. toma; refresco   6. estudian; universidad

Lección 2

A. 1. (Nosotros) necesitamos las sillas blancas y la mesa negra.   2. (Yo) necesito dos lápices rojos.   3. (Yo) estudio con dos chicas (muchachas) muy inteligentes.   4. ¿Necesita (Ud.) las carpetas azules, señorita Vega?

B. 1. bebo; beben   2. leemos; escribimos   3. comes
4. reciben   5. vivo; vive

C. 1. (Yo) deseo visitar a la señorita Arévalo.   2. ¿(Ud.) llama / (Tú) llamas a María?   3. Los estudiantes visitan el museo.

D. 1. bebes; té   2. comemos   3. vivo   4. pluma
5. comprendo   6. quién   7. visitan   8. ómnibus   9. lápiz

Lección 3

A. 1. es   2. eres   3. somos; es   4. son   5. soy; es

B. 1. Carlos es el hijo de María Iriarte.   2. El primo / La prima de Ana es de Colombia.   3. El apellido de la chica / muchacha es Torres.   4. (Ella) necesita el número de teléfono de la señora Madera.   5. La casa de David es verde.

C. 1. ¿(Ud.) necesita / (Tú) necesitas la dirección de él o la dirección de ella?   2. La señorita Vega es nuestra amiga.
3. (Yo) necesito mis cuadernos.   4. ¿(Ud.) necesita hablar con sus hijos, señor Verela?   5. ¿Deseas tus lápices negros, Paquito?

D. 1. da; damos   2. vas; van   3. estoy; están   4. vamos
5. estás

E. 1. es; está   2. somos   3. es; es   4. es   5. estoy
6. son   7. es; es   8. estás

F. 1. argentino(a)   2. abuelo   3. Estados   4. profesión
5. amiga   6. cuaderno   7. dónde   8. quién   9. Cómo
10. difícil

Lección 4

A. 1. (Yo) necesito el número de teléfono del señor Soto.
2. (Ella) va a la universidad los viernes.   3. (Yo) llamo al gerente los martes.   4. (Ella) es la hija del señor Miranda.
5. (Nosotros) vamos al mercado los sábados.

B. 1. (Ella) es tan alta como mi hijo.   2. El Hotel Azteca es el más caro de la ciudad. ¡(Él) es el mejor!   3. ¿(Ella) es menor o menor que David?   4. Colombia es más pequeño que los Estados Unidos.   5. (Yo) tengo poco dinero, pero (él) tiene menos dinero que yo.   6. (Nosotros) estamos tan cansados como tú / Ud., Anita.

C. 1. tiene; tienes   2. vengo; tengo   3. tenemos
4. tienen; venimos   5. vienes

D. 1. (Yo) no tengo hambre, pero tengo mucha sed.
2. Darío tiene diecinueve años. ¿Cuántos años tienes (tú), Paquito?   3. ¿Tiene (Ud.) prisa, señorita Perales?   4. ¿(Tú) tienes frío, Papá? ¡(Yo) tengo calor!   5. (Nosotros) tenemos mucho sueño.   6. ¡(Ud.) tiene razón, señora Vega! Paquito tiene mucho miedo.

E. 1. barato 2. pensión 3. pequeño / pequeña 4. menor
5. mejor 6. piscina 7. cuántos 8. hambre 9. sed
10. frío

Lección 5

A. 1. a las siete y media de la mañana 2. por la tarde
3. a las nueve y cuarto de la noche 4. las siete menos
veinticinco 5. la una

B. 1. quieres; prefiero 2. cierra; empieza 3. entienden;
entendemos

C. *(Possibilities; answers may vary.):* 1. Tú vas a leer el
libro. 2. Nosotros vamos a comer los sándwiches. 3. Ellos van
a estudiar la lección dos. 4. Yo voy a tomar / beber café.
5. Ella va a estudiar francés.

D. 1. ¿Cuántos estudiantes hay en la clase? 2. No hay
reunión mañana. 3. Hay un vuelo a Caracas a las siete y media.
4. Hay cinco teatros en la ciudad.

E. 1. tercer 2. primero 3. quinta; sexta 4. octavo
5. séptima

F. 1. desayunamos 2. revista 3. cuánto 4. noche
5. prefieres 6. entiendes 7. vuelos 8. piso 9. reunión /
junta 10. qué

Lección 6

A. 1. Hoy es miércoles. 2. Las mujeres quieren igualdad
con los hombres. 3. La educación es importante.
4. (Nosotros) vamos a la cárcel la semana próxima. 5. (Yo) no
tengo clases los viernes.

B. *(Possibilities; answers may vary.):* 1. (Yo) vuelvo a mi
casa a las cinco y media. 2. Cuando (nosotros) vamos a México,
volamos. 3. Sí, (nosotros) recordamos los verbos irregulares.
4. (Yo) duermo ocho horas. 5. No, (nosotros) no podemos ir a
la iglesia hoy.

C. 1. Ellos recuerdan algo. 2. Hay alguien en la escuela.
3. Yo quiero volar también. 4. Recibimos algunos regalos.
5. Siempre tiene éxito.

D. 1. Para tener éxito, hay que trabajar. 2. (Ud.) tiene
que volver la semana próxima, señor Vega. 3. (Ella) tiene que
trabajar mañana. 4. Hay que comenzar temprano.
5. ¿(Nosotros) tenemos que empezar a los ocho?

E. 1. ¿(Ud.) puede / (Tú) puedes venir conmigo?   2. ¿(Ud.) va / (Tú) vas a trabajar con ellos?   3. El dinero es para ti, Anita. 4. El regalo no es para mí. Es para ella.   5. No, Paco, (yo) no puedo ir contigo.

F. 1. agencia de viajes   2. iglesia   3. educación   4. viene 5. ida; vuelta   6. éxito   7. duerme   8. próxima

Lección 7

A. *(Possibilities; answers may vary.):* 1. (Nosotros) servimos sopa.   2. (Yo) pido Coca-Cola para beber.   3. No, (yo) no digo mi edad.   4. Sí, (yo) sigo en la universidad.   5. Sí, (nosotros) siempre pedimos postre.

B. 1. conduzco   2. salgo   3. pongo   4. traduzco 5. conozco   6. traigo   7. hago   8. veo   9. sé

C. 1. (Yo) conozco a su hijo.   2. (Él) no sabe francés. 3. ¿Sabe (Ud.) nadar, señorita Vera?   4. ¿Conoce (Ud.) al instructor?   5. ¿Conocen los estudiantes las novelas de Cervantes?

D. *(Possibilities; answers may vary.):* 1. En los Estados Unidos se habla inglés.   2. Se dice *a menudo / muchas veces*. 3. La librería se cierra a las diez.   4. Mi apellido se escribe S-M-I-T-H.   5. Las oficinas se abren a las diez.

E. 1. Yo las conozco. 2. Uds. van a comprarlo. 3. Nosotros no queremos verte.   4. Ella la sirve.   5. ¿Ud. no me conoce?   6. Él los escribe.   7. Carlos va a visitarnos. 8. Nosotros no lo vemos.

F. 1. coche   2. llevar   3. memoria   4. sábanas   5. vez 6. todos   7. poema   8. muchas veces

Lección 8

A. 1. (Yo) necesito estas pelotas y aquéllas.   2. ¿Quiere (Ud.) este cuaderno o ése?   3. (Yo) prefiero estos periódicos, no aquéllos.   4. Papá, ¿quieres (tú) comprar esta raqueta o ésa? 5. (Yo) no quiero comer en este restaurante. (Yo) prefiero aquél. 6. (Yo) no entiendo eso.

B. 1. está estudiando   2. está comiendo   3. estamos leyendo   4. estás diciendo   5. estoy bebiendo.

C. 1. Me va a comprar unos patines.   2. Le doy el diario. 3. Nos habla en español.   4. Les voy a decir la verdad.   5. Les pregunto la dirección de la oficina.   6. Le estamos escribiendo a nuestro padre.   7. Le escribo los lunes.   8. Le doy la información al presidente. 9. Te hablo en inglés. 10. No me compran nada.

D. 1. ¿El dinero? (Yo) se lo doy mañana, señor Peña.
2. (Yo) sé que necesitas un diccionario, Anita, pero (yo) no puedo prestártelo. 3. (Yo) necesito mi mochila. ¿ Puede (Ud.) traérmelo, señorita López? 4. ¿Las plumas? (Ella) nos las trae.
5. Cuando (yo) necesito patines, mi mamá me los compra.

E. 1. (Yo) voy a preguntarle dónde vive. 2. (Yo) siempre le pido dinero a mi esposo. 3. (Ella) siempre pregunta cómo está usted, señora Nieto. 4. (Ellos) me van a pedir los libros de español. 5. (Yo) quiero preguntarle cuántos años tiene (él).

F. 1. deportiva 2. quién 3. pelota; raqueta 4. hijos
5. periódico 6. tío 7. comida 8. parque

Lección 9

A. 1. No, no son mías. 2. No, no son de ella. 3. No, no es mío. 4. No, no es nuestra. 5. No, no es de ellos. 6. No, no son míos. 7. No, no es nuestra. 8. No, no es de ustedes.

B. 1. (Yo) me levanto a las siete, me baño, me visto y salgo a las siete y media. 2. ¿A qué hora se despiertan los niños?
3. (Ella) no quiere sentarse. 4. (Él) se afeita todos los días.
5. ¿(Tú) te acuerdas de tus maestros, Carlitos? 6. (Ellos / Ellas) siempre se están quejando. 7. Primero (ella) acuesta a los niños, y entonces (ella) se acuesta. 8. ¿Quiere (Ud.) probarse estos pantalones, señorita? 9. ¿Dónde van a poner (Uds.) el dinero, señoras? 10. Los estudiantes siempre se duermen en esta clase.

C. 1. Abra 2. Hablen 3. Traiga 4. Vengan 5. Cierre
6. Doblen 7. Siga 8. Den 9. Estén 10. Sean 11. Vaya
12. Vuelva 13. Sirva 14. Pongan 15. Escriban

D. 1. Dígales la verdad, señor Mena. 2. ¿El postre? No me lo traiga ahora, señorita Ruiz. 3. No se lo diga a mi vecino(a), por favor. 4. Traigan las bebidas, señores. Tráiganlas a la terraza. 5. No se levante, señora Miño. 6. ¿El té? Tráigaselo a las cuatro de la tarde, señor Vargas.

E. 1. cintas 2. diversiones 3. tintorería 4. tarjeta de crédito 5. izquierda 6. bebidas 7. acostar 8. derecho

Lección 10

A. 1. Ayer ella entró en la cafetería y comió una ensalada.
2. Ayer María le escribió a su suegra. 3. El viernes pasado ella me prestó su abrigo. 4. El año pasado ellos fueron los mejores

estudiantes.   5. El sábado pasado ellos te esperaron cerca del cine.   6. El verano pasado mi hijo fue a Buenos Aires.   7. Ayer por la mañana le di el impermeable.   8. El lunes pasado nosotros decidimos comprar la aspiradora.   9. Anoche le pregunté la hora.   10. Anoche tú no pagaste por el queso. 11. El jueves pasado fuimos los primeros.   12. Ayer me dieron muchos problemas.   13. Anoche mi suegro no bebió café. 14. Ayer yo no fui a esquiar.   15. La semana pasada te dimos el suéter.

B. 1. El ladrón entró por la ventana.   2. (Ella) pasó por mi casa.   3. (Ella) no vino por la lluvia.   4. Hay vuelos para México los sábados.   5. (Nosotros) vamos por avión.   6. El límite de velocidad es cincuenta y cinco millas por hora.   7. (Yo) necesito la lección de economía para mañana.   8. ¿Para quién es el paraguas?   9. (Yo) necesito el dinero para pagar el impermeable.   10. (Ella) pagó doscientos dólares por ese aspiradora.

C. 1. Hace mucho viento hoy.   2. Hace mucho frío, y también nieva / está nevando.   3. Hace mucho calor en Cuba. 4. ¿Qué tiempo hace hoy?   5. ¿Hace sol o está nublado? 6. No hay vuelos por la niebla.

D. 1. abrigo / suéter   2. límite   3. impermeable   4. uvas 5. escoba   6. plancha   7. cocinera   8. tiempo

Lección 11

A. 1. ¿Cuánto tiempo hace que (Uds.) trabajan en San Juan? 2. Hace cinco años que (nosotros) trabajamos en San Juan. 3. ¿Cuánto tiempo hace que (ellos) esperan?   4. Hace tres horas que (ellos) esperan.   5. ¿Cuánto tiempo hace que (ella) estudia español?   6. Hace dos años que (ella) estudia español.

B. 1. Ayer María estuvo en la tienda.   2. Anoche no pudieron venir.   3. El mes pasado puse el dinero en el banco. 4. El domingo pasado no hiciste nada.   5. Ayer ella vino con Juan.   6. El lunes pasado no quisimos venir a clase.   7. Anoche yo no dije nada.   8. Ayer trajimos la aspiradora.   9. Anoche yo conduje mi coche.   10. Ayer ellos tradujeron las lecciones.

C. 1. Vivíamos en Alaska.   2. Hablaba inglés.   3. Veía a mi abuela.   4. Depositábamos el dinero en el Banco de América.   5. Se acostaban a las nueve.   6. Iba a la zapatería. 7. Compraba pollo.   8. Gastábamos nuestro dinero en libros.

D. 1. Ven acá, por favor.   2. Habla con la maestra. 3. Dime tu dirección.   4. Lávate las manos.   5. Ponte el abrigo.   6. Tráenos la limonada.   7. Termina el trabajo.

8. Hazme un favor.   9. Apaga la luz.   10. Ve de compras hoy.
11. Sal temprano.   12. Aféitate aquí.   13. Ten paciencia.
14. Sé buena.   15.   Cena con nosotros.

E. 1. No se lo digas (a él).   2. No salgas ahora.   3. No te
levantes.   3. No traigas los guantes ahora.   4. No bebas la
limonada.   6. No lo rompas.   7. No les hables.   8. No vayas a
la tienda.   9. ¿Ese vestido? ¡No te lo pongas!   10. No hagas
eso.

F. 1. compras   2. apaga   3. arroz   4. limonada
5. liquidación / venta   6. época   7. caminar   8. nunca
9. cuando   10. vez

Lección 12

A. 1. estábamos comiendo   2. estabas haciendo   3. estaba
escribiendo   4. estaba hablando   5. estaban comprando
6. estaba leyendo   7. estaban estudiando   8. estaba trabajando

B. 1. (Nosotros) nos acostamos a las once anoche.   2. (Ella)
estaba escribiendo a máquina cuando la vi.   3. (Nosotros)
íbamos a Lima todos los veranos.   4. Eran las diez y media
cuando (yo) llamé a mi cuñada.   5. (Ella) dijo que quería leer.

C. 1. conocía; conocí   2. sabíamos; supimos   3. podía /
quería   4. pudieron   5. quiso / pudo   6. quería; supe

D. *(Possibilities; answers may vary.)* 1. Nosotros llegamos
al aeropuerto a las seis y media.   2. Mi cuñada está en casa.
3. Ellos están en la joyería.   4. La fiesta es a las doce.   5. Yo
estoy en la farmacia.

E. 1. traje   2. vidriera   3. quedarnos; todo   4. máquina
5. farmacia   6. vacaciones   7. juntos / juntas   8. aeropuerto
9. cuñado   10. examen

Lección 13

A. 1. Ayer él sintió mucho dolor.   2. Anoche Marta no
durmió bien.   3. Ayer no le pedí nada.   4. La semana pasada
ella te mintió.   5. El sábado pasado ellos sirvieron los refrescos.
6. Ayer no lo repetí.   7. Anoche ella siguió estudiando.   8. El
lunes pasado tú no conseguiste nada.

B. 1. Sí, acabo de encontrarlo.   2. Sí, acabo de tomársela.
3. Sí, acaban de comprarlos.   4. Sí, acabamos de medirla.
5. Sí, acabo de bañarme.   6. Sí, acaban de llegar.

C. 1. me gustan   2. le hace falta   3. le duele   4. nos hace
falta   5. Le gusta   6. Le hace falta   7. Me duele   8. le (te)
gusta

D. 1. ¿Qué es una batería / un acumulador? 2. ¿Cuál es su / tu dirección? 3. ¿Qué es un termómetro? 4. ¿Cuál es su / tu número de teléfono? 5. ¿Cuáles son sus ideas sobre esto?

E. 1. aspirina; duele 2. termómetro 3. falta 4. acaba; estación 5. muela 6. neumáticos / gomas 7. divertimos 8. mecánico 9. acumulador 10. despedimos

Lección 14

A. 1. (a) Hace tres meses que nosotros llegamos a California. (b) Nosotros llegamos a California hace tres meses. 2. (a) Hace dos horas que el niño tomó un poco de café. (b) El niño tomó un poco de café hace dos horas. 3. (a) Hace dos días que ellos terminaron el trabajo. (b) Ellos terminaron el trabajo hace dos días. 4. (a) Hace veinte años que ella lo vio. (b) Ella lo vio hace veinte años. 5. (a) Hace quince días que tú viniste a esta ciudad. (b) Tú viniste a esta ciudad hace quince días.

B. 2. recibido 3. volver 4. usado 5. escrito 6. ir 7. aprendido 8. abrir 9. cubierto 10. comido 11. ver 12. hecho 13. sido 14. decir 15. cerrado 16. morir 17. romper 18. dormido 19. estado 20. poner

C. 1. El libro está escrito en inglés. 2. (Él) tiene una pierna rota. 3. La puerta está abierta. 4. ¿Están cerradas las ventanas? 5. El trabajo está terminado.

D. 1. he venido 2. han terminado 3. hemos hablado 4. han dicho 5. has escrito 6. hemos hecho / hemos tenido 7. ha abierto 8. ha puesto 9. se han casado 10. me he roto

E. 1. (Yo) ya había traído los boletos. 2. (Ellos) nos habían dado (el) treinta por ciento de descuento. 3. (Ellos) habían roto los lápices. 4. (Él) ya había visto al profesor. 5. Había cubierto (Ud.) las mesas, señorita Peña?

F. 1. Perdió; llegó 2. cola; boletos 3. casarse 4. pierna 5. descuento; ciento 6. itinerario 7. matemáticas 8. vuelto / cambio

Lección 15

A. 1. Hacía diez horas que yo no comía. 2. Hacía media hora que nosotros lo esperábamos. 3. Hacía dos meses que yo estudiaba español. 4. Hacía dos horas que la paciente no bebía. 5. Hacía tres años que nosotros trabajábamos en la sala de emergencia.

B. 1. La fiesta del hospital será el sábado. 2. Los análisis

estarán listos la semana que viene.   3. (Yo) enseñaré el español.
4. Para esa fecha (nosotros) estaremos en Florida.   5. (Nosotros)
le diremos que sí.   6. (Yo) no haré nada el domingo.
7. (Nosotros) sabremos el resultado de los análisis hoy.   8. El
mecánico arreglará el coche.   9. Los paramédicos podrán venir.
10.   La enfermera le pondrá la inyección.   11. Los niños
volverán de México el sábado.   12. La ambulancia vendrá en
una hora.   13. (Nosotros) tendremos que estudiar para el
examen.   14. (Yo) le daré las radiografías mañana sin falta.
15. (Nosotros) saldremos con Raúl y con Mario el sábado.

   C. 1. iríamos   2. venderían   3. habría   4. serviría
5. trabajarías   6. pondría   7. preferirían   8. seguirían   9. Te
levantarías   10.   nos quejaríamos

   D. 1. (Nosotros) no llegaremos a la universidad a tiempo.
2. ¿Llevaste (tú) a tu perro al veterinario, María?   3. Después
(nosotros) viajaremos en avión.   4. (Ella) está en el hospital.
(Ella) está mejorando.   5. ¿De qué están hablando (ellos)?

   E. 1. veterinario   2. emergencia   3. inyección   4. puntos
5. listos; falta   6. ambulancia   7. resultado   8. mejorar

Lección 16

   A. 1. aconsejemos   2. alquile   3. escriban   4. vivas
5. diga   6. cierre   7. vengan   8. se levante   9. pida
10. hagan   11. traiga   12. recomiende ˙   13. gastemos
14. vaya   15. se afeite   16. durmamos   17. dé   18. sepan
(conozcan)   19. salga   20. tengas

   B. 1. (Ella) quiere que yo traiga los paquetes.   2. (Yo)
prefiero que (nosotros) vayamos a la oficina de correos.   3. ¿A
qué hora quiere (Ud.) que (yo) esté allí mañana, señor Acevedo?
4. Pídale que alquile el carro / coche / auto, señora Portillo.
5. Dígales que se laven la cara ahora.   6. Que lo haga tu novio.
7. Que pasen / entren.   8. (Él) quiere que (yo) sea su novia.
9. ¿(Ud.) necesita que le traigan los muebles, señor?   10. (Yo)
no quiero que (tú) hagas nada, Juancito.

   C. 1. ¡Ah, sí! Es altísimo.   2. ¡Ah, sí! Es carísima!   3. ¡Ah,
sí! Son lentísimos.   4. ¡Ah, sí! Es buenísima.   5. ¡Ah, sí! Es
dificilísima.   6. ¡Ah, sí! Es bellísima.   7. ¡Ah, sí! Es facilísimo.
8. ¡Ah, sí! Estoy ocupadísimo.

   D. 1. alquilar; mecánicos; gastan   2. cara   3. muebles
4. correos   5. ocupado(a)   6. asegure   7. bella

Lección 17

A. 1. (Yo) espero que (tú) puedas hablar con tu consejero(a) hoy, Ana.   2. (Yo) me alegro de que su mamá se sienta mejor, Sr. Gómez.   3. (Yo) temo que (nosotros) no podamos firmar el contrato mañana, señora Herrero.   4. (Nosotros) nos alegramos de estar aquí hoy.   5. (Ella) espera salir mañana por la mañana. 6. (Yo) espero que (Ud.) pueda venir a la conferencia, señor Peña.   7. (Nosotros) tememos no poder terminar el trabajo esta noche.   8. (Yo) siento que (Ud.) esté tan enferma, señora Treviño.

B. 1. se matriculen   2. estudiar   3. escribir 4. terminamos   5. esté   6. sacar   7. llegan   8. firmar

C. 1. felizmente   2. especialmente   3. rápidamente 4. fácilmente   5. lenta y cuidadosamente

D. 1. matrícula   2. abogado(a)   3. nota   4. conferencia; parcial   5. beca   6. consejero(a)   7. química   8. noche 9. lástima   10. cuidadosamente

Lección 18

A. 1. Estoy seguro(a) de que el café ya está frío.   2. No creo que Pedro vaya con nosotros.   3. No es verdad que María esté muy enferma.   4. Dudo que la criada esté aquí.   5. Es cierto que ella quiere huevos fritos.   6. No es cierto que ella almuerce aquí.

B. 1. Busco una casa que quede cerca del centro.   2. Aquí hay una chica que sabe escribir a máquina.   3. No hay nadie que pueda arreglar el fregadero.   4. Tengo una empleada que puede trabajar los domingos.   5. Hay dos personas que pueden poner la mesa ahora.   6. Busco un restaurante que sirva comida mexicana.

D. 1. arbolito   2. hermanita / Teresita   3. vestidito / hijita   4. Juancito   5. cochecito

E. 1. criada; limpiar   2. libre   3. poner   4. mundo 5. árbol   6. queda   7. almorzamos   8. frito

Lección 19

A. 1. (Yo) le hablaré tan pronto como (yo) vea al cirujano. 2. Quédese aquí en caso de que él tenga fiebre, señora Ortega. 3. (Él) me escribió en cuanto (él) llegó.   4. (Nosotros) vamos a esperar hasta que (él) venga.   5. (Yo) no puedo ir sin que lo sepan mis padres.   6. (Nosotros) iremos al oculista cuando (nosotros) tengamos dinero.

B. 1. haya visto   2. hayan hecho   3. hayas aprendido
4. hayan firmado   5. haya arreglado   6. hayamos bajado
7. haya vuelto   8. se haya acostado

C. 1. Ellos sienten que ustedes hayan estado enfermos.
2. Rosa no cree que yo lo haya hecho.   3. Nosotros tememos
que él haya muerto.   4. No es verdad que nosotros nos hayamos
puesto a dieta.   5. Ojalá que papá haya hecho ejercicio hoy.

D. 1. oculista   2. cirujano   3. fiebre   4. peso; dieta;
ejercicio   5. correo; copia   6. autopista; horrible
7. testamento   8. ayudante   9. sobrevivieron   10. pastillas;
pronto

Lección 20

A. 1. asistiéramos   2. dejaras   3. se lavaran   4. recogiera
5. pudiera   6. trajera   7. devolvieran   8. tuviera

B. 1. Le pedí que viniera en seguida.   2. Me alegro de que
pudieras terminarlo anoche.   3. No creí que ella lo hiciera.
4. No es verdad que ellos celebraran su aniversario de bodas
ayer.   5. Temían que ella no dejara propina anoche.   6. Dudo
que el banquete fuera el sábado pasado.

C. *(Possibilities; answers may vary.)*   1. tuviera dinero
2. tenemos tiempo   3. estuviera enfermo   4. no llueve
5. pudieran   6. lo vemos   7. tuviera sueño   8. tenemos
hambre

D. 1. celebrar; bodas   2. asado   3. consulado   4. cordero;
ostras   5. puré   6. propina   7. asistir   8. devolver
9. recoger   10. raro

Spanish-English Vocabulary

A

a   to, 3[1]; at, 12; in, 15
¿a dónde?   where to?, 3
a casa   (toward) home, 6
a la derecha   to the right, 9
a la izquierda   to the left, 9
a menos que   unless, 19
a menudo   often, 7
¿a quién?   to whom?, 4
a tiempo   on time, 15
abogado(a) *(m., f.)*   lawyer, 17
abrigo *(m.)*   coat, 10
abril   April, PII
abrir   to open, 2
abuela *(f.)*   grandmother, 3
abuelo *(m.)*   grandfather, 3
acabar   to finish, 14
acabar de   to have just, 13
accidente *(m.)*   accident, 14
aceite *(m.)*   oil, 13
aconsejar   to advise, 16
acordarse (o:ue) (de)   to remember, 9
acostar(se) (o:ue)   to put to bed, to go to bed, 9
acumulador *(m.)*   battery, 13
adentro   inside, 18
adiós   goodbye, PII
aeropuerto *(m.)*   airport, 12
afeitar(se)   to shave (oneself), 9
afuera   outside, 18
agencia *(f.)*   agency, 6

—de viajes   travel agency, 6
agosto   August, PII
ahora   now, 3
alegrarse (de)   to be glad, 17
alemán(a) *(m., f.)*   German, 2
algo   something, anything, 6
alguien   someone, anyone, 6
alguna vez   ever, 6
algunas veces   sometimes, 6
alguno(a)   any, some, 6
almorzar (o:ue)   to have lunch, 18
almuerzo *(m.)*   lunch, 18
alquilar   to rent, 16
alto(a)   tall, 2
allá   over there, 8
allí   there, 11
ambulancia *(f.)*   ambulance, 15
americano(a) *(m., f.)*   American, PII
amigo(a) *(m., f.)*   friend, 3
amistad *(f.)*   friendship, PI
análisis *(m.)*   test, analysis, 15
anillo *(m.)*   ring, 12
aniversario *(m.)*   anniversary, 20
—de bodas *(m.)*   wedding anniversary, 20
anoche   last night, 10

---

[1] Numbers in Spanish-English and English-Spanish vocabularies refer to chapter numbers.

antes de   before, 9
antes de que   before, 19
año *(m.)*   year, PII
apagar   to turn off, 11
apellido *(m.)*   surname, P2
  —de soltera   maiden
    name, PI
aprender   to learn, 2
aquel(los), aquella(s) *(adj.)*
  that, those *(distant)*, 8
aquél(los), aquélla(s) *(pron.)*
  that (one), those *(distant)*,
  8
aquello *(neuter pron.)*   that,
  8
aquí   here, 6
árbol *(m.)*   tree, 18
aretes *(m.)*   earrings, 12
argentino(a) *(m., f.)*
  Argentinian, 3
arreglar   to fix, 5
arroz *(m.)*   rice, 11
  —con pollo   chicken and
    rice, 11
asado(a)   roast, 20
asegurar   to insure, 16
asistir   to attend, 20
aspiradora *(f.)*   vacuum
  cleaner, 10
aspirina *(f.)*   aspirin, 13
auto *(m.)*   car, automobile, 3
autobús *(m.)*   autobus, bus,
  2
automóvil *(m.)*   automobile,
  car, 3
autopista *(f.)*   freeway, 19
avión *(m.)*   plane, 10
ayer   yesterday, 10
ayudante *(m., f.)*   assistant,
  19
ayudar (a)   to help, 2
azul   blue, 2

B

bajar   to go down, 19
banco *(m.)*   bank, 7

BASTANTE - ENOUGH

banquete *(m.)*   banquet, 20
bañar(se)   to bathe (oneself),
  9
barato   cheap, 4
barrer   to sweep, 10
batería *(f.)*   battery, 13
beber   to drink, 2
bebida *(f.)*   drink, 9
beca *(f.)*   scholarship, 17
bello(a)   pretty, 16
biblioteca *(f.)*   library, 3
bien   well, fine, PII
billete *(m.)*   ticket (for
  transportation), 6
blanco(a)   white, 2
boleto *(m.)*   ticket (e.g., bus,
  train), 14
bonito(a)   pretty, 3
brazo *(m.)*   arm, 14
buenas noches   good
  evening, good night, PII
buenas tardes   good
  afternoon, PI
bueno(a)   good, 4; kind, 16
buenos días   good morning,
  good day, PII
buscar   to look for, 15

C

cabeza *(f.)*   head, 13
café *(m.)*   coffee, 2
cafetería *(f.)*   cafeteria, 1
calamidad *(f.)*   calamity,
  disaster, PI
calle *(f.)*   street, PI
cama *(f.)*   bed, 7
cambiar   to change, 7
cambio *(m.)*   change, 14
caminar   to walk, 11
cansado(a)   tired, 4
cara *(f.)*   face, 16
cárcel *(f.)*   jail, 6
carne *(f.)*   meat, 7
caro(a)   expensive, 4
carpeta *(f.)*   folder, 2
carro *(m.)*   car, 7

carta *(f.)* letter, 7

casa *(f.)* house, PI

casado(a) married, PII

casarse (con) to get married, 14

casi nunca hardly ever, 11

celebrar to celebrate, 20

cena *(f.)* dinner, 5

cenar to have supper, 18

centro *(m.)* downtown (area), 18

cerca de near, 9

cerrar (e:ie) to close, 5

cerveza *(f.)* beer, 1

cine *(m.)* movie theater, 5

cina *(f.)* tape, 9

cirujano(a) *(m., f.)* surgeon, 19

cirujía *(f.)* surgery, 19

ciudad *(f.)* city, PI

clase *(f.)* class, 4; kind, type, 18

clima *(m.)* climate, PI

cobija *(f.)* blanket, 7

cocina *(f.)* kitchen, 10

concinero(a) *(m., f.)* cook, 10

coctel *(m.)* cocktail, 11

coche *(m.)* car, 7

comenzar (e:ie) to begin, to start, 5

comer to eat, 2

comida *(f.)* food, dinner, meal, 8

¿cómo? how?, 3

¿cómo es? what is (it, she, he) like?, 3

compañía *(f.)* company, 2

comprar to buy, 5

comprender to understand, 2

con with, 4

¿con quién? with whom?, 3

concierto *(m.)* concert, 5

conducir to drive, to conduct, 7

conferencia *(f.)* lecture, 17

conocer to know, to be acquainted with, 7

conseguir (e:i) to obtain, to get, 7

consejero(a) *(m., f.)* adviser, 17

consulado *(m.)* consulate, 20

contento(a) happy, content, 14

contrato *(m.)* contract, 17

conversación *(f.)* conversation, PI

conviene it is advisable, 17

cordero *(m.)* lamb, 20

correo *(m.)* post office, 16

creer to believe, 8

criado(a) *(m., f.)* servant, maid, 18

cuaderno *(m.)* notebook, 3

¿cuál (es)? what?, which (one)?, 3

¿cuándo? when?, 4

¿cuánto(a)? how much?, 5

¿cuánto tiempo? how long?, 11

¿cuántos(as)? how many?, 4

cuarto *(m.)* room, 4

cuarto(a) fourth, 5

cubrir to cover, 14

cuchara *(f.)* spoon, 1

cuenta *(f.)* bill, account, 19

cuidadoso(a) careful, 17

cuñada *(f.)* sister-in-law, 12

cuñado *(m.)* brother-in-law, 12

CH

cheque *(m.)* check, 2

chequear to check, 19

chica *(f.)* girl, young woman, 4

chico *(m.)* boy, young man, 4

chocar to collide, 19

D

dar to give, 3
de of, from, 3; about, 6
deber must, should, 3
de cambios mecánicos with standard shift, 16
¿de dónde? where from?, 3
de ida one way, 6
de ida y vuelta round-trip, 6
de memoria by heart, 7
de nada you're welcome, PII
¿de quién? whose?, 3
de vez en cuando once in a while, 11
decidir to decide, 2
décimo(a) tenth, 5
decir (e:i) to say, to tell, 7
decisión (f.) decision, PI
dejar to leave (behind), 20
dentista (m., f.) dentist, 13
desayunar to have breakfast, 5
descuento (m.) discount, 14
desear to want, to desire, 1
desinfectar to disinfect, 15
despedirse (e:i) to say goodbye, 13
despertar(se) (e:ie) to wake up, 9
después afterwards, later, 15
devolver (o:ue) to return (something), to give back, 20
día (m.) day, PI
diario (m.) newspaper, 8
diccionario (m.) dictionary, 4
diciembre December, PII
difícil difficult, 3
dinero (m.) money, PI
dirección (f.) address, PII

director(a) (m., f.) director, 6
disco (m.) record, 9
divertirse (e:ie) to have a good time, 13
divorciado(a) divorced, PII
doblar to turn, 9
doctor(a) (m., f.) doctor, PI
documento (m.) document, 9
dólar (m.) dollar, 5
doler (o:ue) to hurt, to ache, 13
dolor (m.) pain, 13
domicilio (m.) address, PII
domingo Sunday, PII
¿dónde? where?, 2
dormir(se) (o:ue) to sleep, 6; to fall asleep, 9
dormitorio (m.) bedroom, 9
dudar to doubt, 18

E

economía (f.) economics, 10
echar al correo to mail, 19
edad (f.) age, PII
edificio (m.) building, 13
educación (f.) education, 6
él he, 1
elegir (e:i) to choose, to select, 13
ella she, 1
ellas (f.) they, 1
ellos (m.) they, 1
emergencia (f.) emergency, 15
empezar (e:ie) to begin, to start, 5
empleado(a) (m., f.) attendant, clerk, 13
en in, at, 1; on, 6; inside, over, 15
en casa at home, 12

G

gasolina *(f.)* gasoline, 16
gasolinera *(f.)* gas station, 13
gastar to spend, to use, 16
generalmente generally, 9
generoso(a) generous, 8
gerente *(m., f.)* manager, 4
gimnasio *(m.)* gym, 4
goma *(f.)* tire, 13
grande big, 2
guantes *(m.)* gloves, 11
guapo(a) handsome, 2
guía *(m.)* guide, 9
gustar to be pleasing, to like, 13

H

Habana *(f.)* Havana, 11
haber to have *(aux.)*, 5
habitación *(f.)* room, 4
hablar to speak, to talk, 1
hacer to do, to make, 6
—**calor** to be hot
—**frío** to be cold
—**sol** to be sunny
—**viento** to be windy, 10
—**falta** to need, to lack, 13
—**cola** to stand in line, 14
—**ejercicio** to exercise, 19
hasta (que) until, 19
hasta luego I'll see you later, PII
hasta mañana see you tomorrow, PII
hay there is (are), 5
herida *(f.)* wound, 15
hermana *(f.)* sister, 6
hermano *(m.)* brother, 6
hija *(f.)* daughter, 3
hijo *(m.)* son, 3
hijos *(m.)* children, kids, 8
hombre *(m.)* man, PI
horario *(m.)* schedule, 14

horrible horrible, 19
hospital *(m.)* hospital, 3
hotel *(m.)* hotel, 3
huevo *(m.)* egg, 18

I

idea *(f.)* idea, PI
idioma *(m.)* language, PI
iglesia *(f.)* church, 6
igualdad *(f.)* equality, 6
impaciente impatient, 9
impermeable *(m.)* raincoat, 10
importante important, 6
imposible impossible, 17
información *(f.)* information, 8
informe *(m.)* report, 19
ingeniero(a) *(m., f.)* engineer, 3
inglés *(m.)* English (language), 1
instructor(a) *(m., f.)* instructor, 4
instrumento *(m.)* instrument, 13
inteligente intelligent, 2
invierno *(m.)* winter, PII
inyección *(f.)* injection, shot, 15
ir to go, 3
—**a esquiar** to go skiing, 8
—**de compras** to go shopping, 11
—**de vacaciones** to go on vacation, 12
irse to leave, to go away, 9
italiano(a) Italian (language), 1
itinerario *(m.)* schedule, 14

J

jabón *(m.)* soap, 5
jamás never, 6

jefe(a) *(m., f.)* boss, chief, 18

joyería *(f.)* jewelry store, 12

jueves Thursday, PII

jugar to play (a game), 8

julio July, PII

junio June, PII

junta *(f.)* meeting, 5

juntos(as) together, 12

L

la *(pl.* **las)** the *(f.)*, PI

la *(dir. obj. pron.)* her, it *(f.)*, you *(formal f.)*, 7

ladrón(ona) *(m., f.)* thief, 10

lámpara *(f.)* lamp, PI

lápiz *(m.)* pencil, PI

las *(dir. obj. pron.)* them *(f.)*, you *(formal f.)*, 7

lavar(se) to wash (oneself), 9

le *(ind. obj. pron.)* to him, her, it, you *(formal f.)*, 8

lección *(f.)* lesson, PI

leer to read, 2

lengua *(f.)* language, PI

lento(a) slow, 16

les *(ind. obj. pron.)* to them, you *(formal, pl. m., f.)*, 8

levantar(se) to lift, to raise, to get up, 9

libertad *(f.)* liberty, PI

libre free, 18

librería *(f.)* bookstore, 7

libro *(m.)* book, PI

límite *(m.)* limit, 10
   —**de vebcidad** speed limit, 10

limonada *(f.)* lemonade, 11

limpia parabrisas *(m.)* windshield wiper, 13

limpiar to clean, 18

liquidación *(f.)* sale, 11

lo *(dir. obj. pron.)* him, it, *(m.)*, you *(formal m.)*, 7

lo siento I'm sorry, PII

los *(dir. obj. pron.)* them, you *(m. pl.)*, 7

lugar *(m.)* place
   —**de nacimiento** place of birth
   —**donde trabaja** place of work, PII

lunes Monday, PII

luz *(f.)* light, 1

LL

llamar to call, 2

llanta *(f.)* tire, 13

llegar to arrive, 4
   —**tarde** to be late, 14

llevar to take (something or someone to someplace), 7; to carry, 10

llover (o:ue) to rain, 10

lluvia *(f.)* rain, 10

M

madera *(f.)* wood, 3

madre *(f.)* mother, mom, 3

maestro(a) *(m., f.)* teacher (elementary school), 7

mal badly, 4

maleta *(f.)* suitcase, 9

malo(a) bad, 4

mamá mom, mother, 3

mandar to order, 16

mano *(f.)* hand, PI

manta *(f.)* blanket, 7

mantel *(m.)* tablecloth, 1

mañana *(f.)* morning, 5

mañana tomorrow, 6

máquina de escribir *(f.)* typewriter, 12

martes Tuesday, PII

marzo March, PII

más more, 4

masculino masculine, PII

matemáticas *(f.)* mathematics, 14

matrícula *(f.)* tuition, 17; registration, 20

matricularse to register, 17
mayo May, PII
mayor oldest, biggest, 4
me *(obj. pron.)* me, to me, (to) myself, 7
me *(refl. pron.)* myself, (to / for) myself, 9
mecánico *(m., f.)* mechanic, 13
media hora half an hour, 11
medianoche *(f.)* midnight, 9
medicina *(f.)* medicine, 8
médico(a) *(m., f.)* medical doctor, PI
medir (e:i) to measure, 13
mejor better, 4
mejorar to improve, 15
menor younger, smaller, 4
menos less, 4
mentir (e:ie) to lie, 13
mercado *(m.)* market, 4
mes *(m.)* month, 6
mesa *(f.)* table, PI
metal *(m.)* metal, 3
mi *(adj.)* my, 2
mi *(obj. of prep.)* me, 6
miércoles Wednesday, PII
mil thousand, PII
milla *(f.)* mile, 10
mío(a) *(adj.)* my, of mine, 9
mio(a) mine, 9
mirar to look at, 12
modelo *(m.)* model, 13
momento *(m.)* moment, 8
morir (o:ue) to die, 13
mover (o:ue) to move, 16
mozo *(m.)* waiter, 20
muchacha *(f.)* girl, young woman, 2
muchacho *(m.)* boy, young man, 2
muchas gracias thank you very much, PII
muchase veces often, 7
mucho(a) much, 4

mucho gusto how do you do, much pleasure, PII
muebles *(m.)* furniture, 16
muela *(f.)* tooth (molar), 13
mujer *(f.)* woman, PI
museo *(m.)* museum, 2
muy very, 3

N

nacionalidad *(f.)* nationality, PII
nada nothing, 6
nadar to swim, 7
nadie nobody, no one, 6
necesario necessary, 17
necesitar to need, 1
negar to deny, 16
negro(a) black, 2
neumático *(m.)* tire, 13
nevar (e:ie) to snow, 10
ni neither, nor, 6
niebla *(f.)* fog, 10
ninguno(a) no, none, not any, 6
niña *(f.)* girl, child, 11
niño *(m.)* boy, child, 11
no no (not), PII
noche *(f.)* late evening, night, 5
nombre *(m.)* name, PII
norteamericano(a) *(m., f.)* North American, PII
nos *(obj. pron.)* us, to us, (to) ourselves, 9
nos *(refl.)* (to / for) ourselves, 9
nosotros(as) we, us, 1
nota *(f.)* grade, 17
novela *(f.)* novel, 7
noveno(a) ninth, 5
novia *(f.)* girlfriend, 3
novio *(m.)* boyfriend, 3
noviembre November, PII
nublado(a) cloudy, 10

nuestro(s), nuestra(s) *(adj.)*
  our, 3
nuestro(s), nuestra(s), *(pron.)*
  ours, 9
nuevo(a) new, 12
número *(m.)* number, PII
  —de la licencia para
    conducir license
    number, PII
  —de seguro social social
    security number, PII
  —de teléfono telephone
    number, PII
nunca never, 6

O

o or, 2; either, 6
octavo(a) eighth, 5
octubre October, PII
oculista *(m., f.)* eye doctor,
  19
ocupación *(f.)* occupation,
  PII
ocupado(a) busy, 16
oficina *(f.)* office, 5
  —de correos *(f.)* post
    office, 16
ojalá if only . . . , I hope,
  17
ómnibus *(m.)* bus, 2
operación *(f.)* surgery, 19
ostra *(f.)* oyster, 20
otoño *(m.)* fall, PII
otra vez again, 11
otro(a) other, another, 13

P

paciente *(m., f.)* patient, 15
padre *(m.)* father, dad, 3
padres *(m.)* parents, 3
pagar to pay, 8
pantalones *(m.)* trousers, 9
papá *(m.)* dad, father, 3
paquete *(m.)* package, 16

para to, in order to, 5; for,
  by, 10
para que in order that, 19
¿para quién? for whom?, 8
paraguas *(m.)* umbrella, 10
paramédico *(m., f.)*
  paramedic, 15
parque *(m.)* park, 8
parque de diversiones *(m.)*
  amusement park, 9
pasado(a) last, 6
pasaje *(m.)* ticket (for
  transportation), 6
pasajero(a) *(m., f.)*
  passenger, 19
pasaporte *(m.)* passport, 7
pasar (por) to go by, 10
pase come in, PII
pastilla *(f.)* pill, 19
patines *(m.)* skates, 8
pedir (e:i) to ask for, to
  request, to order, 7
peine *(m.)* comb, 9
pelota *(f.)* ball, 8
pensión *(f.)* boarding house,
  4
peor worse, 4
pequeño(a) small, little
  (size), 4
perder (e:ie) to lose, 5
perder to miss (e.g., a
  train), 14
periódico *(m.)* newspaper, 8
pero but, 1
perro *(m.)* dog, 15
peso *(m.)* weight, 19
pierna *(f.)* leg, 14
piscina *(f.)* swimming pool,
  4
piso *(m.)* floor (story), 5
planchar to iron, 10
plástico *(m.)* plastic, 15
playa *(f.)* beach, 17
pluma *(f.)* pen, PI
poco(a) little (quantity), 4

poder (o:ue) to be able to, 6
poema *(m.)* poem, 7
pollo *(m.)* chicken, 11
poner(se) to put, to place, 7; to put on, 9
poner la mesa to set the table, 18
poner una inyección to give a shot, 15
ponerse a dieta to go on a diet, 19
por around, along, by, for, through, 10
por ciento percent, 14
por eso that's why, therefore, 14
por favor please, PII
por lo menos at least, 19
¿por qué? why, 5
porque because, 5
posible possible, 17
postre *(m.)* dessert, 7
precio *(m.)* price, 15
preferir (e:ie) to prefer, 5
preguntar to ask (a question), 8
presidente(a) *(m., f.)* president, 8
prestar to lend, 8
primavera *(f.)* spring, PII
primero(a) *(m., f.)* first, 5
primo(a) *(m., f.)* cousin, 3
probable probably, 17
probar(se) (o:ue) to try, to taste, to try on, 9
problema *(m.)* problem, PI
profesión *(f.)* profession, 3
profesor(a) *(m., f.)* professor, PI
programa *(m.)* program, PI
progreso *(m.)* progress, PI
pronto soon, 15
propina *(f.)* tip, 20
próximo(a) next, 6
puerta *(f.)* door, 9
puntos *(m.)* stitches, 15

puré de papas *(m.)* mashed potatoes, 20

Q

que than, 4; that, which, 8
¿qué? what?, 2
que viene next, coming, 6
quedarse to stay, to remain, 12; to be located, 18
quejarse (de) to complain, 9
querer (e:ie) to want, 5
querido(a) dear, 9
queso *(m.)* cheese, 10
¿quién(es)? who?, whom?, 2
química *(f.)* chemistry, 17
quinto(a) fifth, 5
quitar(se) to take away, to take off, 9

R

radiografía *(f.)* x-ray, 15
rápido(a) fast, 17
¡Rápido! Quick!, 11
raqueta *(f.)* racket, 8
—de tenis tennis racket, 8
raro(a) rare, 20
recepcionista *(m., f.)* receptionist, 3
recibir to receive, 2
reciente recent, 17
recoger to pick up, 20
recomendar (e:ie) to recommend, 16
recordar (o:ue) to remember, 6
refresco *(m.)* soft drink, soda, 1
regalo *(m.)* gift, present, 6
repetir (e:i) to repeat, 7
requisito *(m.)* requirement, 17
restaurante *(m.)* restaurant, 1
resultado *(m.)* result, 15
reunión *(f.)* meeting, 5

revisar to check, 19
revista (*f.*) magazine, 5
rogar to beg, 16
rojo(a) red, 2
romper to break, 14

S

sábado Saturday, PII
sábana (*f.*) sheet, 7
saber to know a fact, to know how, 7
sacar to take out, 13
—copia de to photocopy, 19
sala de emergencia (*f.*) emergency room, 15
salir to go out, to leave, 7
se (*refl.*) (to / for) himself, herself, etc., 9
sección deportiva (*f.*) sports section, 8
secretario(a) (*m., f.*) secretary, PI
seguir (**e:i**) to follow, to continue, 7
—derecho to continue straight ahead, 9
sentar(se) (**e:ie**) to sit, to sit down, 9
sentir (**e:ie**) to regret, to be sorry, 17
sentir(se) (**e:ie**) to feel, 12
señor (*abbr.* **Sr.**) Mr., sir, gentleman, PI
señora (*abbr.* **Sra.**) Mrs., madam, lady, PI
señorita (*abbr.* **Srta.**) Miss, young lady, PII
separado(a) separated, PII
septiembre September, PII
séptimo(a) seventh, 5
ser to be, 3
servilleta (*f.*) napkin, 1
servir (**e:i**) to serve, 7
sexo (*m.*) sex, PII
sexto(a) sixth, 5

sí yes, 1
siempre always, 2
silla (*f.*) chair, PI
sin falta without fail, 15
sin que without, 19
sistema (*m.*) system, PI
sobre about, 13
sobrevivir to survive, 19
sobrina (*f.*) niece, 3
sobrino (*m.*) nephew, 3
solamente only, 12
solo only, 12
solo(a) alone, 4
soltero(a) single, PII
sopa (*f.*) soup, 7
su his, hers, its, your (*formal*), their, 3
suegra (*f.*) mother-in-law, 10
suegro (*m.*) father-in-law, 10
suéter (*m.*) sweater, 10
sugerir (**e:ie**) to suggest, 16
sumamente extremely, highly, 16
supervisor(a) (*m., f.*) supervisor, 4
suyo(s), suya(s) (*pron.*) yours (*formal*), his, hers, theirs, 9

T

también also, too, 4
tampoco neither, 6
tan so, 9
—pronto como as soon as, 19
tarde (*f.*) afternoon, 5
tarde late, 2
tarea (*f.*) homework, 12
tarjeta (*f.*) card
—de crédito credit card, 9
taxi (*m.*) taxi, 2
te (*pron.*) you (*fam.*), to you, (to / for) yourself, 9
té (*m.*) tea, 2

teatro (*m.*)   theater, 2
teléfono (*m.*)   telephone, PI
telegrama (*m.*)   telegram, PI
televisión (*f.*)   television, PI
temer   to fear, 17
temperatura (*f.*)
   temperature, 13
temprano   early, 2
ten paciencia   be patient, 11
tenedor (*m.*)   fork, 1
tener   to have, 4
   —**... años**   to be . . .
      years old
   —**calor**   to be warm
   —**éxito**   to succeed, 6
   —**frío**   to be cold
   —**hambre**   to be hungry
   —**miedo**   to be afraid
   —**prisa**   to be in a hurry
   —**que**   to have to, 6
   —**razón**   to be right
   —**sed**   to be thirsty
   —**sueño**   to be sleepy, 4
tenis (*m.*)   tennis, 8
tercero(a)   third, 5
terminar   to finish, 14
termómetro (*m.*)
   thermometer, 13
terraza (*f.*)   terrace, 9
testamento (*m.*)   testament,
   will, 19
tía (*f.*)   aunt, 8
tiempo (*m.*)   weather, 10
tienda (*f.*)   store, 4
tintorería (*f.*)   cleaner, 9
tío (*m.*)   uncle, 8
toalla (*f.*)   towel, 5
todavía   yet, 9
todo(a)   all, 11
   —**el día**   all day, long, 12
todo el mundo   everybody,
   18
todos(as)   every, 11
   —**los días**   every day, 7
tomar   to drink, 1; to take
   (e.g., the bus), 2

tome asiento   sit down (take
   a seat), PII
trabajar   to work, 1
trabajo (*m.*)   work, job, 14
traducir   to translate, 7
traer   to bring, 7
traje (*m.*)   suit, outfit, 13
   —**de baño**   bathing suit,
      12
tren (*m.*)   train, 14
tres reyes magos   three wise
   men, 8
tu   your (*fam.*), 1
tú   you (*fam.*), 1
tuyo(s), tuya(s) (*pron.*)   yours
   (*fam. sing.*), 9

U

una vez por semana   once a
   week, 7
universidad (*f.*)   university,
   PI
usar   to use, 13
usted (*abbr.* **Ud.**)   you
   (*formal*), 1
ustedes (*abbr.* **Uds.**)   you
   (*pl.*), 1
uvas (*f.*)   grapes, 10

V

vacaciones (*f.*)   vacation, 12
valija (*f.*)   suitcase, 9
vecino(a) (*m., f.*)   neighbor,
   7
velocidad (*f.*)   velocity,
   speed, 10
vender   to sell, 13
venir   to come, 4
venta (*f.*)   sale, 11
ventana (*f.*)   window, 9
ver   to see, 7
verano (*m.*)   summer, PII
verdad (*f.*)   truth, 7
verde   green, 2
vestido (*m.*)   dress, 9

vestir(se) (e:i)   to dress, to get dressed, 9
veterinario(a) *(m., f.)* veterinarian, 15
viajar   to travel, 5
viajero(a) *(m., f.)*   traveller, 18
vidriera *(f.)*   store window, 12
viernes   Friday, PII
visitar   to visit, 2
viudo(a) *(m., f.)*   widower, widow, PII
vivir   to live, 2

volar (o:ue)   to fly, 6
volver (o:ue)   to return, to come (go) back, 6
vuelo *(m.)*   flight, 5
vuelto *(m.)*   change, 14

Y

ya   already, now, 7
yo   I, 1
yo creo que sí   I think so, 15

Z

zapatería *(f.)*   shoe store, 11

A

about de, 6; sobre, 13
accident accidente (*m.*), 14
account cuenta (*f.*), 19
ache doler (o:ue), 13
address dirección (f.), PII;
  domicilio (*m.*), PII
advise aconsejar, 16
adviser consejero(a) (*m.*, *f.*),
  17
afternoon tarde (*f.*), 5
afterwards después, 15
again otra vez, 11
age edad (*f.*), PII
agency agencia (*f.*), 6
airport aeropuerto (*m.*), 12
all todo(a), 11
  —day long todo el día, 12
alone solo(a), 14
along por, 10
also también, 4
always siempre, 2
ambulance ambulancia (*f.*),
  15
American americano(a)
  (*m.*, *f.*), PII
amusement park parque de
  diversiones (*m.*), 9
analysis análisis (*m.*), 15
anniversary aniversario
  (*m.*), 20
another otro(a), 13
any alguno(a), 6
anyone alguien, 6
anything algo, 6
April abril, PII

Argentinian argentino(a)
  (*m.*, *f.*), 3
arm brazo (*m.*), 14
around por, 10
arrive llegar, 14
as soon as en cuanto, 19;
  tan pronto como, 19
ask (a question) preguntar,
  8
ask (for) pedir (e:i), 7
aspirin aspirina (*f.*), 13
assistant ayudante (*m.*, *f.*),
  19
at en, 1; a, 12
at home en casa, 12
at least por lo menos, 19
attend asistir, 20
attendant empleado(a)
  (*m.*, *f.*), 13
August agosto, PII
aunt tía (*f.*), 8
autobus autbús (*m.*), 2
automobile auto (*m.*), 3;
  automóvil (*m.*), 3

B

bad(ly) malo(a) (*adj.*), 4; mal
  (*adv.*), 4
ball pelota (*f.*), 8
bank banco (*m.*), 7
banquet banquete (*m.*), 20
bathe (oneself) bañarse, 9
bathing suit traje de baño
  (*m.*), 12

battery acumulador (m.),
13; batería (f.), 13
be estar, 3; ser, 3
—**afraid** tener miedo
—**cold** tener frío
—**hot** tener calor
—**hungry** tener hambre
—**in a hurry** tener prisa
—**right** tener razón
—**sleepy** tener sueño
—**thirsty** tener sed
—**. . . years old** tener
(cumplir) años, 4
—**able** poder (o:ue), 6
—**acquainted with**
conocer, 7
—**cold (weather)** hacer
frío
—**hot (weather)** hacer
calor
—**windy** hacer viento
—**sunny** hacer sol, 10
—**patient** ten paciencia,
11
—**pleasing** gustar, 13
—**late** llegar tarde, 14
—**ready** estar listo(a), 15
—**glad** alegrarse (de)
—**sorry** sentir (e:ie), 17
—**located** quedarse, 18
beach playa (f.), 17
because porque, 5
bed cama (f.), 7
bedroom dormitorio (m.), 9
beer cerveza (f.), 1
before antes de, 9; antes de
que, 19
beg rogar, 16
begin comenzar (e:ie), 5;
empezar (e:ie), 5
believe creer, 8
better mejor, 4
big grande, 2
biggest mayor, 4
bill cuenta (f.), 19

black negro(a), 2
blanket cobija (f.), 7;
frazada (f.), 7; manta (f.), 7
blue azul, 2
boarding house pensión (f.),
4
book libro (m.), PI
bookstore librería (f.), 7
boss jefe(a) (m., f.), 18
boy muchacho, 2; chico, 4;
niño, 11
boyfriend novio (m.), 3
break romper, 14
bring traer, 7
broom escoba (f.), 10
brother hermano, 6
brother-in-law cuñado (m.),
12
building edificio (m.), 13
bus autobús (m.), 2;
omnibus (m.), 2
busy ocupado(a), 16
but pero, 1
buy comprar, 5
by para, 10; por, 10
by heart de memoria, 7

C

cafeteria cafetería (f.), 1
calamity calamidad (f.), PI
call llamar, 2
car auto (m.), automóvil
(m.), 3; carro (m.), 7; coche
(m.), 7
card tarjeta (f.), 9
careful cuidadoso(a), 17
carry llevar, 10
celebrate celebrar, 20
certain seguro(a), 17
chair silla (f.), PI
change cambiar (verb), 7;
cambio (m.), 14
cheap barato, 4
check cheque (m.), 2

check chequear, 14; revisar, 19

cheese queso *(m.)*, 10

chemistry química *(f.)*, 17

chicken pollo *(m.)*, 11

chicken and rice arroz con pollo, 11

chief jefe(a) *(m., f.)*, 18

child niño(a) *(m., f.)*, 11

children hijos *(m.)*, 8

choose elegir (e:i), 13

church iglesia *(f.)*, 6

city ciudad *(f.)*, PI

class clase *(f.)*, 4

clean limpiar, 18

cleaner tintorería *(f.)*, 9

clerk empleado(a) *(m., f.)*, 13

climate clima *(m.)*, PI

close cerrar (e:ie), 5

cloudy nublado(a), 10

coat abrigo *(m.)*, 10

cocktail coctel *(m.)*, 11

coffee café *(m.)*, 2

collide chocar, 19

comb peine *(m.)*, 9

come venir, 4

—**back** volver (o:ue), 6

—**in** pase, PII; entrar, 10

coming que viene, 6

company compañía *(f.)*, 2

complain quejarse (de), 9

concert concierto *(m.)*, 5

conduct conducir, 7

consulate consulado *(m.)*, 20

content contento(a), 14

continue seguir (e:i), 7

—**straight ahead** seguir derecho, 9

contract contrato *(m.)*, 17

conversation conversación *(f.)*, PI

cook cocinero(a) *(m., f.)*, 10

cousin primo(a) *(m., f.)*, 3

cover cubrir, 14

credit card tarjeta de crédito *(f.)*, 9

D

dad papá, padre, 3

date fecha *(f.)*, PII

—**of birth** fecha de nacimiento, PII

daughter hija, 3

day día *(m.)*, PI

dear querido(a), 9

December diciembre, PII

decide decidir, 2

decision decisión *(f.)*, PI

dentist dentista *(m., f.)*, 13

deny negar, 16

desire desear, 1

dessert postre *(m.)*, 7

dictionary diccionario *(m.)*, 4

die morir (o:ue), 13

difficult difícil, 3

dinner cena *(f.)*, 5; comida *(f.)*, 8

director director(a) *(m., f.)*, 6

disaster calamidad *(f.)*, PI

discount descuento *(m.)*, 14

disinfect desinfectar, 15

divorced divorciado(a), PII

do hacer, 6

doctor doctor(a) *(m., f.)*, PI

document documento *(m.)*, 9

dog perro *(m.)*, 15

dollar dólar *(m.)*, 5

door puerta *(f.)*, 9

doubt dudar, 18

downtown (area) centro *(m.)*, 18

dress vestido *(m.)*, 9

dress (oneself) vestir(se) (e:i), 9

drink tomar, 2; beber, 2 *(verb)*; bebida *(f.)*, 9

drive conducir, 7

E

early   temprano, 2
earrings   aretes *(m.)*, 12
easy   fácil, 3
eat   comer, 2
economics   economía *(f.)*, 10
education   educación *(f.)*, 6
egg   huevo *(m.)*, 18
eighth   octavo(a), 5
either   o, 6
emergency   emergencia *(f.)*,
    15
    —room   sala de
        emergencia *(f.)*, 15
engineer   ingeniero(a)
    (m., f.), 3
English (language)   inglés
    (m.), 1
enter   entrar, 10
equality   igualdad *(f.)*, 6
ever   alguna vez, 6
every   todo(a), todos(as), 11
    —day   todos los días, 7
everybody   todo el mundo,
    18
exam   examen *(m.)*, 12
excellent   excelente, 7
exercise   hacer ejercicio, 19
expensive   caro(a), 4
extremely   sumamente, 16
eye doctor   oculista *(m., f.)*,
    19

F

face   cara *(f.)*, 16
fall   otoño *(m.)*, PII
fall asleep   dormirse (o:ue),
    9
family   familia *(f.)*, 16
fast   rápido(a), 17
father   padre, papá *(m.)*, 3
father-in-law   suegro *(m.)*, 3
favor   favor *(m.)*, 11
favorite   favorito(a), 7
fear   temer, 17

February   febrero, PII
feel   sentir(se) (e:ie), 12
feminine   femenino(a), PII
fever   fiebre *(f.)*, 19
fifth   quinto(a), 5
find   encontrar (o:ue), 13
fine   bien, PII
finish   acabar, 14; terminar,
    14
first   primero(a), 5
fix   arreglar, 5
flight   vuelo *(m.)*, 5
floor (story)   piso *(m.)*, 5
fly   volar (o:ue), 6
fog   niebla *(f.)*, 10
folder   carpeta *(f.)*, 2
follow   seguir (e:i), 7
food   comida *(f.)*, 8
for   para, 10; por, 10
for whom?   ¿para quién?, 8
fork   tenedor *(m.)*, 1
fourth   cuarto(a), 5
free   libre, 18
freeway   autopista *(f.)*, 19
French (language)   francés
    (m.), 1
Friday   viernes, PII
fried   frito(a), 18
friend   amigo(a) *(m., f.)*, 3
friendship   amistad *(f.)*, PI
from   de, 3
furniture   muebles *(m.)*, 16

G

gas station   estación de
    servicio *(f.)*, 13; gasolinera
    (f.), 13
gasoline   gasolina *(f.)*, 16
generally   generalmente, 9
generous   generoso(a), 8
gentleman   señor, PI
German   alemán(a) *(m., f.)*,
    2
get   conseguir (e:i), 7
    —dressed   vestirse (e:i)

—**up**   levantarse, 9
—**married**   casarse (con),
  14
gift   regalo (m.), 6
girl   muchacha, 2; chica, 4;
  niña, 11
girlfriend   novia (f.), 3
give   dar, 3
—**a shot**   poner una
  inyección, 15
—**back**   devolver, 20
gloves   guantes (m.), 11
go   ir, 3
—**out**   salir, 7
—**skiing**   ir a esquiar, 8
—**away**   irse, 9
—**by**   pasar, 10
—**shopping**   ir de
  compras, 11
—**on vacation**   ir de
  vacaciones, 12
—**down**   bajar
—**on a diet**   ponerse a
  dieta, 19
good   bueno(a), 4
good afternoon   buenas
  tardes, PII
good day   buenos días, PII
good evening   buenas
  noches, PII
good morning   buenos días,
  PII
good night   buenas noches,
  PII
goodbye   adiós, PII
grade   nota (f.), 17
grandfather   abuelo, 3
grandmother   abuela, 3
grapes   uvas (f.), 10
guide   guía (m.), 9
gym   gimnasio (m.), 4

H

half an hour   media hora, 11
hand   mano (f.), PI
handsome   guapo(a), 2

happy   feliz, 2; contento, 14
hardly ever   casi nunca, 11
Havana   Habana (f.), 11
have   tener, 4; haber, 5
—**breakfast**   desayunar, 5
—**a good time**   divertirse
  (e:ie)
—**just**   acabar de, 13
—**lunch**   almorzar (o:ue)
—**supper**   cenar, 18
he   él, 1
head   cabeza (f.), 13
help   ayudar, 12
her   la (dir. obj.), 7; le (ind.
  obj.), 8
here   aquí, 6
hers   su, 3
hers   suyo(a), suyos(as), 9
herself   se, 9
highly   sumamente, 16
him   lo (dir. obj.), 7; le (ind.
  obj.), 8
himself   se, 9
his   su, 3
his   suyo(a), suyos(as), 9
home   casa, a casa, 6
homework   tarea (f.), 12
hope   esperar, 17
horrible   horrible, 19
hospital   hospital (m.), 3
hotel   hotel (m.), 3
house   casa (f.), PI
how?   ¿cómo?, 3
how do you do   mucho
  gusto, PII
how long?   ¿cuánto tiempo?,
  11
how many?   ¿cuántos(as)?, 4
how much?   ¿cuánto(a)?, 5
hurt   doler (o:ue), 13
husband   esposo (m.), 4

I

I   yo, 1
I hope   Ojalá, 17
I think so   yo creo que sí, 15

idea   idea (*f.*), PI
If only . . .   Ojalá, 17
impatient   impaciente, 9
important   importante, 6
impossible   imposible, 17
improve   mejorar, 15
in   en, 1; a, 15
in case   en caso de que, 19
in order to   para, 5
in order that   para que, 19
in that case   entonces, 17
in those days   en esa época, 11
information   información (*f.*), 8
injection   inyección (*f.*), 15
inside   en, 15; adentro, 18
instructor   instructor(a) (*m., f.*), 4
instrument   instrumento (*m.*), 13
insure   asegurar, 16
intelligent   inteligente, 2
iron   planchar, 10
it   lo (*m.*), 7; la (*f.*), 7; le (*ind. obj.*), 8
it is advisable   conviene, 17
Italian (language)   italiano (*m.*), 1
its   su(s), 3

J

jail   cárcel (*f.*), 6
January   enero, PII
jewelry store   joyería (*f.*), 12
job   trabajao (*m.*), 14
July   julio, PII
June   junio, PII

K

kids   hijos (*m.*), 8
kind   clase (*f.*), 18
kind   bueno(a) (*adj.*), 16
kitchen   cocina (*f.*), 10
know   conocer, saber, 7

L

lack   hacer falta, 13
lady   señora, PI
lamb   cordero (*m.*), 20
lamp   lámpara (*f.*), PI
language   idioma (*m.*), PI; lengua (*f.*), PI
last   pasado(a), 6
last night   anoche, 10
late   tarde, 2
late evening   noche (*f.*), 5
later   después, 15
lawyer   abogado(a) (*m., f.*), 17
learn   aprender, 2
leave   salir, 7; irse, 19; dejar, 20
lecture   conferencia (*f.*), 17
leg   pierna (*f.*), 14
lemonade   limonada (*f.*), 11
lend   prestar, 8
less   menos, 4
lesson   lección (*f.*), PI
letter   carta (*f.*), 7
liberty   libertad (*f.*), PI
library   biblioteca (*f.*), 3
license number   número de la licencia para conducir, PII
lie   mentir (e:ie), 13
lift   levantar, 9
light   luz (*f.*), 1
like   gustar, 13
limit   límite (*m.*), 10
little   pequeño(a) (**size**), 4; poco(a) (**quantity**), 4
live   vivir, 2
look at   mirar, 12
look for   buscar, 15
lose   perder (e:ie), 5
lunch   almuerzo (*m.*), 18

M

madam   señora, PI
magazine   revista (*f.*), 5

maid criado(a) *(m., f.)*, 18
maiden name apellido de
　soltera *(m.)*, PII
mail echar al correo, 19
make hacer, 6
man hombre *(m.)*, PI
manager gerente *(m., f.)*, 4
March marzo, PII
marital status estado civil
　(m.), PII
market mercado *(m.)*, 4
married casado(a), PII
masculine masculino, PII
mashed potatoes puré de
　papas *(m.)*, 20
mathematics matemáticas
　(f.), 14
May mayo, PII
me me *(dir. and ind. obj.)*,
　7
me mi *(obj. of prep.)*, 6
meal comida *(f.)*, 8
measure medir (e:i), 13
meat carne *(f.)*, 7
mechanic mecánico *(m., f.)*,
　13
medical doctor médico
　(m., f.), PI
medicine medicina *(f.)*, 8
meet encontrarse (con), 12
meeting reunión *(f.)*, 5;
　junta *(f.)*, 5
metal metal *(m.)*, 3
midnight medianoche *(f.)*, 9
midterm exam examen
　parcial *(m.)*, 17
mile milla *(f.)*, 10
mine mío(a), 9
miss (e.g., a train) perder,
　17
Miss señorita, PII
model modelo *(m.)*, 13
mom madre, mamá, 3
moment momento *(m.)*, 8
Monday lunes, PII

money dinero *(m.)*, PI
month mes *(m.)*, 6
more más, 4
morning mañana *(f.)*, 5
move mover (o:ue), 16
movie theater cine *(m.)*, 5
mother madre, mamá, 3
mother-in-law suegra *(f.)*,
　10
Mr. señor, PI
Mrs. señora, PI
much mucho(a), 4
　—pleasure mucho gusto,
　　PII
museum museo *(m.)*, 2
must deber, 3
my mi *(adj.)*, 2; mío(a)
　(adj.), 9
myself me, 9

N

name nombre *(m.)*, PII
napkin servilleta *(f.)*, 1
nationality nacionalidad *(f.)*,
　PII
near cerca de, 9
necessary necesario, 17
need necesitar, 1; hacer
　falta, 13
neighbor vecino(a) *(m., f.)*,
　7
neither tampoco, 6
neither ni, 6
nephew sobrino *(m.)*, 3
never nunca, 6; jamás, 6
new nuevo(a), 12
newspaper diario *(m.)*, 8;
　periódico *(m.)*, 8
next próximo(a), 6; que
　viene, 6
niece sobrina *(f.)*, 3
night noche *(f.)*, 5
ninth noveno(a), 5
no no, PII; ninguno(a), 6
no one nadie, 6

nobody   nadie, 6
none   ninguno(a), 6
North American
    norteamericano(a) *(m., f.)*,
    PII
not any   ninguno(a), 6
notebook   cuaderno *(m.)*, 3
nothing   nada, 6
novel   novela *(f.)*, 7
November   noviembre, PII
now   ahora, 3
number   número *(m.)*, PI
nurse   enfermero(a) *(m., f.)*,
    PI

O

obtain   conseguir (e:i), 7
occupation   ocupación *(f.)*,
    PII
October   octubre, PII
of   de, 3
office   oficina *(f.)*, 5
often   a menudo, 7; muchas
    veces, 7
oil   aceite *(m.)*, 13
older   mayor, 4
on   en, 6
on time   a tiempo, 15
once a week   una vez por
    semana, 7
once in a while   de vez en
    cuando, 11
one way   de ida, 6
only   sólo, solamente, 12
open   abrir, 2
or   o, 2
order   pedir (e:i), 7; mandar,
    16
our   nuestro(a), nuestros(as)
    (adj.), 2
ours   nuestro(a), neustros(as)
    (pron.), 9
ourselves   nos. 9
outfit   traje *(m.)*, 13
outside   afuera, 18

over   en, 15
over there   allá, 8
oyster   ostra *(f.)*, 20

P

package   paquete *(m.)*, 16
pain   dolor *(m.)*, 13
paramedic   paramédico
    (m., f.), 15
parents   padres *(m.)*, 3
park   parque *(m.)*, 8
party   fiesta *(f.)*, 3
passport   pasaporte *(m.)*, 7
passenger   pasajero(a)
    (m., f.), 19
patient   paciente *(m., f.)*, 15
pay   pagar, 8
pen   pluma *(f.)*, PI
pencil   lápiz *(m.)*, PI
percent   por ciento, 14
pharmacy   farmacia *(f.)*, 12
photocopy   sacar copia, 19
physics   física *(f.)*, 17
pick up   recoger, 20
pill   pastilla *(f.)*, 19
pity   lástima, 17
place   lugar *(m.)*, PII
    —of birth   lugar de
        nacimiento
    —of work   lugar donde
        trabaja, PII
place   poner, 7
plane   avión *(m.)*, 10
plastic   plástico, 15
play (a game)   jugar, 8
please   por favor, PII
poem   poema *(m.)*, 7
possible   posible, 17
post office   correo *(m.)*, 16;
    oficina de correos *(f.)*, 16
prefer   preferir (e:ie), 5
present   regalo *(m.)*, 6
president   presidente(a)
    (m., f.), 8

pretty bonito(a), 3; bello(a), 16
price precio (*m.*), 15
probably probable, 17
problem problema (*m.*), PI
profession profesión (*f.*), 3
professor profesor(a) (*m., f.*), PI
progress progreso (*m.*), PI
put (on) poner, 7; ponerse, 9
 —**to bed** acostar(se) (o:ue), 9

Q

Quick! ¡Rápido!, 11

R

racket raqueta (*f.*), 8
rain llover (o:ue), 10
rain lluvia (*f.*), 10
raincoat impermeable (*m.*), 10
raise levantar, 9
rare raro(a), 20
read leer, 2
receive recibir, 2
recent reciente, 17
receptionist recepcionista (*m., f.*), 3
recommend recomendar (e:ie), 16
record disco (*m.*), 9
red rojo(a), 2
register matricularse, 17
registration matrícula (*f.*), 20
regret sentir (e:ie), 17
remain quedarse, 12
remember acordarse (de) (o:ue), 9; recordar (o:ue), 6
rent alquilar, 16
repeat repetir (e:i), 7
report informe (*m.*), 19
request pedir (e:i), 7

requirement requisito (*m.*), 17
restaurant restaurante (*m.*), 1
result resultado (*m.*), 15
return (something) devolver, 20
rice arroz (*m.*), 11
right away en seguida, 17
ring anillo (*m.*), 12
roast asado(a), 20
room cuarto (*m.*), 4; habitación (*m.*), 4
round trip de ida y vuelta, 6

S

salad ensalada (*f.*), 7
sale liquidación (*f.*), 11
Saturday sábado, PII
say decir (e:i), 7
 —**goodbye** despedirse (e:i), 13
schedule horario (*m.*), 14; itinerario (*m.*), 14
scholarship beca (*f.*), 17
school escuela (*f.*), 6
secretary secretario(a) (*m., f.*), PI
see ver, 7
 —**you later** hasta luego
 —**you tomorrow** hasta mañana, PII
select elegir (e:i), 13
sell vender, 13
separated separado(a), PII
September septiembre, PII
servant criado(a) (*m., f.*), 18
serve servir (e:i), 7
set the table poner la mesa, 18
seventh séptimo(a), 5
sex sexo (*m.*), PII
shave (oneself) afeitarse, 9
she ella, 1

sheet   sábana (f.), 7
shoe store   zapatería, 11
shot   inyección (f.), 15
should   deber, 3
sick   enfermo(a), 3
sign   firmar, 17
single   soltero(a), PII
sink   fregadero (m.), 18
sir   señor, PI
sister   hermana, 6
sister-in-law   cuñada (f.), 12
sit (down)   tome asiento, PII,
   sentar(se) (e:ie), 9
sixth   sexto(a), 5
skates   patines (m.), 8
ski   esquiar, 8
sleep   dormir (o:ue), 6
slow   lento(a), 16
small   pequeño(a), 4
smaller   menor, 4
snow   nevar (e:ie), 10
so   tan, 9
soap   jabón (m.), 5
social security number
   número de seguro social,
   PII
soda   refresco (m.), 1
soft drink   refresco (m.), 1
some   alguno(a), 6
someone   alguien, 6
something   algo, 6
sometimes   a veces, 6
son   hijo, 3
soon   pronto, 15
sorry   lo siento, PII
soup   sopa (f.), 7
Spanish (language)   español
   (m.), PI
speak   hablar, 1
special   especial, 17
speed   velocidad (f.), 10
   —limit   límite de
   velocidad, 10
spend   gastar, 16
spoon   cuchara (f.), 1

sports section   sección
   deportiva (f.), 8
spring   primavera (f.), PII
stage   escenario (m.), 9
stand in line   hacer cola, 14
standard shift   de cambios
   mecánicos, 16
start   comenzar (e:ie), 5;
   empezar (e:ie), 5
station   estación (f.), 14
stay   quedarse, 12
stitches   puntos (m.), 15
store   tienda (f.), 4
street   calle (f.), PI
student   estudiante (m., f.),
   2
study   estudiar, 1
succeed   tener éxito, 6
suggest   sugerir (e:ie), 16
suit   traje (m.), 13
suitcase   maleta (f.), 9
summer   verano (m.), PII
Sunday   domingo, PII
supervisor   supervisor(a)
   (m., f.), 4
surgeon   cirujano(a) (m., f.),
   19
surgery   cirujía (f.), 19;
   operación (f.), 19
surname   apellido (m.), PII
survive   sobrevivir, 19
sweater   suéter (m.), 10
sweep   barrer, 10
swim   nadar, 7
swimming pool   piscina (f.),
   4
system   sistema (m.), PI

T

table   mesa (f.), PI
tablecloth   mantel (m.), 1
take   tomar, 2; llevar, 7
   —away   quitar
   —off   quitarse, 9
   —out   sacar, 13

tall alto(a), 2
talk hablar, 1
tape cinta *(f.)*, 9
taste probar (o:ue), 9
taxi taxi *(m.)*, 2
tea té *(m.)*, 2
teach enseñar, 15
teacher (elementary school)
  maestro(a), 7
telegram telegrama *(m.)*, PI
telephone teléfono *(m.)*, PI
  —number número de
    teléfono *(m.)*, PII
television televisión *(f.)*, PI
tell decir (e:i), 7
temperature temperatura
  (f.), 13; fiebre *(f.)*, 19
tennis tenis *(m.)*, 8
tennis racket raqueta de
  tenis *(f.)*, 8
tenth décimo(a), 5
terrace terraza *(f.)*, 9
test análisis *(m.)*, 15
testament testamento *(m.)*,
  19
than que, 4
thank you very much
  muchas gracias, PII
that *(adj.)* *(near person*
  addressed) ese, esa(os,
  as); *(distant)* aquel,
  aquella(os, as); *(pron.)* ése,
  ésa(os, as), aquél,
  aquélla(os, as); *(neuter)* eso,
  aquello; *(rel. pron.)* que, 8
that's why por eso, 14
the la *(pl.* las), PI
theater teatro *(m.)*, 2
their su(s), 3
theirs suyo(a), suyos(as), 9
them los, las *(dir. obj.)*, 7;
  les *(ind. obj.)*, 8
then entonces, 17
there allí, 11
there is *(are)* hay, 5

therefore por eso, 14
thermometer termómetro
  (m.), 13
they ellos(as), 1
thief ladrón(ona) *(m., f.)*, 10
third tercero(a), 5
this *(adj.)* este, esta; *(pron.)*
  éste, ésta; *(neuter)* esto, 8
thousand mil, PII
through por, 10
Thursday jueves, PII
ticket billete *(m.)*, 6; pasaje
  (m.), 6; entrada *(f.)*, 9;
  boleto *(m.)*, 14
tip propina *(f.)*, 20
tire goma *(f.)*, llanta *(f.)*,
  neumático *(m.)*, 13
tired cansado(a), 4
to a, 3; para, 5
  —my / myself me, 7
to the left a la izquierda, 9
to the right a la derecha, 9
together juntos(as), 12
tomorrow mañana, 6
tonight esta noche, 17
too también, 4
tooth muela *(f.)*, 13
towel toalla *(f.)*, 5
train tren *(m.)*, 14
translate traducir, 7
travel viajar, 5
travel agency agencia de
  viajes, 6
traveller viajero(a) *(m., f.)*,
  18
tree árbol *(m.)*, 18
trousers pantalones *(m.)*, 9
truth verdad *(f.)*, 7
try; try on probar(se) (o:ue),
  9
Tuesday martes, PII
tuition matrícula *(f.)*, 17
turn doblar, 9
turn off apagar, 11
type clase *(f.)*, 18

type escribir a máquina, 12
typewriter máquina de
escribir (*f.*), 12

U

umbrella paraguas (*m.*), 10
uncle tío (*m.*), 8
understand comprender, 2;
entender (e:ie), 5
United States Estados
Unidos (*m.*), 3
university universidad (*f.*),
PI
unless a menos que, 19
us nos (*dir. and ind. obj.*),
9; nosotros(as), 1
use usar, 13; gastar, 16

V

vacation vacaciones (*f.*), 12
vacuum cleaner aspiradora
(*f.*), 10
very muy, 3
veterinarian veterinario(a),
15
visit visitar, 2

W

wait for esperar, 2
waiter mozo (*m.*), 20
wake up despertar(se) (e:ie),
9
walk caminar, 11
want desear, 1; querer
(e:ie), 5
wash (oneself) lavar(se), 9
we nosotros(as), 1
weather tiempo (*m.*), 10
wedding anniversary
aniversario de bodas (*m.*),
20
Wednesday miércoles, PII
weight peso (*m.*), 19

well bien, PII
what? ¿qué?, 2; ¿cuál(es)?, 3
what is (it, she, he)
like ¿cómo es?, 3
when? ¿cuándo?, 3
where? ¿dónde?, 2
where from? ¿de dónde?, 3
where to? ¿a dónde?, 3
which (one)? ¿cuál?, 3; que,
8
white blanco(a), 2
who? ¿quién?, ¿quiénes?, 2
whom? ¿quién?, 2; ¿a
quién?, 4
whose? ¿de quién?, 3
why? ¿por qué?, 5
widow viuda, PII
widower viudo, PII
wife esposa (*f.*), 4
will testamento (*m.*), 19
window ventana (*f.*), 9
windshield wiper limpia
parabrisas (*m.*), 13
winter invierno (*m.*), PII
with con, 4
—whom? ¿con quién?, 3
without sin que, 19
without fail sin falta, 15
woman mujer (*f.*), PI
wood madera (*f.*), 3
work trabajo (*m.*), 14
work trabajar, 1
worse peor, 4
wound herida (*f.*), 15
write escribir, 6

X

X-ray radiografía (*f.*), 15

Y

year año (*m.*), PII
yes sí, 1
yesterday ayer, 10
yet todavía, 9

you *(fam. sing.)*   tú; *(dir. and ind. obj.)* te, 9
you *(formal) (subj. pron.)*   usted (Ud.), ustedes (Uds.), 1; *(dir. obj.)* la, le, lo, los, las; *(ind. obj.)* les, 8
young lady   señorita, PII
young man   chico *(m.)*, 4
young woman   muchacha *(f.)*, 2; chica *(f.)*, 4
younger   menor, 4

your *(fam.)*   tu(s), 1; *(formal)*, su(s), 3
you're welcome   de nada, PII
yours *(pron.) (fam.)*   (el) tuyo, (la) tuya, (los) tuyos, (las) tuyas; *(formal)* (el) suyo, (la) suya, (los) suyos, (las) suyas, 9
yourself   *(fam)* te, 9

Index